Strategies of Multinationals in Central and Eastern Europe

First published 2009 by
PALGRAVE MACMILLAN

Palgrave Macmillan in the UK is an imprint of Macmillan Publishers Limited,
registered in England, company number 785998, of Houndmills, Basingstoke,
Hampshire RG21 6XS.

Palgrave Macmillan in the US is a division of St Martin's Press LLC,
175 Fifth Avenue, New York, NY 10010.

Palgrave Macmillan is the global academic imprint of the above companies
and has companies and representatives throughout the world.

Palgrave® and Macmillan® are registered trademarks in the United States,
the United Kingdom, Europe and other countries.

ISBN 978–0–230–23055–2

This book is printed on paper suitable for recycling and made from fully
managed and sustained forest sources. Logging, pulping and manufacturing
processes are expected to conform to the environmental regulations of the
country of origin.

A catalogue record for this book is available from the British Library.

A catalog record for this book is available from the Library of Congress.

10 9 8 7 6 5 4 3 2 1
18 17 16 15 14 13 12 11 10 09

Printed and bound in Great Britain by
CPI Antony Rowe, Chippenham and Eastbourne

Strategies of Multinationals in Central and Eastern Europe

Innovation Systems and Embeddedness

Yordanka Chobanova

To all the people I love

Contents

List of Tables, Figures and Boxes

Tables

Figures

Boxes

List of Abbreviations

AGRI	Directorate-General for Agriculture and Rural Development
AIESEC	Association Internationale des Etudiants en Sciences Economiques et Commerciales
AMC	Agricultural Marketing Centre (Hungary)
AMET	Africa, Middle East and Turkey
AOA	Asia–Oceania–Africa region
APKs	agro-industrial complexes
ARIS	Romanian agency for foreign investment
BGN	Bulgarian lev
BSMEPA	Bulgarian small and medium-size enterprise agency
CAGR	compound annual growth rate
CAPs	agricultural production cooperatives
CEE	Central and Eastern Europe
CEECs	Central and Eastern European countries
CEFTA	Central European Free Trade Agreement
CHF	Swiss Franc
CIAA	Confederation of the Food and Drink Industries
CMEA	Council for Mutual Economic Assistance
CRC	cooperative research centres
CSF	community support framework
CSPAS	Czech Beer and Malt Association
CZK	Czech Koruna
EBRD	European Bank for Reconstruction and Development
ECR	efficient customer response system
EFTA	European Free Trade Association
EIS	European Innovation Scoreboard
EU	European Union
FABs	flavoured alcoholic beverages
FDI	foreign direct investment
FTAs	Free Trade Agreements
FYROM	former Yugoslav Republic of Macedonia
GERD	gross expenditure on R&D
HACCP	Hazard Analysis and Critical Control Point System
HQ	headquarters
HUF	Hungarian Forint

IAESTE	International Association for the Exchange of Students for Technical Experience
IB	international business literature
IMF	International Monetary Fund
IPR	intellectual property right
ISO	International Organization for Standardization
ISTP	Integrator Supplier Target Programme
ITDH	Hungarian Investment and Trade Development Agency
LAOUL	Law for Agricultural Land Ownership and Land Use
MAF	Ministry of Agriculture and Forestry
MER	Ministry of Education, Research and Youth (Romania)
MNE	multinational enterprise
MFN tariffs	most favoured nation tariffs (WTO definition)
NIF	National Innovation Fund
NIS	National Innovation Strategy
NGO	non-governmental organization
NORT	National Office of Research and Technology (Hungary)
OECD	Organisation for Economic Co-operation and Development
R&D	research and development
RDI	research, development and innovation
RTDI	research, technology, development and innovation
SAB	South African Breweries
SI	systems of innovation
SII	Summary Innovation Index
SME	small and medium-sized enterprise
SOE	state-owned enterprises
UBF	Unilever Bestfoods Food
VAT	value added tax
WTO	World Trade Organization

Acknowledgements

This book is the result of my doctoral dissertation presented to the European University Institute, Florence, Italy. I would like to thank all the people, institutions and companies whose support made it possible.

First, the person to whom I am most in debt is Professor Martin Rhodes, who has been my supervisor at European University Institute. Martin Rhodes has the gift to motivate and encourage his supervisees and to give them the freedom to express their ideas, gently guiding them with his advice and comments. Thank you, Martin. I have been blessed to have you as my supervisor.

I remember the months, which I spent in Bulgaria, Romania, the Czech Republic and Hungary, where I interviewed the CEOs of Nestlé, Unilever and InBev. I would like to say that without their extremely generous support this book simply would not exist. All the three companies have been very open, friendly and transparent. I am especially grateful to the management staff at the various headquarters, who provided me with all the information I needed.

It has been a great pleasure to spend four years of my life at the EUI, Florence and I will never forget this time. The institute has just been everything I could have wished for from an academic institution: excellent facilities, friendly and open colleagues from all over Europe and the world, and of course, the amazing picturesque view of Fiesole.

I wish to express my thanks to the Austrian authorities who gave me a grant for the first three years at EUI and to the EUI itself for its financial support in my fourth year.

I would like to extend my gratefulness to Professor Rajneesh Narula, whose impressive and innovative range of publications on innovation systems inspired me to set up the theoretical foundations of my book. The Business School of the University of Reading made an important contribution to my academic development. I cannot mention how warmly I was accepted at the Business School and I would like to thank them for the opportunity they gave me to freely use their rich library facilities and electronic resources, which enriched my book largely.

I owe a lot to Professor Mihaly Laki, for his great help while doing my field research in Hungary. I am thankful to Professor Mladen Velev for his encouragement and support.

I would like to thank all the people whom I met from 2003 to 2009 and who helped me in the different stages of the book; sorry that I cannot mention all of you.

Brussels   YORDANKA CHOBANOVA

Foreword

The last two decades has seen a burgeoning of studies of multinational enterprises (MNEs). This is not just a reflection of academic fashion, but is indicative also of the central role that MNEs play in economic globalization. Globalization is about growing cross-border interdependence, as well as the intertwining of political and economic actors. Globalization is a process, and certainly not a recent phenomenon, but its effects have become especially noticeable since the early 1990s, and it draws the attention of all: everyone – from the average citizen to the politician – has been affected by it, and all have opinions on its consequences and benefits.

Europe is at the epicentre of this brave new world, perhaps initially by accident, but certainly by design since the Maastricht Treaty. Europe has responded proactively (aided sometimes by fortuitous circumstances!) to global-integration-through-globalization. Europe has accelerated, channelled and harnessed a variety of synergies – some internal to the European landscape, others exogenous and driven by globalization – through the process of sustained political and economic integration.

Most obviously, these last two decades have seen the virtual doubling of EU members and candidate countries with the westward shift of a number of Central and Eastern European states. MNEs have played an important – and not always positive – role in this rather large political, economic and social restructuring.

Since the beginning of the new millennium, Europe has sought to consolidate its future by continuing to co-opt and internalize opportunities through an explicit focus on innovation, and this has – whether explicitly or otherwise – involved the MNE. Many academic contributions have sought to understand the MNE's role in promoting innovation in the enlarged and 'new' Europe, but these have tended to take a more macro-view, and neglect to see the MNE as an organic and evolving set of operations, which have themselves responded in specific ways to globalization. Dr Chobanova's study is therefore timely – she has taken the time to understand how the MNE affiliate interacts with the innovation milieu in these countries, using firm-level and affiliate-level information. She has painstakingly interviewed managers and key decision-makers at the corporate and subsidiary level, as well as policy-makers and other key decision-makers, in order to understand how EU membership has affected the nature of their operations and, most importantly, their propensity to engage with local partners in their various host countries.

Her findings provide a sharp contrast to the aggregated and more macro-economic studies in this area. Aggregation has its advantages, but it also obfuscates important nuances. Yordanka's findings, for instance, show us that, when left to their own devices, and unrestricted by distortions in markets introduced by regulation, MNEs prefer to create economies of scale and scope in their existing activities within the core EU countries despite the low cost advantages the new member states offer. In many cases, the competition with other locations in the EU was too strong for MNE subsidiaries to survive in many of the new member states after accession. She also discusses the benefits of passive versus active promotion of MNE embedding measures, and this provides a number of interesting insights, contrasting Bulgaria and Romania with the Czech Republic and Hungary. There are many other profoundly interesting observations, but I will not give these away, and leave it to the readers to discover these on their own!

This is an excellent study, and deserves to be read not just by academic scholars, but also by policy-makers in Brussels, as well as the member states. It is even-handed and carefully considered, and a number of findings will give even the most seasoned expert in this field cause to pause and reflect.

I congratulate Dr Chobanova on what I hope will be the first of many books. She is a young and enterprising person, with diverse interests. Her active participation in policy issues as a member of the Bulgarian delegation to the European Union is a good sign that Europe is moving in the right direction!

RAJNEESH NARULA
Director, John H. Dunning Centre for International Business
University of Reading, UK

Part I
The Nature of the Study

Introduction

One of the ideas driving European integration and enlargement is that a wider Europe enjoys more economic growth and political stability. However, what has been observed until now is mostly divergence rather than convergence between East and West. Effective progress in catching up has occurred in only a few of the acceding Central and Eastern European countries (CEECs). Yet, if we wish to have a strong and dynamic Europe, the benefits of enlargement need to be secured across the region as a whole.

This study focuses on the industrial integration of the CEECs into the EU at the firm and inter-organizational levels. The major actors of the study are multinational enterprises (MNEs), as they link the host country economy with the global economy by participating in the emergence and development of the networks at global, national and local levels through the resources and capabilities embodied in them. Moreover, MNEs are the subject of the following research, as they contribute to the catching-up of the CEECs' economies by transferring technological know-how, implementing advanced management structures, and modernizing manufacturing sectors. As Lall and Narula (2004: 3) point out:

> The role of the MNE as a source of capital and technology has grown over time, as other sources of capital have become scarcer or more volatile and technical change has accelerated. MNEs continue to dominate the creation of technology; indeed, with the rising costs and risks of innovation their importance has risen (with the exception of very new technology areas).

In brief, the expansion and successful embeddedness of Western European multinational firms is crucial for the industrial integration of CEECs into the EU.

The participation of CEE firms in multinational networks depends on the policies of national economic actors and institutions. Liberalization is no longer enough to attract and retain foreign direct investment (FDI) in the host country. As Lall and Narula (2004: 4) argue, 'The removal of restrictions on FDI does not create the complementary factors that MNEs need; it only allows them to exploit existing capabilities more freely'. Thus, in a free trade regime such as the one provided by EU integration, MNEs should contribute to local development only in those places where local capabilities are strong. Put differently, the creation of linkages and the internationalization of spillovers from MNE activities depend on local absorptive capacity. As Narula (2005: 12) concludes, 'FDI *per se* does not provide growth opportunities unless a domestic industrial sector exists which has the necessary technological capacity to profit from the externalities from MNE activity.'

Therefore, the major question that motivates this study is:

What determines beneficial MNE embeddedness in CEECs?[1]

In other words, are MNEs embedded in CEECs with high absorptive capacities (Czech Republic, Hungary) but not embedded in the others (Romania and Bulgaria), which have weak local capacity?

The purpose of this volume is to investigate the shaping of the microeconomic architecture – in particular, the strategies and structures of the firms playing an active role in economic development, chief among which are the major multinationals, often linked through a variety of equity and non-equity links with local enterprises. On the one hand, the focus will be on the networks of these multinational enterprises (MNEs) and the degree to which they reflect the 'shallow'[2] aspects of integration, or are providing a mechanism towards 'deepening' integration in the context of the EU. On the other hand, this project is about national institutions and actors, and their growing discretion to act as direct intermediaries for the introduction of catch-up policies, and their dependence on the provision of new systems of economic governance. In the course of EU integration, the growth of competitive export industries and positive spillover effects for economic development depend to a great extent on the backward and forward linkages already in existence in particular sectors (where MNEs are present) with the local and the global economy.

How deeply embedded are the multinational companies in the national economic systems of governance?

How deeply do they lay the foundations for market/product/technology expansion in post-socialist countries (present members of the EU), thus shaping the opportunities for industrial upgrading and increased competitiveness?

What global strategies do MNEs follow, and how do these strategies shape their CEE policies?

How do MNEs' entry strategies shape their behaviour in CEE?

What is the impact of EU membership on the level of embeddedness of MNEs?

It is questions such as these that this book seeks to address. It discusses industrial development and company embeddedness using the Systems of Innovation (SI) approach. The essence of the 'systems' approach is to analyze the technological development of domestic firms, considering the environment in which they operate: firms' networks of direct customers and suppliers, the institutional and organizational framework, infrastructure, and institutions that create and diffuse knowledge (Freeman, 1987; Lundvall, 1992; Niosi *et al.*, 1993; Patel and Pavitt, 1994; Narula, 2004). 'The concept of a national system of innovation is the key to explaining the behaviour and the performance of the set of institutions on which long-term economic growth and sustainable development are based' (Niosi, 2002: 300). In order to understand the efficiency of economic actors – firm or non-firm – one has to examine how much and how efficiently they interact amongst themselves (Narula, 2004).

To respond to the above questions, the book also refers to international business (IB) literature, which underlines the role of motives for investment with regard to the quality of MNEs' spillovers and embeddedness (Dunning, 1993, 2000, 2002). Simply put, whether a company follows market-seeking, resource-seeking or knowledge-seeking investment strategy matters with regard to the level of embeddedness of the subsidiaries. Using strategic management literature (Ghoshal, 1987; Bartlett and Ghoshal, 1989; Yip, 1989), I also argue that the strategy of the company – whether global, multi-domestic or transnational – has an impact on the embeddedness of MNE subsidiaries.

In particular, I focus on Western European MNEs investing in the packaged food industry in CEECs. The agro-food sector is selected as it fits several criteria:

- It allows for possible inter-sectoral comparisons across countries
- It is important in the process of EU integration

Table I.1   MNEs and their subsidiaries in this research

MNE	Country	Bulgaria	Czech Republic	Hungary	Romania
Nestlé	Switzerland	✓	✓	✓	✓
Unilever	UK/The Netherlands	✓	✓	✓	✓
InBev	Belgium	✓	✓	✓	✓

- It is involved in global production networks
- It is significant for the CEE economies (in terms of employment and contribution to industrial value-added)
- It is a high-tech sector where the role of innovation and knowledge is clearly observed.

The headquarters and subsidiaries of Nestlé (Switzerland), Unilever (UK/Holland) and InBev (Belgium) in CEECs are the key objects of this study (see Table I.1). These are the largest food MNEs in Europe and the world; that is, companies with global strategies and networks. They are the best representatives of the current and near-future level of industrial integration between Eastern and Western Europe.

Country and sector selection

Country selection

Comparative analysis[3] is applied in order to study the diversity of MNE behaviour in the CEECs. Two groups of countries are compared: (1) Hungary and the Czech Republic; and (2) Bulgaria and Romania.

The common characteristic of both groups is that the agro-food industry, in which there has been MNE investment, has a significant place in the economy[4] (Table I.2). All four countries have high value-added, created by the food industry. In Hungary and the Czech Republic, the figure is 13–14 per cent of total industrial value-added. The figure is higher in the second pairing of countries: Romania 30 per cent, and Bulgaria 16.2 per cent. At the same time, the food industry provides 13 per cent of the industrial jobs in Hungary, 11 per cent in the Czech Republic and 10.2 per cent in Romania. For Bulgaria, this figure is even higher, at 15 per cent. Moreover, the agricultural sector – the supplier of raw materials – generated 9.4 per cent of GDP for Bulgaria in 2004 and 13 per cent of GDP for Romania, compared with figures of 4–5 per cent for the Czech Republic and 3.3 per cent for Hungary. Yet, despite the fact that, for

Table I.2 Significance of the agro-food industry in CEECs, 2004

	Percentage of industrial jobs	Contribution of agriculture to GDP (%)	FDI (% of total FDI 1990–2004)	Percentage of total industrial value-added
Bulgaria	15.0	9.4	10.0	16.2
Romania	30 (Agriculture) +10.2 Food industry	13.0	12 (Agriculture) +6.5 Food industry	30.0
Hungary	13.0	3.3	28.0 of FDI to industry	13–14 + 3.3 – Agriculture
The Czech Republic	11.0	4–5	11	13–14 + 3.0 – Agriculture

Source: based on OECD Investment Reports and National Central Bank statistics.

Romania and Bulgaria, agriculture is a much more important sector because of its scale, it is less developed than in Hungary and the Czech Republic. Although very similar, the two groups of countries are also very different.

The first group, the Czech Republic and Hungary, represents macro-economically stable countries that have attracted most of the FDI in CEE. They are characterized by innovation systems that perform relatively well, and their local and national authorities have developed different policies to embed the foreign capital. The second group, Bulgaria and Romania, represent the opposite situation.

Sectoral analysis

In the early 1990s, there were concerns that political and economic restructuring would have dramatic regional impacts in Europe. An integrated European Community 'will be defining underdeveloped areas and problem regions quite differently from the nation states' (Bergman *et al.*, 1991: 1). This would be even more visible after the entry of the new members from the East into the European Union.

This book aims to identify the factors that influence the level of embeddedness of MNEs from the food industry in Hungary, the Czech Republic, Romania and Bulgaria. It does so by analyzing MNEs' global strategies and regional strategies towards CEE subsidiaries. A special focus is given to the national innovation systems of the countries as a factor that shapes the strategies of the companies in CEE. Building the analysis on first- and second-wave accession countries allows the reader to project the behaviour of MNEs in the countries that have recently entered the EU.

Criteria for sector selection

The criteria for sector selection are:

- the ability for inter-sectoral comparisons to be made across countries in order to capture the diversity in MNE behaviour
- sector importance in the process of EU integration
- sector involvement in global production networks
- sector significance to the CEE economies and EU[5]
- focus on high-tech sectors, as the role of innovation and knowledge is important to the study of networks.

The agro-food sector overwhelmingly corresponds to these criteria. First, it allows for inter-sectoral comparisons across countries (Hungary and the Czech Republic compared with Romania and Bulgaria). The food industry is traditionally a local industry and, from a regional policy perspective, very strategic for CEE. As a result of the process of globalization, it is becoming more and more internationalized, and the establishment of multinational companies and their international production networks is becoming increasingly significant.

Second, it is important for EU membership. EU accession requires quality and sanitary standards[6] to be met, intensification of marketing activities, implementation of the internal market mechanisms, the CAP, EU structural policy, and institution building, and so on. Hence, greater emphasis should be put on developing high value-added products and export markets. To respond to these challenges, high-level managerial skills, concentration on production efficiency, cutting surplus capacity, and investment in equipment and technology is required. In this context, FDI from Western multinationals tends to play a significant role, as it contributes to the modernization of the agro-food industry.[7] 'With a population of 100 million people, the CEECs represent a large market for agricultural and food products, and an important region for agricultural production and trade' (OECD, 2001).[8] The export of agricultural products plays a considerable economic role in all CEECs. Yet, the OECD report underscores that CEE agricultural exports are mainly low value-added products – dairy products, pig meat, grains, fruit and vegetables, and wine. At the same time, imports consist of high value-added foodstuffs.

Third, the research focus is on the relationships between different actors in the agro-food industry – agricultural producers (suppliers); food processors and retailers; and how the relevant factors, such as FDI and institutions, contribute to the integration of local firms and markets into the global market. If an enlarged Europe is to enjoy long-term political and economic stability, then there should be strong industrial and innovation networks at local and regional levels to match national and global production networks. State governments, local governments from CEE, multinational corporations, domestic firms, international agencies, EU policy communities, and educational organizations all influence the alignment of networks. The more networks grow to complement each other, the broader and deeper economic integration will be between East and West.

Fourth, the agro-food industry is a significant sector in CEE, creating around 15 per cent of the industrial value-added of the countries. According to the Confederation of the Food and Drink Industries (CIAA), the food and drink industry is the largest manufacturing sector in the EU-25, accounting for 13.6 per cent of total manufacturing turnover. The food and drink industry is the leading employer in the manufacturing sector, with 3.8 million workers in 282,600 companies. Again, according to the CIAA, with a turnover reaching €836 billion, the food and drink industry ranks at number one, ahead of the automobile and chemical industries.[9]

Fifth, the significance of the agro-food industry comes also from the fact that it is a high-tech sector that uses recent achievements in biotechnology, informatics, genetic engineering, and so on. Food and beverage MNEs do not only innovate in the food field; they are also extremely diversified and innovate in a variety of areas, such as chemistry, bioengineering, machinery, and pharmacy (Alfranca *et al.*, 2005). Although, European multinationals are among the biggest R&D investors in the world, they locate a large share of their research activities in the USA. This might reflect inadequacies in European systems of innovation and 'is a matter of concern given the importance of this industry for EU trade and FDI' (Alfranca *et al.*, 2005: 140). In 2004, EU-15 R&D intensity was 0.24 per cent of the food and drink industry output, which is below the spending by the food and drink industry in the United States (0.35 per cent), Australia (0.40 per cent), and Japan (1.21 per cent) (CIAA, 2006: 18). Hence, special attention should be paid by European authorities on how to increase the competitiveness of the food industry, considering that the EU is the number one exporter of food and drink products worldwide.

As one of the key priorities for a united Europe is to become a strong, knowledge-based economy, then 'it will be extremely important to observe knowledge-based East–West networks' (CIAA, 2006: 5). The food markets in Western Europe are mature, and it is difficult for a company from France to go to the UK because existing competition costs for the marketing and branding of food products are very high. That is why, when the Eastern European market was liberalized in the early 1990s, many Western European multinationals preferred to invest there, because they could swiftly obtain a high market share and these markets offered the potential of faster rates of growth. In addition, they could easily compete with local companies in the new market because these state-owned enterprises (SOEs) and small private companies lacked resources, managerial skills, technology and know-how. It is important to note that a small number of MNEs operate in the food and drink sector. Their contribution to local economic development varies. The type of relationship between small and large firms in the sector also varies across regions.

The liberalization of markets in the new globalization era brought with it the need for a proliferation of product supply, especially important for the agro-food industry, which, to a great extent, responds to the growing differentiation of consumer tastes in contemporary societies. This requires companies to respond quickly to product innovation and new technologies (for example, biotechnology, ecological products, and so on). These circumstances resulted in the need for a transfer of technology, know-how, and skills from West to East in order to close the gap between production in developed economies and production in economies in transition. We could have expected the integration process, in the light of future EU membership, to bring better opportunities for local companies to develop. Otherwise, once CEE companies became part of the EU market, it would be difficult for them to sustain production levels and quality requirements. Moreover, EU regulation specifications would incur additional costs for the local producers. The question, then, is:

> What kind of EU can we envisage for the future? Are CEE countries going to be transformed into the Eastern backyard of the core where raw materials and low value-added products will be exported or is there an observable catch-up of the economies from the East that are successfully climbing the 'chain' ladder, thus upgrading their local industries?

This book contributes to answering this question.

Methodology and sources

The book draws on research conducted between 2004 and 2006. The core of this study concerns food MNEs in Bulgaria, Romania, Hungary and the Czech Republic. The author conducted face-to-face interviews and, in some cases, telephone interviews with the regional presidents responsible for CEE at the headquarters of Nestlé in Vevey, Switzerland; Unilever in Rotterdam, Holland; and InBev in Leuven, Belgium. In 2004, at the beginning of the research, the managers of the three companies were contacted and then, two years later, in 2006, they were interviewed again in order to update and elaborate on the information they had provided earlier. The interviews were organized around a semi-structured questionnaire consisting of closed and open-ended questions (see the Appendix), which allowed for better management of the conversation.

Interviews were also conducted with the executive directors and/or external communications officers at the subsidiaries of Nestlé, Unilever, and InBev in each of the four CEE countries – Bulgaria, Romania, the Czech Republic and Hungary – for the period 2004–6. The interviews were based on an open questionnaire, thanks to which it was possible to obtain a deeper understanding of the companies' activities in CEE. During the study period, there had been gradual changes in most of the management staff of the three companies; some managers had retired, others had moved up in the corporate hierarchy or had been appointed to different geographical regions. In this sense, when companies were contacted for the second time in 2006, the interviews involved different people. Their answers complemented the previous findings. It should be noted that, in all the cases, the final drafts of interviews were discussed and approved by the companies' executives.

As this study touches on the national innovation systems of Romania, Bulgaria, Hungary and the Czech Republic, and analyzes the absorptive capacities of these countries, interviews were conducted at the Ministries of Economy in the four countries; at the Foreign Direct Investment Agencies (CzechInvest, the Hungarian Investment and Trade Development Agency (ITDH), the InvestBulgaria Agency, and the Romanian Agency for Foreign Investment (ARIS)); and at the Food and Agricultural Associations in the four countries. The interviews were open, the basic focus being on the role of these institutions in the embedding of MNEs in the host country through different initiatives and programmes.

This book also uses secondary sources such as OECD investment reports, UN reports, company reports and country reports, which contribute to the discussion of firm embeddedness. The marketing reports for the analysis are derived from the Euromonitor database, which contains considerable information on all countries all over the world, including CEE. Sources such as the WTO trade policy reviews and the Trend Chart

Country reports of the EU commission were essential for an understanding of the role of governments in the locking in of MNEs in CEE.

The remainder of this introduction briefly highlights the main features of each chapter in this volume.

Chapter 1 covers the theoretical part of the study by looking at the insights from the SI approach and the IB literature. It presents the causality of the theoretical argument and draws hypotheses from the literature.

Chapter 2 deals extensively with the strategies of the food MNEs. It presents and analyzes the global business strategies of Nestlé, Unilever, and InBev. The chapter then examines the implications of these strategies on the CEE subsidiaries, using in-depth interviews conducted at the headquarters of the three companies.

Chapter 3 provides a description of the privatization and restructuring policies in the agro-food industries in the four countries that are the object of the research in this book. It tests the first and second hypotheses of the study, which argue that the preservation of previously existing supplier networks is important for the creation of strong linkages between MNEs and domestic suppliers. The chapter proves the argument that the local absorptive capacity of the country is crucial for the positive spillovers of FDI.

Chapter 4 is an in-depth study analyzing the national innovation system of Hungary and the governmental policies that encourage linkages between FDI and local suppliers, on the one hand, and linkages between industry and academia, on the other. It also examines the role of private actors such as business organizations and chambers of commerce in the process of industrial upgrading. This chapter describes the strategies of Nestlé, Unilever, and InBev in Hungary, and reveals the role of their subsidiaries in local development. It explores relations between affiliates, local suppliers, and distributors; between subsidiaries and local research institutes and universities; and discusses companies' plans to internationalize their R&D activities in the country. The chapter also presents the impact of the global strategies on the policies of the Hungarian subsidiaries.

Chapter 5, Chapter 6 and Chapter 7 have the same structure as Chapter 4, presenting the activities of Nestlé, Unilever, and InBev in the Czech Republic, Bulgaria and Romania, respectively.

The final chapter, Chapter 8, draws conclusions from the comparative case studies, and relates the studies to the literature on MNEs, regional integration, and national innovation systems. It highlights the role of national innovation systems in the attraction of FDI; however, it questions their role in the embedding of MNEs. The book highlights the importance of factors such as regionalization and globalization, which shape MNEs' strategies.

***

This study analyzes MNEs' strategies in the agro-food sector in the context of EU integration. Despite the importance of this sector, the literature on the globalization of food companies is very limited. Most of the research is on a highly aggregated level, and there is a lack of empirical research at a company level. As far as CEE is concerned, the companies in this sector are unexplored to an even greater degree. In this sense, the major contribution of this book is in the combining of the SI approach and IB literature in order to capture the complex interplay of a variety of forces that determine the embeddedness of food MNEs in CEE.

1
The Analytical Framework

Introduction

The theoretical approach that this study applies to explain the embed-dedness of food MNEs in CEE is based on the systems of innovation (SI) approach and on the international business (IB) literature. SI gives a macro-level view, as it stresses the role of institutions and economic actors for the embeddness of FDI, while IB literature explains that phenomenon from a micro-level perspective, using firm strategies and investment motives. As the host country capabilities and government regulations have an impact on firms' strategies, I use a synthesis of both SI and IB literatures in order to explain the level of embeddedness of MNEs in CEE.

* * *

Lall and Narula (2004: 20) argue that MNEs and FDI can contribute to increased productivity and exports, 'but they do not necessarily result in increased competitiveness of the domestic sector or increased indus-trial capacity, which ultimately determines economic growth in the long run'. The point they are suggesting is that what matters for increased competitiveness is the ability of the country not only to attract, but also to lock in FDI. In general, the more embedded the foreign subsidiary, the greater the intensity of the value-added activity and the greater the amount of R&D activity. Hence, the question is: Which factors determine the embeddedness of MNEs in the host economy? Two groups of factors can be suggested: internal to the company, and external to the company (Narula, 2005). The global strategy of company headquarters, the role of the subsidiary in the company's global organization, and the firm's investment motives are among the internal factors. IB literature focuses upon explanations for these factors. The external factors are the market size, local content regulations, the size and technological capability of local firms, and so on. The SI approach helps with understanding the role of these forces. The next sections elaborate on these two groups of factors.

Theoretical backbone

Systems of innovations (SI) approach

External factors that influence the embeddedness of MNEs

Narula (2005) shows that, without the appropriate domestic absorptive capacity[1] – whether in the form of knowledge, infrastructure or an efficient domestic industrial sector – FDI is unlikely to become embedded. As stated in the *World Investment Report 2001*, 'Mobile factors only go to and "stick" in those places where efficient complementary factors exist' (UNCTAD, 2001: 7). Public and private institutions, and economic actors play a crucial role in this process. As Nelson (2006: 5) highlights, ' "institutions" came to be used as the term to characterize the fundamental factors shaping economic productivity, and progressiveness'. Rodrik *et al.* (2002) argue that efficient institutions contribute more to economic growth than location or trade. Institutions are not organizations; institutions are all the laws, social rules, cultural norms, routines, habits, and technical standards that form the institutional context within which organizations interact (Edquist, 2002). Institutions are the rules of the game that shape the behaviour of firms and other organizations with regard to whether they innovate or not (North, 1990). Institutions are also the governing structures that make or enforce rules (Williamson, 1975). In this sense, the creation or redesign of organizations and institutions might be more important policy instruments in the encouragement of innovation than subsidies and other financial instruments (Edquist, 2002).

Rodrik *et al.* (2002) distinguish between formal and informal institutions. As formal institutions, they classify the intellectual property regime, competition policy, technical standards, taxation, incentives for innovation, education, and so on. Informal institutions are those that create and promote links between the various actors; for example, the governmental programmes that encourage firm collaboration with universities or promote entrepreneurship. Xu (2000) and Lundvall (2002) emphasize the importance of human capital as a crucial condition for a country to benefit from the technology spillovers from MNEs. Borensztein *et al.* (1998) show that, at country level, a minimum threshold of absorptive capacity is necessary for FDI to contribute to higher productivity growth. At the firm level, Narula and Marin (2003) argue that FDI spillovers only occur where firms demonstrate high investment in absorptive capacities. Put briefly, the factors external to the company – such as the absorptive capacity of the country – pre-determine the extent to which the host economy will benefit from MNE spillovers.

Firms do not operate independently but in close partnership with their suppliers, distributors, and so on. They are part of a network of other firms and institutions that make up an SI, and this shapes the firm's behaviour (Narula, 2002). The strongest channel for diffusing skills, knowledge and technology from foreign affiliates is the linkages they build with local firms and institutions. Such linkages can contribute to the growth of a vibrant domestic enterprise sector (UNCTAD, 2001). Over time, the extent of linkages between foreign and local firms increases as the skill level of local entrepreneurs grows and new suppliers emerge that are more competitive. However, Narula (2002) highlights that lock-in can be an efficient outcome under certain circumstances, particularly in sectors in which SI is competitive and which are evolving gradually. In some cases, lock-in can also have negative consequences; this is when radical innovations are created externally and the domestic SI cannot respond to this challenge effectively – that is, the domestic economy does not have the required absorptive capacity to accumulate this knowledge. However, taking the example of Norway, Narula (2002) argues that firms can react to this situation either by modifying the existing SI or by looking for alternative SI in different locations where they can find the necessary technological capacity.

In order to test whether food MNEs are embedded in CEE, this book uses the concept of an innovation system as suggested by scholars such as Freeman (1987) and Freeman and Louca (2001), Nelson (1993, 2002), Lundvall (1992), Edquist (1997). 'Systems of innovation' is a new approach that has emerged only during the last decade. It reflects the significance of knowledge for country competitiveness. 'SI is simply at the centre of modern thinking about innovation and its relation to economic growth, competitiveness, and employment' (Edquist, 2002: 225). As Edquist argues, the strongest asset of the SI approach is that it encompasses all the important factors that influence the development, diffusion, and use of innovations, as well as the relations between these factors. Even more important, it focuses not only on the elements of the system, but also on the interactions among these elements. As the

OECD (1997) report underscores, innovation and technological development are the result of a complex set of relationships among actors in the system. In the centre of this system are the firms. However, firms do not innovate in isolation but, rather, in interaction with other organizational actors (other firms, universities, standard-setting agencies, and so on) and this interaction is shaped by, and shapes, the framework of existing institutions and rules (laws, norms, technical standards, and so on). In brief, innovations emerge in systems where organizational actors and institutional rules are important elements (Edquist, 2002: 226–7). Therefore, policies relating to regulations, taxes, financing, competition and intellectual property can ease or block the various types of interactions and knowledge flows (OECD, 1997: 13).

Lundvall (1992) distinguishes between 'narrow' and 'broad' national systems of innovation. A narrow system of innovation he describes as one that consists of institutions that deliberately promote the acquisition and dissemination of knowledge, and that are the main sources of innovation. The 'broad' approach recognizes that these 'narrow' institutions are embedded in a much wider socio-economic system in which political and cultural factors, as well as economic factors, help to define the pattern, nature and extent of knowledge accumulation within a given industry. These political, cultural, and economic factors also define the extent and nature of industrial innovation within its borders (Freeman, 2002; Narula, 2002). For example, public research institutes and laboratories are more important as developers and diffusers of applied technologies in Europe than in the United States, where universities are the core around which technology based firms and research institutes gather in more informal localized innovation centres (OECD, 1997).

In this sense, this book focuses on the national SI of Bulgaria, Romania, Hungary, and the Czech Republic, and, in particular, analyzes the strength of linkages existing between food MNEs and the domestic, knowledge and financial institutions;[2] public sector organizations; and governments (Figure 1.1). A special focus is given to government efforts to attract and retain FDI in the host economies, and to the initiatives that encourage the partnership between knowledge institutions and industry. Attention is paid to the programmes that promote cooperation between the MNEs and domestic suppliers. The linkages between food MNEs and domestic actors in CEE are analyzed by three types of knowledge flows: (1) interactions between MNEs and domestic companies – suppliers and retailers; (2) interactions among MNEs, universities and public research institutes, including joint research, co-patenting, co-publications and more informal linkages; and (3) investments by

19

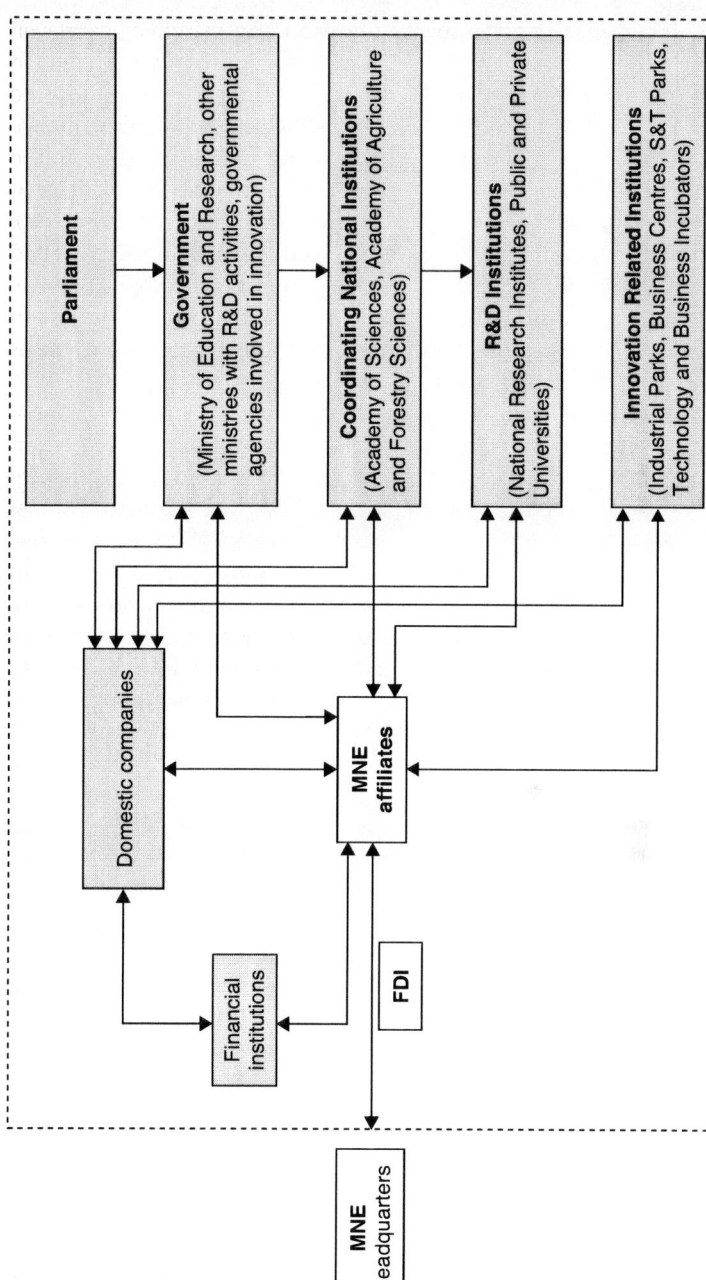

Figure 1.1 MNEs, domestic suppliers, and the linkages between the different actors of the National innovation system

MNEs in R&D laboratories in the host country. The effective interaction between the different actors in the innovation system is a key to the successful embeddedness of MNEs.

Along these lines, Rasiah (1994) shows that the role of governments is critical to providing the necessary technological infrastructure. The government can enhance the development of local technology by offering incentives to MNEs and imposing tariffs selectively to promote the diffusion of technology across different sectors and industries. Narula and Marin (2003) conclude that governments have a responsibility to create policies that promote linkages, encourage the development of local firms, and foster the development of important infrastructure, all of which provide the raw material for absorptive capacity. David Mowery and Timothy Simcoe (2002) show that the role of government is especially important in the early stages of the emergence of critical innovations. They analyze the emergence of the world largest computer network – the Internet – and prove that the USA played the leading role in its development and commercialization, thanks to the far-sighted policies of the Department of Defense and the National Science Foundation. These bodies supported the development of fundamental inventions, post-graduate training, prototypes, infrastructure, and the adoption of open standards and flows of information. Narula (2005) argues that the development of a strong domestic industrial policy requires systemic long-term investments in developing public infrastructure and in promoting domestic suppliers. For example, he points out CEE countries, which are characterized by a qualified work force; however, this does not mean that these countries have efficient absorption of knowledge, or efficient use of industrial development. A number of CEE countries invested in R&D; however, the majority of the formal R&D efforts were conducted by SOEs and the non-firm sector: 'While the role of the state must necessarily remain a significant investor in innovation, these policies need to be orchestrated with the private firm sector, whether domestic or foreign' (Narula, 2005: 12).

One of the EU's strategic economic goals for the decade to 2010 is 'to become the most competitive and dynamic knowledge-based economy' (Sapir *et al.*, 2003), as industries depend more on innovations than on a mass labour force, which was not the case some time previously. Moreover, the most profitable and fastest growing companies are those that are based on knowledge capital. In that respect, the role of micro-regional authorities is crucial in encouraging the creation of knowledge-based networks, between private firms, universities, colleges, government agencies, NGOs, and so on. Yet, the question as to the extent to which the government should interfere in industrial relations is 'hotly debated today' (Dunning, 2002: 67). On the one hand, markets became liberalized, while central planning was discredited. On the other hand, the role of the state became crucial, in that the economic prosperity of firms and nations became more dependent on the continual upgrading of indigenously created assets – innovatory capacity, human resources and the commercial and communications infrastructure – many of which it is within the power of governments to influence. Globalization is not reducing the role of government, 'but it is changing its *"raison d'être and its content"*, and it is doing so within the context of structural integration, the growing importance of public goods, greater mobility within and across firms, greater flexibility of labour markets, greater reliance on market finance and higher investment in both R&D and higher education, and the increasing ease with which the corporations can "vote with their feet"' (Dunning, 2002: 67).

International economics and neo-classical economics neglected the macro-organizational role of government (Dunning, 2002). This analytical lacuna has been recently taken over by two groups of scholars. The first group, following the writing of Paul Krugman (1986, 1994), injected new life into international trade theory as it attempted to explain how strategic trade policy by governments might affect the location of economic activity. The second group involved the work of US scholars such as Ray Vernon, Fred Bergsten, Gary Hufbauer and Monty Graham, on the changing interface between trade, FDI and global business activity, and its implications for a range of domestic economic and other issues. However, as Dunning (2002: 181) points out, 'neither group of scholars gave much attention to the ways in which governments might interact with firms and markets to lessen the failure of different organisational forms of economic activity'. That is why political scientists, economists and organizational scholars are more closely examining the concept of government as a superintendent of the organization of economic activity and the instruments it uses to facilitate an efficient market system.[3] Moreover, in recent work on the determinants of the locational preferences of MNEs, the role of host governments – and particularly their ability to affect the co-ordinating and transaction costs of economic activity – has been shown to be a critical one.[4] The EU accession countries from CEE are especially useful examples for understanding whether Dunning and others are correct. These countries experienced a transformation of their economies and political change that necessitated state withdrawal, while, at the same time, they were trying (and still are trying) to converge on a moving target – the EU: and building the necessary institutional arrangements and regulations becomes a must.

Apart from organizations and institutions, the other factor that might influence the level of embeddedness of MNEs is the period of investment in a particular country. The logic is that MNEs build on the locational advantages of the host economy and, as those advantages develop over time, companies' embeddedness increases relatively. The research of Rasiah (1994) and Narula and Marin (2003) shows that this phenomenon was observed in East Asia. As will be revealed later, the CEOs of Nestlé and Unilever admitted that the duration of investment in Hungary was among the factors that influenced their decision to invest in the country. The good contacts Unilever had with the Hungarian factory before the 1990s were crucial in determining the amount of investment for the acquisition of the plant. However, Lall and Narula (2004) note that a period of investment does not always result in deeper embeddedness. They conclude that there are probably many more cases where linkages and spillovers did not substantially increase over time. This reflects, *inter alia*, the kind of subsidiaries and companies' entry strategies.

To summarize, external factors play a crucial role in shaping MNEs' strategies. An economy with a strong knowledge capacity has greater opportunities to attract and retain FDI. Yet, whether or not a particular MNE would embed in the host economy is very much an internal company decision. The internal factors for company determinants that influence the level of embeddedness in the host economy include MNEs' entry strategies and entry modes into CEE, and their business strategies.

International business literature

Entry strategy and entry modes

MNEs' headquarters define company strategy and map the global priorities and goals. Foreign subsidiaries have different strategic roles in the implementation of the firm's overall international strategy (Ghoshal and Nohria, 1989; Gupta and Govindarajan, 1991; Roth and Morrison, 1992). Birkinshaw (1996) demonstrates that foreign subsidiaries are an important source of strategic resources for the parent company and play a crucial role in the MNE's international competitiveness. In this sense, from the position of the subsidiary in the global production chain, one can conclude the propensity of an MNE to settle in the host economy. Subsidiary autonomy allows the subsidiary manager to deal more easily with the demands of the local market and task environment (O'Donnell,

2000). The more independent the subsidiary is from the parent company, the greater the opportunities to source locally and cooperate with the local institutions. Birkinshaw and Hood (2000) support this argument, explaining that subsidiaries established in leading edge[5] clusters usually embed themselves strongly in the local environment in order to benefit from local knowledge. To do that 'requires a significant level of decision-making autonomy' (Birkinshaw and Hood, 2000: 144). However, it should be noticed that the subsidiary mandates[6] and autonomy are earned through the entrepreneurial efforts of the subsidiary's management, and are not simply given by the parent company's management (Birkinshaw 1996).

Birkinshaw and Bouquet (2006) investigate the positive attention between foreign subsidiaries and company headquarters; that is, the extent to which the parent company recognizes and gives credit to the subsidiary for its contribution to the MNE as a whole. Using detailed questionnaire and archival data on 283 subsidiaries in multinational enterprises, they find strong evidence that the attention given to the foreign subsidiary is not simply influenced by structural considerations of weight, the 'voice' of a subsidiary matters as well. Birkinshaw and Bouquet's analysis also reveals that specific aspects of the subsidiary's historical situation moderate the relationship between the subsidiary 'voice' and headquarters' attentiveness. O'Donnell (2000) proves that relationship between company headquarters and the subsidiary is characterized less by hierarchy and control, and more by mutual interdependence and learning. Thus, he suggests consideration of multiple intrafirm relationships when examining management issues in MNEs that compete on a global basis.

The entry strategy in a given market can say a great deal about the company's plans in a particular economy. Estrin and Meyer (2004) conclude that, to understand the mechanisms of spillovers, it is important to understand processes within the investing MNE. As Narula (2005: 4) argues, the motive for investment is crucial in determining the extent to which linkages and externalities develop. He explains that the motive for an investment helps to determine the potential for spillovers. Scholars (White and Poynter, 1984; Dunning, 1993)[7] have identified four main motives for investment: (1) market seeking; (2) resource seeking; (3) efficiency seeking; and (4) strategic asset seeking. The relative importance of each is a function of the stage of economic development, which itself is a function of the quality of its absorptive capacity. Companies following an asset-seeking strategy have the greatest willingness to lock into a particular economy. Birkinshaw and Hood (2000) show that subsidiaries in leading-edge clusters are strongly embedded in the local network in terms of strong relationships with local customers, suppliers, and contacts with government and local universities; they are more autonomous and more internationally oriented. In contrast, the authors argue that subsidiaries in other industry sectors do not develop the same network of relationships, either because such partner firms and institutions are not present locally or because the subsidiary was established for different reasons (for example, low labour costs, or market access). However, as pointed out in the previous section, effective national institutions are capable of locking in companies that follow any of the other three entry strategies.

As far as food MNEs are concerned, they followed market-seeking strategies when they penetrated CEE market. In general, food companies have been interested in the extension of production into a new country or region. Hence, their focus has been on the status of the local market (the size and income level of the population) and its growth potential. The opening up of CEE offered possibilities for growth for Western multinationals that operate in mature Western European markets.[8] As Meyer and Tran (2006: 3) outline, 'the main attraction of emerging economies is their high economic growth and the corresponding expectation of rapidly increasing demand of consumer goods'.

Dunning (2000: 37) argues that market-seeking FDI can contribute to the upgrading of the host country in several ways:

- It provides complementary assets (technology, management and organizational competence)
- It fosters backward supply linkages and clusters of specialized labour markets and agglomerative economies
- It raises standards of product quality, and also raises domestic consumers' expectations of indigenous competitors
- It stimulates local entrepreneurship and domestic competition.

Among the objectives of this study is an empirical check as to the extent to which food MNEs contributed to local economies in such ways. In addition, this study observes the impact of MNEs' global strategies on their CEE subsidiaries. It also presents the way in which MNEs adapt their strategies according to the CEE environment.

Limited research has been conducted on the micro-level in CEECs. Deniz Yoruk and Nick von Tunzelmann (2002) have worked on a project related to network formation by both domestic and foreign actors in the food processing industry in some CEECs.[9] The primary object of their study is 'what foreign multinationals are and are not doing in reorganizing and updating the CEE food industry'. Their paper's assessment is that Western food MNEs have been interested in market opportunities rather than the knowledge capabilities of the region; that is, they have market-seeking investment strategies rather than efficiency-seeking strategies. The basic findings are that Western companies largely ignored upstream segments[10] of food processing, but, recently, they have been 'dragged into reconstituting them in order to raise the quality of local raw materials'. In the downstream agro-food sector, where MNEs are mainly to be found, the priority has been market control achieved by technologies that are brought from the home country – ignoring domestic sources of technology in the host countries. Yoruk and Tunzelmann claim that there is a network failure in CEECs, and that foreign MNEs bring upgrading but 'mesh less adequately with domestic capabilities and resources at this national level, where there continues to be much catching-up still to be taken on'. The 'network failure', they argue, varies from one country to another, depending on its circumstances. In Romania, for example, the main problem is found to be on the supply side in agriculture, whereas in Poland it seems to be on the demand side, in marketing. In short, Yoruk and Tunzelmann conclude that foreign companies strengthened some networks that were previously weak, but at some cost to the networks that were previously strong; the reason for this being the global context in which the MNEs operate. Although very inspiring, their paper on the food industry in CEE has some shortcomings. The authors talk about networks, but they do not define precisely what a network is for them and which actors it includes. They discuss socialist networks as a whole, and do not investigate the networks of the particular MNEs as an object of their research. The explanation that the global environment influences the network formation of MNEs in CEE is reasonable, but it needs to be further elaborated. In fact, the evidence has shown that a certain MNE might have stronger networks in some CEECs than in others. Moreover, the authors themselves argue that the reason for network failure varies from country to country. Therefore, further research is needed in this direction and the present study attempts to address these issues.

The early years of investment in CEE economies have been characterized by unique challenges for MNEs, as there were no sophisticated institutions or well-developed supplier networks. Packaged-food MNEs, which are the focus of this study, were faced with a bunch of macroeconomic risks: a non-functioning market economy, no stable legislative framework, poorly developed marketing infrastructure, price conscious and not very brand-loyal consumers, and intense competition. In addition, the average consumption of typical consumer products – such as toiletries, beverages, confectionery, detergents and household cleaners – was well below Western levels. However, the potential for growth offered by CEE markets has been a very strong stimulus for the MNEs to undertake the risks and invest in the region. Moreover, early entrance into the region, ahead of other competitors, has been vital to success (Quelch *et al.*, 1991; Schuh and Damova, 2001). 'First mover advantage' gave foreign investors the unique chance to buy leading local firms (this is a policy of Nestlé, for example), to be the first to bring their brands to consumers' attention, to access marketing and distribution channels, and to sign contracts with the best suppliers. Apart from these advantages, production oriented considerations also played a role in the decision for investment in the region, as the lower local production costs allowed Western firms to service price sensitive mass markets that could not be covered by exporting.

The major entry modes popular among Western firms for CEE were exporting, forming a joint venture with a local partner, acquiring a local firm in course of the privatization process, and greenfield investments. The entry mode is an important part of a company's global strategy as it influences a firm's efficiency and competitiveness. CEE was a risky and unexplored market, which made companies cautious when investing. In this respect, forming joint ventures between Western companies and CEE partners has been very popular (Shama, 1995). This form of cooperation was mutually beneficial for both foreign investors and local firms, as foreign investors could avoid market risks, as well as reduce costs arising from greenfield investments, and local firms could benefit from the knowledge and capital of the foreign firm. In particular, food MNEs brought along their global brand names, worldwide reputations, and global distribution networks. In return, the local companies provided them with their local distribution channels and their knowledge of the local market, as well as know-how concerning local tastes and preferences, and industrial processing techniques. These local market specific assets helped the food MNEs to keep pace with local market conditions, which could have otherwise been particularly difficult to deal with. An example of how difficult it might be for a company to become familiar with local tastes and preferences is the case of Nestlé, Bulgaria. The CEE manager of Nestlé, Mr Gallagher, in an interview that is presented later in this book, revealed that understanding local consumer tastes was among the greatest obstacles to the success of the company in Bulgaria. Nestlé was reporting losses for years and management could not figure out what was wrong. Finally, when the local management team was changed, the problem was solved. It became clear that local confectionery products, which Nestlé adopted and had given its brand name to, were low quality. For years, the company had been mistaken in thinking that this was the local preference and had done nothing to improve the products.

Inviting FDI to Hungary, mainly in the form of joint ventures, was a major policy aim during the 1980s, and a large number of joint ventures were established. Because of the general openness of the Hungarian and Czech economy, these two countries attracted most of the FDI in the CEE region (see Figure A.1 in the Appendix). In addition, long-term cooperation links were frequently developed with major MNEs. However, most of the joint ventures in CEE were only temporary in nature. The major restructuring efforts occurred only after the foreign investor had obtained a qualified majority or full ownership of the firm (Szanyi, 2001). Examples of such cases are Danone and Nestlé in the Czech Republic.

When the privatization of state-owned companies began in the early and mid-1990s, the sale of large national companies offered a unique opportunity for established foreign companies to expand their market position, and for new entrants to become major players in the market. For packaged food MNEs, the most common entry mode in CEE was the acquisition of plants through privatization. Chocolate, dairy products and beer are traditional, culturally embedded products. This fact made local producers attractive takeover candidates for foreign companies, and major players such as Nestlé, Unilever, Kraft Foods and Interbrew (now InBev) seized the opportunity offered by the privatization process to establish a presence in the region. In the case of the acquisition of a former state-owned company, the new management team, controlled by the parent company, had to initiate and quickly implement an integration programme, with particular attention being paid to the timely integration of the local unit into the corporate group. The task of management was to implant a market and profit orientation, improve overall productivity, optimize the product portfolio, revitalize sales and develop brand management (Schuh and Holzmüller, 2003: 187). The CEOs of the CEE subsidiaries were Western managers who were appointed by the parent company. Reasons for the appointment of managers from outside CEE include CEE managers' lack of knowledge about the market economy, an absence of foreign language skills, and their lack of familiarity with the code of conduct of the parent company. An 'army' of Western experts were employed in CEE in order to train a new generation of management, and to help the integration of the local affiliate to the global production network of the company. The managers of Unilever, for example, revealed in interviews with the author that they consider the investment in their CEE personnel as an equally strong contribution to the local development as the high standards that they introduced to consumer goods.

To summarize, the literature identifies market-seeking, resource-seeking, efficiency-seeking and strategic-asset seeking as entry strategies. Companies looking for strategic assets have the greatest willingness to embed in the local economy, as they are attracted by the knowledge that the country offers. Food MNEs, as already shown, are interested in the growth opportunities of local markets and follow market-seeking strategies. Therefore, one can expect that these companies do not have high propensity to lock into the host economies and to link with the domestic actors. However, a supportive national innovation system might influence the policies of MNEs and make them contribute to industrial upgrading.

Apart from entry strategy, the other factor that defines the extent to which a subsidiary creates linkages in the local economy is the business strategy of the company.

The business strategy of the MNE

The business strategy that an MNE follows gives a picture of the organizational structure of the company, the way it functions, its willingness to embed in a particular economy, and its current aims and long-term plans. Hence, the question is: 'What strategies drive food MNEs and how do they affect CEE subsidiaries?'

Seeking efficiency in continuously globalizing markets becomes a condition for worldwide competitiveness. Only those enterprises that manage to organize their international business activities within global networks have opportunities to attain durable worldwide competitiveness. To achieve global competitive advantage, 'costs and revenues have to be managed simultaneously, efficiency and innovation are both important, and innovations can arise in many different parts of the organization' (Bartlett and Ghoshal, 1989: 60).

The subsidiaries of multinational companies operate in different national environments. In each country, they have to be responsible to the local consumers, business agencies and governments. Ghoshal and Nohria (1993: 26) name these factors 'forces for national responsiveness'. The companies whose activity is strongly influenced by local factors follow a multidomestic strategy. Birkinshaw and Morrison (1995) name these subsidiaries 'local implementers'. The multi-domestic strategy that they pursue has the following characteristics:

- The product is customized for each market
- Control is decentralized; that is, decision-making is undertaken at the local level
- It is effective when large differences exist between countries
- It results in the following advantages: product differentiation, local responsiveness, minimized political risk, minimized exchange rate risk.

However, it should be noted that the different local environments might have something in common – such as, for example, common consumer tastes. Ghoshal and Nohria (1993) describe the linkages across national borders that press MNEs to coordinate their activities as 'forces for global integration', and the strategy that the companies pursue is called a 'global strategy'. Global strategy stimulates MNEs to integrate their overseas subsidiaries with the parent company. Therefore, whereas in a multi-domestic strategy the managers in each country react to competition without considering what is taking place in other countries, in a global strategy, competitive manoeuvres are integrated across nations. As Yip (1989: 31) puts it, the aim of the multi-domestic strategy is to maximize worldwide performance by maximizing local competitive advantage, revenue or profits, while a global strategy seeks to maximize worldwide performance through sharing and integration. Yip argues that, in a multi-domestic strategy, all or most of the value chain is reproduced in every country. In a global strategy, costs are reduced by breaking up the value chain so that each activity can be conducted in a different country. One value chain strategy is partial duplication and partial concentration. The literature (see Bartlett and Ghoshal, 1989) defines a third type of strategy; this is a mixture of the multi-domestic and global strategies and is called a transnational strategy;[11] this is the strategy that global food MNEs follow.

What is a transnational strategy? It tries, simultaneously, to be globally efficient and locally responsible. Knowledge is spread throughout the organization with large flows of people, know-how and products between subsidiaries. Products and marketing are adapted to local markets, and the proportion of local production and R&D is higher than in subsidiaries of global companies. Subsidiaries are more dependent on other subsidiaries for their inputs/outputs than on the parent company. In order to develop a transnational strategy, companies are 'building organizations in which multidimensional management perspective and capabilities are kept legitimate and viable, dispersed assets and resources are developed in a differentiated and interdependent network, and the whole system is integrated with a flexible coordinating process' (Bartlett and Ghoshal, 1989: 210).

Using Unilever as an example of a transnational company, Bartlett and Ghoshal (1989) shed light on the reasons that provoked the company to develop from a multi-domestic organization into a transnational company. They showed that the trend towards converging consumer tastes and the lowered barriers between markets, especially in Europe, made it possible for Unilever to develop and diffuse innovations in a more coordinated way, and to capture more of the scale economies gained by means of integrated operations. In other words, the factor that encouraged Unilever to globalize was the market. Apart from the market, three other industry drivers can be identified as providing the opportunity for a company to globalize: cost drivers, governmental drivers, and competitive drivers (Yip, 1989).

Market drivers depend on customer behaviour and the structure of distribution channels. When customers in different countries want the same type of product or service, there are greater opportunities for a product to be standardized. The existence of global customers both requires and allows a uniform marketing programme. Global and regional channels of distribution allow purchase at a lower price in one country and sale at a higher price in another country. Global channels are rare, but regional channels are increasing in number and are typical for European grocery and retailing.

For food multinationals, the significant factors are the globalized urban lifestyles, the increasing proportion of economically active females, the increasing number of people living on their own, and childless families. All these globalizing drivers bring the populations towards standardized processed products. As Tozanli (2005) notes, markets are often fragmented and MNEs face a difficult dilemma of choosing between local and global brands. The combination of local and global brands satisfies different market segments and leads to market leadership; that is why this combination is usually chosen by large MNEs. A diversified brand portfolio can also help to secure economies of scope in local production and logistics, to strengthen bargaining power with regard to suppliers and retailers, and to fund the introduction of international brands to the local market (Schuh, 2000).

In strongly culturally bound product categories, such as beer and confectionery, the major demand is still for local brands; international brands are less popular in most CEE countries. Therefore, MNEs often retain local brands. InBev, for example, kept the famous Staropramen brand in the Czech Republic and several other smaller brands such as Branik and Kelt.[12] However, the sales volume of a local brand is often too small to generate sufficient profits to cover the cost of upgrading and relaunching the brand, especially when it is aimed at the lower end of the market. Regionalization is often seen as a solution to this problem. Common regional strategy produces synergies and economies of scale;[13] such as, for example, Staropramen beer, which has been distributed around the whole CEE region. Centralized production for a group of countries allows firms to realize economies of scope and scale. Research and development centres are normally situated in MNEs' home countries. In order to improve efficiency, production locations are specialized by product line and are integrated into the regional or global production network of the multinational group (Schuh and Holzmüller, 2003).

Cost drivers actively affect business concentration. As consumers' needs are irrevocably homogenized, they result in internationally standardized products (Levitt, 1983). Economies of scale can be increased by participation in multiple markets where a standardized product is offered. Such an example is the electronics industry, where the economic advantages have shifted to companies that can produce the lowest cost components (Yip, 1989). Even if economies of scale and scope are exhausted, expanded market participation can accelerate the accumulation of learning and experience. Centralized purchasing can lower costs significantly. Rationalization of raw material orders significantly strengthens a firm's low-cost production advantage. Moreover, if the transportation costs are not very high, this might increase the opportunities for a firm's concentration. Of course, the absence of time pressure is also an important factor that affects the decision with regard to concentration. The difference in country costs and skills also has an impact on a firm's concentration capabilities. Concentration in low-cost or high-skill countries can increase productivities and reduce costs (Yip, 1989: 37). Product development costs can be reduced by developing several global or regional products and only a few national products.

The search for synergies between different business units leads to many restructuring operations. Those activities that do not correspond to a targeted profitability or return on investment ratio calculated on a mid-term or long-term basis are considered to be outlying activities and are sold as soon as possible. Duplication of a number of functions by these hundreds of subsidiaries and dozens of divisions that comprised these giant multi-product multinationals (for example, Unilever, Nestlé, Sara

Lee Corp.) reduced the firms' profitability and economic efficiency. For example, Nestlé launched an efficiency initiative called '2004+', which led to divestitures across company divisions. These include the German distribution company Trinks; the Eisman group of companies, which carried out home delivery of frozen foods; cocoa processing activities in York and Hamburg; the Goplana chocolate business in Poland; non-core sugar confectionery businesses; a biscuit business in Central America; mashed potato producers in Germany and the Netherlands; French fries businesses in Canada and the USA, which were sold to McCain; a milk powder business in the Netherlands; and a chilled dairy business in Turkey.[14]

Using empirical evidence, Tozanli (2005) shows the move of the largest 100 food-processing MNEs towards globalization. She concludes that it is no longer the company's size or the breadth of activities in its portfolio that determine the efficiency of a multinational food-processing enterprise but, rather, it is a delicate combination of core activities and their geographical spread across the world that is significant.

Competitive drivers are a question of competitor choice; while market, cost and governmental globalization drivers are fixed for an industry at any given time. Competitors can, themselves, raise the potential of their industry for globalization. Let us take the automotive industry, for example. If certain leading European car companies concentrate production and become more competitive with American manufacturers, for instance, the Americans are pressed to enter more markets so that increased production volume lowers costs (Yip, 1989).

Government globalization drivers depend on the rules set by the national governments. Host governments influence MNEs' globalization plans through trade policies, technical standards and marketing regulations. Measures such as high import tariffs and quotas, non-tariff barriers, export subsidies, local content requirements, currency and capital flow restrictions, and requirements on technology transfer affect MNEs' globalization strategies. The easing of government restrictions, Yip argues, 'can set off a rush for expanded market participation' (1989: 38).

EU membership is an example of such an easing of government restrictions. Are the outcomes an expanded market participation and concentration of production? Meyer and Jensen (2003) analyze the effect of EU membership on the corporate strategies of FDI in CEE. They confirm the argument that the removal of trade barriers, and the consequent economic integration, facilitates the access of Western European businesses to CEE. As trade barriers no longer exist, 'operations across Europe will be integrated to a higher degree, which in turn may lead to centralization of production facilities and therefore closure of peripheral operations' (Meyer and Jensen, 2003: 295). Eden (2001) arrives at the same conclusion, arguing that regional integration leads to improved economies of scale and scope, increased efficiency through the rationalization and reallocation of firms' activities, and improved inter-regional linkages. Benito *et al.* (2003: 447) present similar findings; namely, that 'regional integration promotes the widening of markets, and because "insiders" have easier access to the larger market they are, all else being equal, in a better position than "outsiders" to exploit economies of scale as well as economies of scope and comparative advantages of the various member countries within the EU'. Benito *et al.* argue that the liberalization of trade and factor movements within an area should also increase the level of competition throughout the area. As a result, actors that are less efficient will leave the market; those that remain in an industry are likely to be the most competitive. In this sense, one can suppose that MNEs, as the strongest competitors in the EU market, will go for restructurings and optimization plans now that CEE countries are joining the EU club.

Crookell (1986) suggests that subsidiaries take on two specialized roles as trade barriers are reduced/removed – rationalization-integration and world product mandate. Rationalization-integration occurs when the subsidiary specializes in a narrow set of value activities (Crookell, 1990). In this case, the parent company is responsible for all associated activities; such as, for example, contracts with suppliers and distributors, product development, and R&D (Birkinshaw and Morrison, 1995). By contrast, the world product mandate occurs when the subsidiary has the 'responsibility for product renewal and export marketing' (Crookell 1986: 1061). The subsidiary is responsible for the R&D, manufacturing and marketing of a product or product line globally (Crookell 1986, 1990). As such, the subsidiary works with the parent company to develop and implement corporate strategy. Subsidiaries under world product mandate are relatively autonomous, and there is a significant likelihood of being embedded in the host economy.

Subsidiary management literature (see Gupta and Govindarajan, 1991; Martinez and Jarillo, 1991; Roth and Morrison, 1992; Birkinshaw and Morrison, 1995) offers several typologies of MNEs subsidiary roles that hint at companies' willingness to embed in the host economies. According to Gupta and Govindarajan (1991), an MNE is a network of capital, product, and knowledge flows. Knowledge flows are a characteristic of the modern global company and comprise the magnitude of transactions (the extent to which subsidiaries engage in knowledge transfer) and the directionality of the transactions (whether subsidiaries are the provider

or receiver of knowledge). Based on these two dimensions of knowledge flows, Gupta and Govindarajan define four generic subsidiary roles:
(1) global innovator, (2) integrated player, (3) implementer, and (4) local
innovator. All the four types of subsidiary differ on autonomy, capabilities and product inflows. This suggests that the level and direction
of knowledge flows is an important factor in differentiating subsidiary
roles (Harzing and Noorderhaven, 2006). MNEs that follow transnational
strategies (in the way defined by Bartlett and Ghoshal, 1989) have subsidiaries responding to the role of global innovators, as inter-subsidiary
flows are more important than flows between the parent company and
the subsidiaries (Harzing and Noorderhaven, 2006). These subsidiaries
are less embedded in the local milieu than the local innovators. The
implementer subsidiaries might be expected to dominate in global MNEs,
as the flows go from the parent company to the subsidiaries. Harzing and
Noorderhaven (2006) tried to identify whether, within the group of local
innovators (typical for MNEs following multi-domestic strategies), there
were subsidiaries that were virtually completely isolated from the parent
company. They discovered that the local innovator type of subsidiary
consists of two rather different groups of subsidiaries. The first group
possesses an average level of capabilities, which, however, are not shared
to a significant degree with other parts of the MNE network through
knowledge flows, probably because they are locally bound. The second
group has a very low level of capabilities and seems almost completely
isolated from the remainder of the MNE network, which could lead to a
self-reinforcing cycle. Overall, Harzing and Noorderhaven's study (2006)
indicates that subsidiary knowledge inflows and outflows have increased
substantially since the 1990s. It would therefore seem that more and
more companies are becoming closer to the ideal type of transnational
corporation (Bartlett and Ghoshal, 1989), and that differentiation in
subsidiary roles within the MNE has increased.

Depending on their level of competence, foreign affiliates might serve
a strategic or operational role. Strategic activities include R&D activities
and parent company functions, while operational activities are those
related to sales and manufacturing. According to the scope of their activities, subsidiaries are classified as miniature replicas, rationalized affiliates
and single activity affiliates.

Miniature replicas are established in order to avoid tariffs and as a
means of placating the host governments. They are a duplication of
the parent company, although not with the same scale of production.
These types of subsidiaries are not involved in R&D activities, but might
modify products introduced by the parent company. As Pearce (1999)

points out, these subsidiaries have a large product mix but supply a limited market. They follow market-seeking strategies, and the relationship between the parent company and the affiliates is weakly developed; that is, the subsidiaries are, essentially, independent from the parent company. These types of subsidiary are not considered as being embedded in the host economies. As a result of increasing liberalization of trade between states and regions, these subsidiaries are becoming increasingly uncompetitive and many of them have been closed (Pearce, 1992).

Rationalized subsidiaries are closely integrated in the network of the parent company. They follow an efficiency-seeking strategy, aim at optimizing costs over multiple locations, and often produce a small range of products. Fundamentally, a rationalized production subsidiary is not associated with basic research and its activities are of an operational character, rather than strategic.

Single-activity affiliates are a mixture of rationalized subsidiaries and miniature replicas. On one hand, they undertake a single aspect of a value-added activity; on the other hand, they might be part of the company's rationalized strategy. These affiliates are not involved in strategic planning or decision-making activities (Narula, 2001).

Given the effects of regional integration on economic activities such as reorganization and rationalization, one might conclude that some changes in subsidiary roles are inevitable. As Birkinshaw and Hood (2000) point out, subsidiary roles evolve over time due both to factors internal to the MNE and to the changing external environment – such as regionalization and liberalization. Some of the changes that have happened in CEE MNE subsidiaries are analyzed later in this book. Once an MNE rationalizes its number of subsidiaries or reorganizes activities across borders, the various units are likely to experience changes in their scope and areas of responsibility (Birkinshaw, 1996). Quite often, 'strategic centres' are created. These represent subsidiaries with a wide scope of activities, as well as high competence levels. A good example of the establishment of such a centre is the European Export and Shared Services Centre created by InBev after the Czech Republic entered the EU. The Czech strategic centre aims at handling exports, finance and procurement activities for InBev breweries in 12 European countries.

Regionalization and globalization requires a centralized, vertical coordination of the MNEs' activities worldwide (Tozanli, 2005: 7). These phenomena tend to enhance the forces of centralization, and to shift organizational power from the subsidiaries to company headquarters (Ghoshal, 1987). 'The headquarters has a global responsibility for issues that involve activities crossing national boundaries while the subsidiary's role is limited to local/regional operating environment' (Bartlett and Ghoshal, 1989: 61). Therefore, the subsidiaries have less autonomy and fewer opportunities to take individual decisions and, hence, fewer opportunities to embed in the local economies.

To summarize, the combination of IB literature and the SI approach allows for better understanding of MNE behaviour in CEE and, more precisely, of the forces that determine the embeddedness of food MNEs in the region. The SI approach stresses the importance of a national innovation system to the attraction and embedding of FDI by giving special attention to the role of national institutions and government. IB literature sheds a light on the factors that shape companies' business strategies. The synthesis of these approaches provides a tool with which to explain the level of embeddedness of food MNEs in the first-wave EU accession countries (Hungary and the Czech Republic) and in the second-wave countries (Bulgaria and Romania). A phenomenon such as EU membership, which happened during the period I have been writing this book, significantly helped to identify the factors that have the strongest impact on MNE strategies.

Causality

Variables

The general idea is that if the gap between institutional (macro) and production (micro) integration is too large, this might cause both economic and political costs that would undermine the enlargement process. We might face a variation on the continuum with two extreme positions: technologically stagnant East/West production networks created by MNEs that resemble Mexican *maquilladora* types of relationship, or flexible East/West networks that allow for the transfer of capital, technological innovation, marketing power, management know-how, cultural influences and exchanges that would pave the way for an Eastward deepening of integration on the micro-level. This book attempts to find where EU member CEECs are situated on this continuum in order to be able to provide policy recommendations that could improve the understanding and relevance of the roots of these networks and their influence on states and their sectors.[15]

The pattern of production network is identified as the dependent variable. One can discern strong or weak patterns. The example of a multinational that stands as a 'cathedral in the desert' indicates a weak pattern of production network. The example of a multinational company that is linked to the national innovation system – that is, local agencies, research institutes and regional authorities, creating conditions for an upgrading of local companies and so on – is an example of a strong pattern of production network, and of embeddedness in the local economy.

The independent variables are the local absorptive capacity of the country, the national government and regional policies, the entry strategies of the companies, and MNEs' business strategies, globalization and regionalization of markets.

Therefore, the following hypotheses are derived from the literature:

Generating hypotheses

Hypothesis 1:
The preservation and effective restructuring of existing socialist supplier networks helped the formation of transnational linkages between local companies and multinationals, which created conditions for industrial upgrading.

Under effective restructuring of socialist supplier networks, I understand the processes of land restitution and de-collectivization of state farms happened smoothly and with minimal losses.

In this book, I present the cases of Hungary and the Czech Republic, which are examples of the successful transformation of their supplier networks – that is, agricultural sectors. Since Hungary and the Czech Republic had competitive agricultural producers, they enjoyed benefits from the FDI inflows. In contrast to these successful examples, this book presents the cases of Bulgaria and Romania, where the reforms happened after a significant delay caused by political disagreement and multiple changes in legislation and regulations. Unlike Hungary – where the logic behind privatization was oriented towards the future; that is, considering how to preserve the cooperatives so that they could operate after the reorganization – in Bulgaria and Romania, the only consideration appeared to be the present moment, the outcome of which were massive liquidations and destruction of the cooperative farms. Moreover, land was returned to owners according to historical boundaries and this led to considerable fragmentation of the land, which hampered the modernization of agriculture and the persistence of raw agricultural supplies. Multinational food processing companies had no choice other than to source good quality raw materials abroad, as they could not find local supplies of the required quality. Hence, the opportunities for the MNEs to contribute towards the development of local suppliers were very low in Bulgaria and Romania.

Hypothesis 2:
The duration of investment matters for the level of embeddness of MNEs.

By duration of investment, I mean the length of time for which an MNE has been operating in a given country. The logic is that the longer this period, the greater is the likelihood of the company embedding in the local economy. MNEs in some CEECs (for example, the Czech Republic and Hungary) seemed to be more beneficially embedded in local and national production networks because the privatization process there was initiated much earlier, at the beginning of 1990s, while in Bulgaria and Romania the privatization process began in the mid- and late 1990s. Foreign investors had time to acquaint themselves with the local environment and create relationships with the domestic companies based on mutual trust. However, EU membership seriously questioned these observations. This book disproves this hypothesis, arguing that, no matter how long food companies have been present in a given country, in a free trade regime they can easily leave the country (for example, Unilever Hungary, Kraft Food Hungary).

Hypothesis 3:
The entry strategies of MNEs pre-determine the level of embeddness in the host country.

There are three types of entry strategies: (1) market-seeking; (2) efficiency-seeking; and (3) asset-augmented. Companies interested in the local market – that is, pursuing market-seeking strategies, as do food MNEs – have less willingness to embed in the local economies, compared with those that follow the other two types of strategies. The in-depth case studies of Nestlé, Unilever, and InBev illustrate that, as food MNEs are attracted mainly by the host market, as soon as they find a more efficient way to supply it (for example, by importing) they will close sites and leave the country.

Hypothesis 4:
The higher the absorptive capacity of the local economy, the higher the likelihood of knowledge and technological spillovers from MNEs to local companies.

The ability of the host economy to upgrade its industrial development depends crucially on the relative technological capabilities of recipient and transmitter: the greater the distance between them, the lower the intensity of linkages. By analyzing the innovation policies of the four CEE countries and government policies to embed MNEs through financial measures and linkage creation programmes, this book establishes that countries such as Hungary and the Czech Republic have higher absorptive capacities than Bulgaria and Romania. Hence, they benefited more from the know-how, management skills and technological knowledge of the MNEs than Bulgaria and Romania.

Hypothesis 5:
MNEs' policies of cooperation with local actors and institutions are pre-determined by companies' business strategies.

Companies following global and transnational strategies, such as food MNEs, are highly centralized and integrated compared with those pursing a multi-domestic strategy. Transnational and global companies focus on core brands, have global supply chains and global distribution networks and, hence, there is a lower likelihood of them sourcing locally and internationalizing R&D centres abroad. In order to maximize profit and increase efficiency, global companies follow global restructuring plans, which, as shown in this book, lead to closures of divisions and plants not only in CEE, but also in Western Europe.

Hypothesis 6:
The more that national policies focus on programmes and initiatives to encourage the linkages between MNEs and domestic suppliers, the greater the prospects local companies have to upgrade and catch up with Western companies.

Network support activities involve many different kinds of policy that give support to local and international networking and diffusion activities, including the appropriate use of fiscal incentives and financial institutions, and support for domestic small- and large-firm involvement with foreign company networks. Examples of these are the National Subcontracting Programmes in the Czech Republic and the Hungarian Integrator Programme, which aims at the integration of domestic firms with foreign firms through supply linkages.

Hypothesis 7:
Regionalization and EU integration facilitate MNE restructuring and reorganization plans.

Seeking global and regional competitiveness, MNEs aim at increased efficiency through improved economies of scale and scope. Based on the analysis of interviews at companies' headquarters and subsidiaries, this book shows that the removal of trade barriers as an outcome of EU membership made it easy for MNEs to follow their plans for global optimization, and to divest from all non-profitable activities and to close plants all over Europe. As there are no longer any governmental constraints and logistics are significantly improved, MNEs can easily supply different markets by means of imports.

Conclusion

This chapter outlined the major theoretical contributions that underpin this study. Posing the question as to which factors predetermine the level of embeddedness of food MNEs in CEE, the chapter laid the foundations of an argument that considers the importance of two major variables: (1) the national absorptive capacity of the countries; and (2) the business strategies. It is argued that countries with good absorptive capacity – such as Hungary and the Czech Republic – would embed MNEs more deeply than Bulgaria and Romania, which are characterized by weaker SI. It should be noted that the extent to which subsidiaries cooperate with local economic actors and institutions depends on the strategy that the company follows: multi-domestic, global or transnational. These strategies are shaped by factors such as regionalization (the EU, for example) and globalization, which facilitate MNEs in their efforts to reach worldwide efficiency and competitiveness, and lead to a lower level of embeddedness. The chapter introduced seven hypotheses to be tested in this book.

Part II
CEEC Economies and Global Company Strategies

2
The Global Strategies of Food Companies and their Impact on the CEE Region

Introduction

Truly global companies are characterized by strong centralized management: hence, there is less decision-making authority at the local level; a strong global distribution network and global supply chain; applied R&D; and an absence of innovation from local firms and weak/missing backward linkages with local suppliers. All these features imply weak embeddedness of global MNEs in the host economies. However, there are forces that influence MNEs' strategies; such as government regulations and protectionist measures, the socio-economic and political development of the country, the size of the market, national innovation systems, specificities of the sector where the companies operate, competitors, and so on. Therefore, the question is:

> Do the food MNEs implement their global strategies in the CEE region or there are factors that shape their policies and level of embeddedness?

This chapter answers that question from the point of view of the parent company by analyzing the global strategies of the largest food MNEs in the CEE region: Nestlé (Switzerland), Unilever (UK/Holland) and InBev (Belgium). In-depth interviews were conducted with the managers responsible for the CEE region at the headquarters of these multinationals. The conversations with CEE managers were organized around a semi-open questionnaire (see the Appendix). They reveal the contribution of MNEs to CEE economies and test those companies' affinity for embedding in local economies.

The chapter is divided into two parts. The first part examines the global strategies of Nestlé, Unilever, and InBev, and the second part shows the impact of those global strategies on the performance of their CEE subsidiaries. The final section concludes.

The global strategies of Unilever, InBev, and Nestlé

Unilever

Unilever Group is the third largest packaged food company in the world, with a market share of 2.54 per cent in 2004.[1] The company specializes in a wide range of packaged food categories, including ice cream, soup, frozen food and meal replacement products.[2]

In 2000, Unilever implemented a new global strategy named 'Path to Growth'. The aim of the 'Path to Growth' strategy was to increase global competitiveness. Hence, the management staff of the company made three fundamental decisions.

The first decision was to streamline Unilever's portfolio and activities by focusing on fewer, stronger brands. Amongst the company's best-known global and regional brands are Knorr, Magnum, Bertolli, Findus, Hellmann's, Marmite, Birds Eye, Flora/Becel and Rama. Apart from foods, Unilever is also involved in household and personal care items; the core brands in this field are CIF, Domestos, Omo, Surf, and Radiant.

The second decision was to focus on developing and emerging markets where the company had leading marketing positions.

The third choice was to add vitality to its products. At the heart of the strategy was the concentration of resources behind Unilever's best growth opportunities.

The company was restructured and was split between Unilever Best-foods and home and personal care divisions.

In line with the new strategy, the distribution network of the company was improved; reorganization of the whole production network and divestment of non-performing businesses was undertaken. The supply chain was restructured in order to concentrate on a base of 150 key sites. Patrick Cescau, Unilever Group Chief Executive, explained supply chain reorganization in the following way:[3]

> Our supply chains are becoming more regional or global, with responsibility for managing them shifting away from local markets, so that the people on the ground can concentrate solely on the customer, on delivering the plan. We've started in Europe, with a regional supply chain based in Switzerland.

The IT systems and the management structure of the company were reorganized. Unilever is outsourcing transactional operations in IT, finance and human relations so that it can focus on global brands (Unilever Annual Report, 2006). In short, Unilever is making a fundamental change in the way it operates.

Market share

Unilever has a large and fragmented packaged food portfolio that extends into many sectors and across all major markets. In 2006, Unilever performed strongly in those areas it had identified as growth priorities and where it had invested heavily; namely, developing and emerging markets and the personal care business, which grew by an impressive 6.3 per cent. The global strategy of the company was to invest massively in order to obtain leadership positions in high growth areas, and this strategy has proved to be the right one.

The major share of Unilever sales was derived from Western, Central and Eastern Europe – 38 per cent of company's net sales for 2006.[4] However, the company's performance in Europe had not been good in recent years, as sales in the region were consistently under pressure from competitors and retailers – especially in Western Europe, where operating profit declined by 29 per cent in 2004 (Unilever Annual Review 2004). From then, Unilever redoubled its efforts (innovations and strong marketing support) and this returned the region to modest growth. In 2006, sales grew by 1 per cent – entirely from volume trading. Market shares were broadly stable with gains in ice cream, soups, deodorants, and body care products. However, there were losses in laundry and hair care products, and tea (Unilever Annual Report, 2006: 14).

In 2006, Unilever's performance remained strong in Central and Eastern Europe, driven by double-digit growth in Russia.

Focus on global brands

The global packaged food market is very dynamic. Consolidation is widespread. Companies involved in several business areas are increasingly focusing on core activities. There is ongoing globalization of brands, which allows companies to gain economies of scale in both production and marketing. This trend is set to continue as consumers increasingly opt for high-profile branded products.[5] 'We are passionate about developing great global brands and bringing them to market brilliantly. Our Foods and Home and Personal Care teams invest heavily in world-class innovation in order to create global brand ideas that can be rolled out fast' (Unilever Annual Report, 2006: 20). Unilever has a number of large global brands – including 12 with an annual turnover of over €1 billion – that often depend on global or regional development and supply chains. In 2006, the 12 brands with an annual turnover of over €1 billion grew by 5 per cent, which demonstrates the power of focus.

To increase its growth and competitiveness, Unilever focused on its most powerful brands, reducing its overall portfolio by around 75 per cent – from 1,600 leading brands to around 400. The company was involved in an extensive divestment programme of brands that did not fit within the 'power' brand portfolio – such as Batchelors, Oxo, and the Dutch snacks subsidiary Mora, which was sold in December 2005. As part of this strategy, the company acquired a number of important food companies and brands, such as Bestfoods,[6] Slim Fast, Ben & Jerry's Homemade, and Amora Maille in 2000. Unilever also concentrated in organic products and acquired the Scottish organic company, Go Organic, in 2001.

New product development forms an important part of Unilever's growth strategy. Since 2004, the focus has been on developing healthier eating options, which is reflected in the launch of its Nutrition Enhancement Programme. This initiative, commenced in 2005, looks at the nutritional impact of all its packaged food products. Between 2005 and 2006, Unilever significantly reduced the amount of fats, salt and sugar in its products. In 2006, the company spent over €900 million on R&D worldwide (Unilever Annual Report, 2006: 20).

Functional food is becoming increasingly profitable as companies exploit changing consumer lifestyles and demands. In this way, Unilever joined the trend of other packaged food manufacturers in gaining a stake in functional food sales. This fits in with Unilever's increased focus on functional food, in order to tap into the growing 'wellness' trend as consumers become more health conscious.

Other developments within Unilever include the extension of brands in order to drive growth. For example, within Unilever's biggest brand, Knorr, a number of recent introductions include the launch of Cubitos low-cost seasoning cubes and powdered seasonings, which were designed specifically for low-income families and those in developing markets. In ice cream, innovations such as 'Magnum 7 Sins', 'Magnum Senses', 'Magnum Light', 'Carte d'Or Origin', 'Carte d'Or Fruit & Fresh' and new 'Cornetto' variants were introduced between 2004 and 2005. The nutritional content of ice cream products was improved: artificial colours and flavours were removed, the fruit content increased, and sugar levels reduced in water ices across the children's portfolio in Western Europe.

Restructurings and management changes

The chief executive of the company, in the 2006 Annual Report, underlined:

> Restoring Unilever's competitiveness has involved making a lot of changes to the business. In order to deliver sustained growth and create value for shareholders, we have reformed our governance, over-hauled our organization and put in place a whole new strategy to take the business forward. (Unilever Annual Report, 2006: 11)

The company reorganized or divested under-performing businesses and fully integrated Bestfoods. These processes involved 8,000 redundancies and the sale or closure of some 30 sites. Following the announcement that Procter & Gamble would acquire the Gillette Company in early 2005, which made Procter & Gamble the largest consumer products manufacturer in the world, the pressure has increased on Unilever to fine-tune its restructuring. Within the same month as the 2005 Procter & Gamble acquisition, the company announced sweeping changes to its leadership organization and abandoned its dual chairman/CEO structure, which had been in place for decades.

The 2005 restructuring has led to a number of improvements. The pace of implementation has been rapid: management changes, a clearer separation of responsibilities between regional and brand management, and the disposal of fragrances are key highlights of the first half of 2005. In 2005, Unilever introduced a new, simpler structure that comprises three regions (Europe, the Americas, and Asia/AMET), whose managements are responsible for market operations; and two categories of management (foods; and home and personal care products) responsible for innovation and product management. This is part of the new global 'One Unilever' programme, which commenced in 2004. Its goal is to eradicate duplication; leverage Unilever's scale; and help the company focus on consumers, customers and the marketplace, which will also allow the company to fund future growth largely through cost savings. These latest changes are completely congruent with and build on the 'One Unilever' principles. The company's rationalization continued. After the sale of the Unilever Cosmetics International business[7] to Coty in 2005 for around US$800 million, the company turned its attention to its ailing European operations, and, in particular, its frozen food business, which includes Birds Eye. In February, Unilever closed the Birds Eye plant in Grimsby, UK, with the loss of 620 jobs, and had plans for the possible closures of the Lowestoft site in Suffolk and the Hull site in

East Yorkshire. The launch of a study into its frozen food brands – which include Iglo, Findus and Birds Eye – was announced in September 2005. Given the focus on core business, and following the December 2004 sale of its frozen pizza and baguette business, it was likely that the study's outcome would lead to the ending of Unilever's involvement in this sector. In addition, sales in Europe had been consistently undermined by the development of large-scale retailers, whose private label offers were increasingly sophisticated, as well as the ascendance of hard discounters, particularly in the German market. To this end, the company was seeking to rationalize its portfolio there, and possibly considering selling off its frozen foods business in the region.

Until 2005, the bulk of Unilever's external operations were to do with divestments and, to a lesser extent, acquisitions. However, the company has a few external operations that still impact directly on its core businesses. There were no material acquisitions during 2004. On 18 February 2003, the company announced an agreement to acquire the remaining unheld shares in CPC/Aji Asia (a joint venture with operations in six countries) from Ajinomoto Co. Inc., Japan, for a total of US$381 million (€338 million). Under this agreement, the remaining outstanding shares were purchased as planned in March 2004, and Unilever had full management control of the business with effect from 25 March 2003.

The Pepsi/Lipton Tea Partnership in the USA was formed in 1991 in a bid to give leverage to the Lipton ready-to-drink tea brand. On 14 October 2003, the company announced the creation of Pepsi Lipton International, a 50:50 joint venture between Unilever and PepsiCo, to market and distribute ready-to-drink tea in several international markets outside North America. This business started trading on 1 January 2004, and the scope of the joint venture was expanded to include some additional territories during the year.

The chemicals business in India (Hindustan Lever Chemicals) was merged with Tata Chemicals. The joint venture with Jerónimo Martins in Portugal agreed to acquire the Bestfoods Portugal business. This level of activity might seem extreme but, in 2003, the company disposed of 50 businesses with a total turnover of approximately €1.13 billion.

Distribution network

For the distribution of its products, Unilever mainly uses traditional routes – wholesalers, chains and independent grocery outlets – in addition to Unilever's own sales force and independent distributors. The company has its own distribution centres, satellite warehouses and

Box 2.1   The history of Unilever

Unilever is an English–Dutch multinational company. Its origins go back to the late nineteenth century, in the Netherlands, when Jurgens and Van den Bergh – two family businesses of butter merchants – began to export actively to the UK. In the early 1870s, they became interested in a new product made from beef fat and milk – margarine. They realized that this new product was a very good substitute for butter and could be mass-produced. At approximately the same time (the mid-1880s), in the North of England, a successful wholesale family grocery business run by William Lever started to produce a new type of soap. The addition of copra or pine kernel oil helped it to lather more easily than traditional soaps made from animal fats.

Jurgens and Van den Bergh joined to create Margarine Unie. On 2 September 1929, in one of the largest mergers of that time, Margarine Unie teamed up with Lever Brothers to create Unilever. The reason for this merger was that the tough economic conditions and World War I made trading difficult for everyone. During this period, many businesses formed trade associations to protect their shared interests. With their businesses expanding fast, Margarine Unie and the Lever Brothers started negotiations, intending to stop producing the same types of products; instead, they agreed to merge – and so Unilever was created.

The first decade of Unilever started with the Great Depression and ended with World War II. The business not only rationalized operations, but also continued to diversify. Unilever's operations around the world began to fragment, but the business continued to expand further into the foods market and increased its investment in R&D. Business prospered because of new technologies. The European Economic Community led to rising standards of living in the West, while new markets opened up in emerging economies around the globe. The world economy expanded. Unilever followed the same path. It developed new products, entered new markets and ran a highly ambitious acquisition programme. It survived the hard economic conditions and high inflation of the 1970s. By then, Unilever was one of the world's biggest companies, but it decided to focus its portfolio and rationalize its businesses on core products and brands. In the 1990s, the business expanded into Central and Eastern Europe, and further sharpened its focus on fewer product categories, leading to the sale or withdrawal of two thirds of its brands. In 2000, it launched 'Path to

Growth', a five-year strategic plan, and, in 2004, it further sharpened its focus on the needs of twenty-first century consumers with its 'Vitality' mission (Euromonitor International, Unilever, 2006: 22). Unilever has two headquarters in London (Unilever PLC) responsible for home and personal care products, and Unilever (NV) in Rotterdam dealing with food brands. Unilever NV and Unilever PLC are the twin parent companies of the Unilever group. They have separate legal entities and separate stock exchange listings for their shares, but operate as a single entity.

Source: Unilever, www.unilever.com

storage facilities, and uses public storage facilities when needed (Unilever Annual Report, 2006).

To increase distribution efficiency and obtain the most favourable shelf conditions in-store, Unilever has formed strategic alliances with a number of major retailers in the company's key markets, including Wal-Mart (USA), Tesco (UK), Carrefour (France), and Ahold (the Netherlands). In addition, it has a number of joint ventures that help to widen its distribution channels. One example of this is the Pepsi Lipton International partnership, which ensures the distribution of its key ready-to-drink tea brand outside North America. Unilever intends to find further distribution synergies. The company's 'Path to Growth' initiative is further focused on improving the distribution network and gaining economies of scale through finding global synergies. IT systems have been implemented across many global markets, linking the company's factory systems with those of its key suppliers and stockists, thus allowing suppliers to manage the stock levels by examining factory systems with increased sales as a result. In addition, Unilever has implemented a so-called 'efficient customer response' (ECR) system with the aim of streamlining distribution practices and stock management systems, as well as providing a tool to forecast consumer demand.[8]

Unilever's foodservice division, Unilever Bestfoods Food Solutions (UBF), distributes to large-scale customers such as fast food and hotel chains, restaurateurs and foodservice providers. Operating in 65 countries, UBF ensures that Unilever products are available through a wide range of channels. For example, Hellmann's low-fat dressings are available through branded dispensers placed in salad bars in major fast food chains in North and Latin America, while the Knorr 100% Soup Bar is available to foodservice providers through Knorr Total Soup Solutions.

It has to be heavily underscored that Unilever has a policy of selling its products in nearly all countries throughout the world, and manufactures in many of them. Where it does not have production plants, Unilever supplies the market by importing. For example, in the European Union, where trade barriers do not exist, Unilever makes many of its products in only a few member countries for sale in all the others. 'The chosen manufacturing configuration is generally determined by an optimized regional sourcing strategy, which takes account of requirements for innovation, quality, service, cost and flexibility' (Unilever Annual Report 2006: 6). This strategy explains why Unilever reorganized all its production facilities in CEECs after they entered the EU club.

InBev

InBev is the world's number one brewing company. In addition to its global brands – Stella Artois, Beck's, Leffe, Bass, Hoegaarden and Staropramen – InBev produces and distributes a range of local, private label products. It also has in its product portfolio a small number of flavoured alcoholic beverages (FABs). With the addition of AmBev, InBev is now also involved in the production, distribution and sale of soft drinks, other non-alcoholic beverages, and malt through AmBev's directly or indirectly owned subsidiaries in Brazil and elsewhere in Latin America.[9]

InBev follows a four-pillar 'SuperVoyager' strategy that focuses on a strong brand portfolio, world-class efficiency, winning the consumers at the point of connection, and strong external growth by innovations and financial discipline (InBev, 2006). These goals are operationalized through the model 'cost–connect–win', which means the capture of non-productive money from within overall cost activities and its conversion into productive money by supporting InBev's brands and sales and marketing capabilities.

Market share

InBev is a global market leader by volume, ahead of its global competitors Anheuser-Busch and SABMiller. According to Euromonitor International, InBev owes much of its leader status to the fact that it was born with a very strong presence in non-developed markets – in particular, Latin America.[10] InBev is also a global leader in the beer market, thanks to its lager portfolio – in particular, its global flagship brands range.

Box 2.2   The history of InBev

InBev appeared in 2004, when Interbrew and Companhia de Bebidas das Américas (AmBev) merged to create the world's number one leader in the brewing industry. InBev has 13 per cent of the world beer market, holding the number one or number two position in over 20 key markets around the world, and possesses three global flagship brands: Stella Artois, Brahma and Beck's. The merging of the companies was marked by the combination of the elements of the names of In**terbrew** and Am**Bev**.

Interbrew was born back in 1366. It started from a brewery called Den Horen, located in Leuven. In 1717, Sebastien Artois, master brewer, purchased the brewery and changed its name to Artois. Interbrew was formed in 1987 from the merger of Brasseries Artois, then the second largest brewer in Belgium, and Brasseries Piedboeuf, then the largest brewer in Belgium and the brewer of Jupiler. Both of these brewers had a history of previous acquisitions. Further acquisition continued after the establishment of Interbrew, starting with the purchase of Hoegaarden in 1989 and Belle-Vue in 1990, and continuing through the 1990s and 2000s with takeovers, including that of Labatt in Canada, Oriental Brewery in South Korea, Sun Interbrew in Russia and the Ukraine, Bass Beers and Whitbread Beer in the UK, and Diebels and Beck & Co. in Germany. At the time of the takeover, Interbrew was the world's third largest beer company by volume.

AmBev's origins date back to 1885, but the Companhia de Bebidas das Américas (AmBev) was born when the brewers of Brahma and Antarctica beer in Brazil merged in 1999. While Brazil is the world's fourth largest beer market, and the largest in Latin America, AmBev nevertheless sought to grow beyond its borders into Argentina, Venezuela, Uruguay and Paraguay. It also acquired activities in Central America, Peru and the Caribbean.

Source: InBev, www.inbev.com

Lager is the company's core business interest. InBev is also present in dark beer, stout, and non-/low-alcohol lager; however, these all make small contributions to total revenue. Lager's performance is set to mirror that of beer. Investment in the non-/low-alcohol portfolio might also prove very successful for InBev, as the growth in this sector is expected to be above average – a 5 per cent volume compound annual growth rate (CAGR) between 2005 and 2010.

InBev's outlook in Eastern Europe looks bright. Beer is forecast to post robust growth between 2005 and 2010, with a volume CAGR of 6 per cent. The key category is the premium lager, which is set to post a volume CAGR of 13 per cent over the forecast period. One of the most attractive markets with high growth potential is Russia. InBev intends to continue its interest in Russia, with beer set to post a volume CAGR of 9 per cent between 2005 and 2010. Premium lager offers the greatest rewards, with a volume CAGR of 19 per cent expected over the forecast period, a trend that InBev is well equipped to exploit, having purchased the rights to Lowenbrau and started local production of Hoegaarden in 2005.

The 'early stage' developing markets such as the Ukraine, for example, hold the highest growth potential, with an anticipated volume CAGR of 6 per cent between 2005 and 2010. Romania is another prospective market anticipated to reach 9 per cent growth for this period. In developing markets in the 'latter stage' of development, growth is forecast to be more modest, with a volume CAGR of 3 per cent in Poland and less than 1 per cent in Hungary. The Czech market is set to contract by a negative volume CAGR of 1 per cent between 2005 and 2010. Given this outlook, InBev's strategy is very attentive and, when looking forward, the company focuses on imported lager, as was the case in Poland with the launch of Beck's in 2005.[11]

Part of InBev's international strategy is the licensing of its private label products, in addition to the brewing of a number of partner brands, which ensures its presence in a wide geographical area. The company also has a number of strategic alliances and joint ventures in several markets, which, again, help it to boost its market spread. Amongst its best-known partner-brands are Budweiser (a partnership with Anheuser-Busch) and Cristal (a partnership with Cerveceria Bucanero SA).

The company has extended its agreements with partners in key markets, which has enabled it to increase its market presence. For example, in May 2004, InBev announced that it was to distribute Beck's through its already established alliance with Guangzhou Zhujiang Brewery in China, whilst Carlton & United Breweries in Australia extended its InBev portfolio to include Leffe and Hoegaarden, in addition to its existing agreement for Stella Artois.

Focus on global brands

As a truly global company, InBev focuses on the promotion of its global brands, although it produces and distributes many local brands, as the brewing industry is very much a locally rooted industry.

InBev has more than 200 brands, which are divided into global flagship brands, global speciality brands, multi-country brands and local brands, as well as brands it produces, markets or sells under licence. These individual categories are reflected in the level of marketing support each brand receives, with the greatest investment given to the company's global flagship brands. Global flagship brands are the heart of InBev's portfolio, and they comprise Stella Artois, Beck's, and Brahma. The first two brands came from the Interbrew stable, whilst Brahma is a former AmBev brand that has been given a global launch since the establishment of InBev.

Stella Artois is the company's most successful brand. It received considerable marketing support in recent years, including standardized global packaging and advertising during the fiscal year 2004. Beck's also benefited from an increase in marketing resources beginning in January 2003, which led to an increased share of the global beer market.[12]

Among the global speciality brands are speciality Belgian beers, which are marketed to give international appeal. Hoegaarden is a Belgian wheat (or white) beer with a brewing process that gives it a cloudy-white final appearance, and a sweet yet sour taste. Leffe is a larger brand, comprising Leffe, Leffe Blonde, Leffe Brown, Leffe Triple and Leffe Radieuse/Vieille Cuvée. These beers are promoted as being an alternative to drinking wine with food; with Leffe Blonde is described as being suitable as a drink with everyday meals, whilst Leffe Triple is a stronger beer that is considered to be a good alternative to full-flavoured white wines.

The multi-country brands do not have the global reach of the global flagship brands; neither do they receive the same high level of promotion. Despite this, they are marketed across several countries. Brands in this division include the English ale Bass and Staropramen Czech lager, which is marketed in around 30 countries.

InBev's brand portfolio is dominated by local brands, as beer is very much a locally and regionally rooted product. Many of these brands have particular local appeal and relatively small distribution areas. However, their popularity in these areas is sufficient for them to continue to be produced and marketed by the appropriate subsidiary.

Rather than focusing on the development of new products since the merger, InBev has, instead, concentrated on maximizing the potential of its existing brands, in particular with regard to stimulating growth in the troubled Western European market. This strategy has largely focused on extending key brands belonging to the former Interbrew stable; however, there has been one major exception – the global launch of the former AmBev label Brahma. The company plans to use Brahma to stimulate growth in key mature developed markets where premium/imported lager is one of the few areas displaying discernable forward momentum.

Restructurings and management changes

Pursuing cost efficiencies is a key strategy at InBev. The company completed a range of administrative reforms and continued to overhaul its manufacturing infrastructure, closing a number of facilities following the merger in 2004.

Operational changes, aimed at reducing costs, included the key activities: adoption of longer-term supply contracts; centralization of media, as well as a reduction in the number of creative agencies the company deals with, down from 11 to 2; a reduction in the number of bottle types in circulation from 400 to 100; and supply chain initiatives centred around optimizing the company's brewery network.

During 2004, the company also made changes to its global sponsorship programme and took measures to reduce the cost of raw materials. One such measure involved the establishment of new relationships with new suppliers in low-cost countries.

With regard to the overhaul of its production infrastructure, the company followed the closure of breweries in the Netherlands (Breda), the UK (Manchester, Belfast) and Canada (New Westminster), as well as six facilities in China, with the divestment of its stake in Spanish brewer Damm and the Bosnian beer company Uniline in 2005. The company has downsized its Boddingtons plant in the UK. The sale in Bosnia follows the termination of local production in 2004. In addition, the company consolidated brewing operations in the Czech Republic, with manufacturing at its Branik brewery, which came under the auspices of the Pivovary Staropramen arm in the first quarter of 2007. The outlook for beer in the 'latter-stage' developing markets in Eastern Europe was very modest and the decision to rationalize in the Czech Republic could have been a reaction to this. Looking forward, Inbev has indicated that its restructuring programme will involve further closures and job losses, with cuts expected to affect operations in Belgium, largely as a result of the continued difficulties being experienced in Western Europe.

Distribution network

The creation of InBev has added considerably to the global distribution reach of both Interbrew and AmBev. In particular, InBev opened up Latin America to Interbrew, which previously did not have an extensive presence in this market. At the time of the merger, AmBev had been working towards widening its direct distribution channel. This policy was also adopted by Interbrew, which led to greater use of direct distributors in Western Europe, particularly during the fiscal year 2004. In Russia, InBev increased its number of distributor-employed dedicated sales agents in 2004, enabling wholesalers to focus exclusively on its brand portfolio.

Key to InBev's distribution strategy has been the development of its global field sales force academy, which has been used to train around 5000 sales staff by 2004. This has been developed to make it easier for the company to put as many new coolers in place as possible, mirroring AmBev's use of proprietary freezers, designed to keep beer at the −5°C temperature that Brazilians consider to be perfect for beer drinking, and to capitalize on the Brazilian preference for consumption at the point of sale. By the end of 2003, 193,000 freezers had been installed at the most significant points of sale in the Brazilian beer market. InBev believes that sales from coolers add considerably to volume sales, particularly over the summer; extending the cooler distribution network is therefore a major driver of sales growth.

In October 2004, InBev set up a strategic partnership with Gabriel Sedl-mayr Spaten-Franziskaner Brau. The partnership combines Spaten's beer business with Interbrew Deutschland. The move brought the Lowen-brau and Wissbier brands into Interbrew's portfolio, and consolidated the company's position in Germany (Euromonitor International, 2006a).

InBev is involved in several business agreements to distribute a number of beer and soft drinks products across Latin America. These include two agreements with PepsiCo; one a long-term agreement for the bottling and distribution of PepsiCo's soft drinks (which include Pepsi and the isotonic Gatorade) in Brazil as well as in other Latin American countries, plus a distribution deal whereby PepsiCo distributes AmBev's Guaraná Antarctica soft drink globally.

In July 2005, InBev entered into an agreement with PepsiCo to sell and distribute Beck's in Poland, with InBev using PepsiCo's distribution infrastructure to launch its global flagship brand.

To summarize, InBev has a strong global coverage, comprising extensive exposure to both developed markets and emerging regions. The company has a very strong product mix, with its portfolio comprising a combination of strong international brands and robust local labels. Its Skol label is the number three global beer brand. It invests heavily in marketing and advertising; as a result, its flagship brands enjoy a high profile. The development of globally standardized packaging, such as that for Stella Artois, fosters strong operational strategies. InBev has a very strong distribution network in the key market of Brazil, enjoying universal coverage in an otherwise fragmented sales area. The company has a strong portfolio of strategic alliances, which it has used to penetrate key markets – in particular, emerging markets. A licensing deal with Lion Nathan strengthened InBev's platform in Australasia, from which it has been able to attack both premium and imported lager.

Nestlé

Nestlé is the leading packaged food company in the world, with a large portfolio of brands, including Nescafé, Buitoni, Maggi, Nestea and Perrier. The company's headquarters are in Switzerland, and Nestlé has nearly 140 years' experience in the packaged food market. Originating as a maker of milk-based products, the company has repositioned itself, moving from a straightforward food manufacturer to a health and wellness company.

In addition to food products, Nestlé owns about 75 per cent of the global ophthalmology leader Alcon Inc. (ophthalmic drugs, contact lens solutions, and equipment for ocular surgery) and almost 27 per cent of the global cosmetic leader L'Oréal. The company operates 500 factories in 83 countries, a reduction from 511 in 2003. The company employed 247,000 people in 2004, down from 253,000 in 2003.[13]

Market share

Nestlé is one of very few companies to have a full global presence in a large number of packaged food sectors. Of its peers, only Unilever has a similar reach in terms of geographic markets as well as product sectors. Nestlé is present in Europe, Latin America, Northern America, Africa, the Middle East and the Asia-Pacific Region. The bulk of the company's sales are generated in its domestic regional market of Western Europe. Net sales in the region accounted for 36 per cent in 2004, when it ranked second behind Unilever with a 3.3 per cent share of packaged food. This represents a decline on the 2003 figure of 3.5 per cent, partially a result of a series of regional divestments in 2004, including the German frozen food distributor Eastman and the company's cocoa processing business. Other businesses that were sold include the company's Dutch potato business and powdered milk operation, as well as its chocolate brand Goplana in Poland.

As far as Eastern Europe is concerned, the company's sales in 2004 accounted for only 5 per cent of its turnover, the second lowest regional share after Australasia. The company ranked number one in the region in 2004 and led in dried processed food, soup and confectionery. By far, the biggest value sector for Nestlé in the region is confectionery, which

Box 2.3 The history of Nestlé

The foundations of Nestlé were laid in the 1860s. Henri Nestlé, who was a pharmacist, developed a food for babies who were unable to breastfeed. His first success was with a premature infant who could not tolerate his mother's milk or any of the usual substitutes. People quickly recognized the value of the new product, after Nestlé's new formula saved the child's life, and soon, Farine Lactée Henri Nestlé was being sold in much of Europe. In 1905, Nestlé merged with the Anglo-Swiss Condensed Milk Company. By the early 1900s, the company was operating factories in the United States, Britain, Germany and Spain. World War I created a new demand for dairy products in the form of government contracts. By the end of the war, Nestlé's production had doubled. After the war, governments stopped their orders and consumers switched back to fresh milk. However, Nestlé's management responded quickly, streamlining operations and reducing debt.

The 1920s saw Nestlé's first expansion into new products, with chocolate being the company's second most important activity. Nestlé felt the effects of World War II immediately. Profits dropped from $20 million in 1938 to $6 million in 1939. Factories were established in developing countries, particularly Latin America. Ironically, the war helped with the introduction of the Company's newest product, Nescafé, which was a major drink of the US military. Nestlé's production and sales rose in the wartime economy. The end of World War II was the beginning of a dynamic phase for Nestlé. Growth accelerated and companies were acquired. In 1947, Nestlé merged with Maggi seasonings and soups. Crosse & Blackwell followed in 1950, as did Findus (1963), Libby's (1971) and Stouffer's (1973). Diversification came with the acquisition of a shareholding in L'Oréal in 1974.

Nestlé's growth in the developing world partially offset a slowdown in the company's traditional markets. Nestlé made its second venture outside the food industry by acquiring Alcon Laboratories Inc. Between 1980 and 1984, the company divested a number of businesses. In 1984, Nestlé's improved bottom line allowed the company to launch a new round of acquisitions, the most important being the American food giant Carnation. The first half of the 1990s proved to be favourable for Nestlé: trade barriers crumbled and world markets developed into more or less integrated trading areas. Since 1996, there have been further acquisitions, including San Pellegrino (1997), Spillers Petfoods (1998) and Ralston Purina (2002). There were two

> major acquisitions in North America, both in 2002: in July, Nestlé merged its US ice cream business with Dreyer's, and, in August, a US$2.6bn acquisition was announced of Chef America, Inc.
>
> *Source*: Nestlé, www. nestle.com

accounted for around 57 per cent of the company's regional turnover in 2004. The company's 12 per cent share gave it regional leadership. The market remains relatively fragmented, as large parts of the region, especially in the east, are underdeveloped in terms of large-scale logistical networks.

Focus on global brands

Nestlé has probably the best brand portfolio of any of the major food operators; this has allowed it to build its leading position across several product areas. Its product portfolio is relatively concentrated on a global level, with its top three brands – Nestlé, Maggi and Stouffer's – generating around 22 per cent of its turnover. As with all packaged food manufacturers, Nestlé's product portfolio contains categories where competition from private labels is relatively high, with the exception of baby food, snack bars and convalescence drinks. In addition, Nestlé also owns regional and national brands with which consumers have a close and often long-standing familiarity, thereby recognizing the importance of variations in taste and demand in different markets. The company also is continuously involved in merger and acquisition activity, further expanding its brand portfolio. Nestlé's brand strategies have increasingly tended to focus on its core brands and the development of product line extensions to these brands. The increasing maturity of developed markets and the consequent importance of product innovation in generating value have encouraged the company to concentrate on products offering higher margins in the streamlining of its portfolio.[14] The company is committed to solid expenditure on research and development, and spent CHF 1,413 billion in 2004 in all its areas of activity, a 17 per cent increase on 2003. Since 2004 the focus for the company has been on adding value to its products in terms of health and wellness, and it has spent years since optimizing the nutritional and health value of its entire portfolio.

The company also continued with its strategy of preserving value by repositioning products as premium goods, either by brand extension or by product launch. This is another strategy especially relevant to mature markets in Western Europe and North America.

As with most multinational manufacturers, Nestlé has a strategy of attempting to homogenize its brands – in particular, the development of common packaging/branding. The company sees this as especially important in Western Europe, which is characterized by a large number of distinct national markets exhibiting high levels of maturity.

Restructurings and divestments

Throughout 2004, Nestlé focused consistently on its strategy to improve efficiency and create value. The strategy, involving four pillars, was created to improve operational efficiency, facilitate innovation and renovation, improve consumer communication, and increase product availability.

As in previous years, improved operational efficiency has been carried out under initiatives created by GLOBE (Nestlé's Global Business Excellence Programme, which is a worldwide initiative aiming to implement a single set of procurement, distribution and sales management systems for all Nestlé subsidiaries). At the close of 2004, Operation 'EXCELLENCE 2007' was created to replace 'Target 2004+', which was intended to expand its focus to encompass raw material suppliers and customers, particularly in light of the reversal in falling raw material costs. This was created to run in combination with 'Project FitNes' until 2007.

By the end of 2004, over 10 per cent of the business was running with standard systems, data and processes created under GLOBE. GLOBE was to continue to focus on reducing administrative costs throughout 2005 with the help of a new business technology centre created for GLOBE during 2004.[15]

During 2004, to keep ahead of competitors there was a focus on the renovation of brands such as Nestlé, and, in 2005, the focus also fell on innovations such as organic pet food. Consumer communication continued to receive focus in order to improve payback (efficiency from spend). This focus was to continue in the future in conjunction with a focus on innovation and renovation.

The final pillar in the strategy was the availability of products 'whenever, wherever, however', and 2004 saw a focus on introducing brands into different regions and countries, such as the success of Milo in the Asia-Oceania-Africa (AOA) area and its continued introduction to developing markets.

During 2004, the amount of divestitures (at 3.6 per cent of sales) outstripped that of acquisitions (at 1.2 per cent of sales). The acquisition of

Valio in Finland secured Nestlé the number one position in the Nordic ice cream market while, in the Ukraine, Torchin was acquired, which sold a range of mayonnaise, ketchup and mustard.

As Nestlé's efficiency initiatives such as 'Target 2004+' continued, divestitures across company divisions continued. These include the German distribution company Trinks; the Eisman group of companies, which carried out home delivery of frozen foods; cocoa processing activities in York and Hamburg; the Goplana chocolate business in Poland; the non-core sugar confectionery businesses; a biscuit business in Central America; mashed potato producers in Germany and the Netherlands; French fries businesses in Canada and the USA, which were sold to McCain; a milk powder business in the Netherlands; and a chilled dairy business in Turkey.[16]

The company's packaged food business development, as has its overall strategy, focused on portfolio building, with no single acquisition transforming Nestlé's business. Over the years, the company has predominantly bought large Western European brands – in 1988, for example, it acquired Buitoni-Perugina in Italy and Rowntree in the UK, but other packaged food acquisitions in the recent past include Carnation and Schöller.

In 2003, Nestlé acquired the ice cream and related products of the Swiss Mövenpick Group, which brought the company licensing agreements with companies in Egypt, Finland, Germany, Norway, Sweden and Saudi Arabia.

Nestlé has generally aimed at the acquisition of only the largest and best brands. For example, in 2002, the company, together with Cadbury Schweppes, made a joint US$10.5 billion bid for the Hershey Company; however, Hershey called the sale off later that year. This underlines Nestlé strategy, and explains why the company is perceived as having one of the best food portfolios in the world. However, the company is also perceived as having bought a number of 'clunkers' – Rowntree and Perrier, for example – but even these brands are very well-known.

The company has also redefined its portfolio with judicious disposals. In 2004, Nestlé sold its cocoa processing facilities in Germany and the UK to Cargill. Chocolate is regarded as a core business for the company, but the rise in raw materials and the political instability of the West African cocoa sources meant that the company decided to source its cocoa butter and crumb ready-made.

It also sold its German frozen food distributor Eastman in 2004, as the market came under intense price pressure from discounters. These divestments suggest a company actively guarding its margins.

The company seems keen to shed its reputation as a serial acquirer and, in fact, 2004 was only the third year since 1990 in which disposals outweighed acquisitions. Nestlé claims it has no current interest in larger scale acquisitions – presumably, as it wishes to reassure shareholders that it intends to preserve share value. Alongside its development of its brands in the wealthy markets of the West, the company has always maintained a solid presence in emerging markets such as Latin America, Eastern Europe and Asia-Pacific, although acquisitional activity in these markets over the review period was limited.

Some of these markets were built by means of improved distribution networks, rather than in-market development – the 2002 purchase of the German company Schöller, for example, a producer of ice cream and frozen foods, gave Nestlé an entrepôt into Central and Eastern Europe.

The company has a long history in Africa. It first sold condensed milk in South Africa in the 1880s; opened its first factory in 1927, also in South Africa; and also extended through acquisition, most recently in July 2000, when it acquired two South African mineral water brands – Valvita and Schoonspruit. Valvita was subsequently relaunched as Nestlé Pure Life mineral water and is prominent within the retail sector. This suggests a change in strategy, and that the company's focus for its packaged foods business in future will be based on organic growth, buy-backs and dividends. In 2005, the company announced a CHF1 billion buy-back, and it was anticipated there would be an announcement of another CHF3 billion in 2006.[17]

Distribution strategies

Nestlé's distribution costs fell by almost 1 per cent in 2004, to CHF7,045 million. This was partly a reflection of the divestments undertaken in the course of the year, notably the German frozen food business and the company's cocoa processing businesses.

Distribution costs were expected to rise in 2005, as the savings incurred by divestment were lost. However, the company maintains a very efficient distribution strategy. Nestlé supplies its products both to grocery retailers and wholesalers, although the focus is on delivering direct to retailers, especially in developed markets, to maintain a high speed of stock turnover. Moreover, retailers' depots in developed markets are increasingly larger than those of wholesalers.

In developed markets, such as the UK, multiple grocers constitute the most important distribution format for the company, while in emerging markets, such as Brazil, distribution remains biased towards wholesalers that supply independent retailers across specific countries. Nestlé also focused on the development of other distribution channels, such as direct delivery, and has sought out acquisitions that maintain established distribution systems so that it can readily channel its products into a given market. The acquisition of Schöller Holdings, for instance, gave Nestlé access to a well-developed direct delivery channel in Germany. Nestlé greatly enhanced its US distribution system through the acquisition of the US company Dreyer's Grand Ice Cream, which established one of the most extensive direct delivery networks in the country, tailoring the delivery system to store-specific requirements. Dreyer's is the largest direct distributor of ice cream products, dominant in most major cities. Its refrigerated trucks deliver not only its own brands to supermarkets and convenience stores, but also those of its competitors, including Nestlé and Unilever. The merger gives Nestlé a dominant vertical position, as well as simple product dominance.

Nestlé entered into two important joint ventures during 2004 that helped the company to drive sales in two primary markets: coffee and water. Nestlé joined the Pulmuone Group and long-time partner the Coca-Cola Company to expand water sales in South Korea and Indonesia. This venture was to target two markets: the retail water market, and the home and office water market. The second joint venture came after the relaunching of the Nestlé brand worldwide and the continued success of the Nespresso brand. The joint venture with Miele, Siemens and De Longhi would add to the already expanded Nespresso brand by launching Nespresso coffee machines.

In short, the company has possibly the strongest brand portfolio of any international producer of packaged food products. Nestlé has extensive global coverage, even in the more fragmented developing markets. This global strength diminishes the effects of an economic downturn in any one area. Furthermore, the company's long history gives it solid prowess in product development, which increasingly is the key to sales growth in developed markets. Nestlé's brand strength has allowed it to leverage sales across more than one sector; for example, KitKat, Smarties and Milkybar were successfully extended into ice cream and chilled desserts. Developing existing brands into new sectors prevents cannibalization of the original brand, while maximizing sales of the new product. Nestlé's extensive sectoral coverage enables it to respond quickly to emerging market trends and changing patterns of consumption. Nestlé is not afraid to invest in emerging markets and in new lines of business that have not been immediately profitable but have paid off well in the long term. As a result, the company has sector dominance in developing regions, providing it with high brand recognition and strong retail relationships in those regions. The company's wide product mix enables economies of scale in marketing (through the development of global recognition of the Nestlé trademark) and distribution (as a result of multiple product transport by means of the extensive Nestlé delivery system, which was boosted further by the 2003 acquisition of Dreyer's in the USA). Baby food is Nestlé's core strength. It is a high-margin, good growth business where Nestlé is the global leader and where research and development is important, established brands enjoy strong franchises, and consumers generally stay away from private labels. In short, foods MNEs base their presence beyond their national boundaries on their well-known brands.

The next section outlines how the global strategies of Nestlé, Unilever, and InBev influence the behaviour of their subsidiaries in CEE. Interviews with the presidents of these multinationals were conducted at the head-quarters of the companies. The interviews attempted to find an answer to the questions:

What exactly has motivated food multinationals to invest in CEE?
What were their investment strategies?
Does the parent company consider the subsidiary's work with local suppliers, retailers, banks and research centres important?
What are the long-term plans of the MNEs with regard to their CEE subsidiaries?
Are CEE units independent or highly controlled by companies' headquarters?

Strategies of Unilever, InBev, and Nestlé in the CEECs

Unilever

The CEOs of Unilever[18] that I approached for interviews explained that company strategy in the CEE region is to keep different portfolios in each different CEE country, depending on the potential of the market. In Hungary and the Czech Republic, for example, the company offers a wide variety of products, including global brands, while in Bulgaria and Romania the focus is on local brands. The President of Bestfoods (Europe) underlined that Unilver's policies would also change in Bulgaria and Romania with the development of their consumer markets and the market economy as a whole. According to the interviewed CEOs, market potential is the factor that usually predetermines Unilever's investments in a particular country. In other words, the investment in the country is dependent on the level of the population's purchasing power. To confirm these comments, the Unilever President underlined that, when the company invests, management always looks at the economy of the country. He continued his argument by pointing out that the duration of the partnership is also a factor. With some countries (Hungary was given as example), Unilever had had good business relationship even when the state was under a socialist regime – Rama margarine, for instance, was manufactured under licence before 1989. This fact had an impact on the company's decision to invest in Hungary in the early 1990s. Therefore, the Unilever Group could be described as having followed a market-seeking strategy in entering the CEE region.

Unilever headquarters was asked whether it could close a subsidiary in any CEEC at any point, free from constraints, and, if so, why would that happen. The management answered that the company did not have such plans. However, it was emphasized that, as Unilever possesses a global supply chain, it could be that some of the operations in a CEE subsidiary might be shut down. The reason for this is that the supply chain changes very quickly and nowadays differs considerably from how it used to be ten, or even five, years ago. The trade regulations, and EU and non-EU trade barriers and tariffs are also important, as they influence the company's decisions as to whether certain production processes should be closed or retained. In other words, with regard to the backward linkages of the company with suppliers, Unilever has a mixed strategy: internal and external sourcing. That is the global strategy of the company that is applied to the greatest degree to the CEE region. Unilever Bestfood's President noted that, in general, the high value-added inputs are imported from their global suppliers, as only they can respond to Unilever's high quality and quantity standards. This indicates to host governments and institutions that they should concentrate their efforts on the development of high quality local suppliers.

With regard to product distribution, as a global company Unilever has global retail partners to distribute the firm's products; for example, Tesco. However, in many CEECs the multinational retailers that are Unilever's partners have no presence. In these situations, the company is flexible and open to local retailers, as it aims at achieving a large market share. In the case of Bulgaria and Romania, for example, the company is constrained to work with local retailers, as they have the largest market share and because retail markets there are not yet developed.

Being global requires a very centralized decision-making process. Is this valid for Unilever's subsidiaries in CEE? It emerges from the interviews that the parent company has a very centralized approach towards its subsidiaries. The Unilever Vice-President said that they work within well-defined borders. The subsidiaries are completely dependent on the parent company for strategic decision-making, but independent in the daily decisions relating to marketing, promotion campaigns, and so on. In this sense, the answers to the important questions are determined by the parent company; for example, what is to be produced, at what price, the raw materials to be used, their sources, how much the profit should be, and so on. Some subsidiaries – for example, those in Hungary – are relatively more independent. This is because they have a broader portfolio and so have more decisions to take; these are 'older' subsidiaries that have existed since the early 1990s.

> Do regional public institutions, universities, and research institutes have an impact on Unilever's policies?

The managers interviewed at headquarters said that the company has a policy of cooperating with local universities, as they need to recruit a qualified labour force. However, Unilever has not signed any kind of contract for cooperation, the company does not give grants to Ph.D. students, does not work with university professors on given projects, and so on. As far as collaboration with local research institutes is concerned, Unilever uses local laboratories only for health/sanitary control, which depends on the type of product. CEE laboratories and research centres are used for routine checking only, because the company has a major food research centre in Vlaardingen, near Rotterdam, where investigations and research are carried out. Unilever headquarters also stated that company strategy was to work with branch associations and to collaborate with local firms in the area of health. However, Unilever management admitted that the parent company does not find the relationship with local agencies and business centres particularly important. Local banks are also used to a lesser extent. Unilever has a global partner with which it works, rather than choosing local banks.

Concerning suppliers, there is a strong centralized approach towards them. 'Everything depends on how much you can move the goods. Everything is specific – raw-material-by-raw-material', said Unilever management. For the future, the company intends to make long-term investments to support fast growth. At the same time, it will be making flexible short-term investments depending on the competitors because 'in order to be competitive we have to be flexible', the CEO concluded. According to the managers, Unilever applies its global strategy equally towards all the subsidiaries in the CEE region. There is no differentiated approach; the company has identical rules for all its affiliates. However, not all CEE subsidiaries are equally embedded in the four CEECs that are object of this research: the Czech Republic and Hungary are treated differently compared with Romania and Bulgaria.

> What is the reason for the varying degrees of CEE subsidiaries' embeddedness?

Unilever management underlined that future investments and possible domestic partnerships depend predominantly on the economic development of the countries. For Unilever, regional and local authorities do not have any significant influence over management decisions: the macroeconomic outlook seems to be the most important factor. However, the company does not underestimate the role of national governments and, in particular, the role of governmental regulations and trade measures.

InBev

Interbrew invested in the CEE region in the early and mid-1990s. In 1991, the company acquired the Hungarian brewery 'Borsodi' in Böcs; in 1994, the Romanian breweries in Bianca (Blaj), IEB (Ploiesti), and Proberco (Baia Mare). In 1995, Interbrew invested in Bulgarian breweries in Plovdiv, Haskovo, and Pleven. In 2000, it became an owner of one of the most famous Czech breweries: Staropramen.

In order to understand InBev's strategies in the region, the corporate affairs office at company headquarters in Leuven, Belgium was interviewed.[19] The first question related to whether InBev had an investment strategy plan for Central and Eastern Europe as a whole, and which factors predetermined the level of investments in the different countries. The management explained that the macroeconomic outlook, beer consumption outlook, the competitors and the demographic structure are among the most important factors to have an impact on their decision whether or not to invest in a given country. As an MNE producing goods that are extremely difficult to transport (beer), the company is interested predominantly in the local market and follows a market-seeking strategy. Its entry mode into most CEECs concentrated on privatization deals. Together, these responses reveal that the macroeconomic and political environment in the host country is crucial to attracting market-seeking FDI.

Yet another interesting question arises.

> Are these factors strong enough to embed InBev in the region? Could the company easily close a subsidiary in CEE?

'There are always constraints when closing a subsidiary', corporate management said. However, they explained that this could happen under certain circumstances; for example, following a dramatic increase in the cost of the labour force, a decrease in the purchasing power of the population, or in the presence of very strong local competitors. The political environment, regulatory constraints, and a climate of instability also matter. In some countries, the company has, in the past, closed breweries, which led to redundancies. In sum, for InBev – the present world leader in the brewing industry – the most important factors for the development of a particular subsidiary are the macroeconomic policies pursued by the host government, the quality of national and local infrastructure and institutional regulations, the potential of the local and regional markets, and the availability of a cheap labour force.

Does the company use local distributors or global retailers?

The answer is that InBev adapts its distribution strategy according to a mix of local retailers and wholesalers. The company uses both local and multinational retailers, as every retailer is valuable as a customer in its own right and drives the distribution of InBev beers.

With regard to the partnership of InBev with local universities, the parent company is open to cooperation, as the interviewees underscored. However, InBev management was far from precise as to the extent to which the company is willing to collaborate with the local knowledge institutions. InBev 'does not rely on CEE research institutes for elaborated research and for ideas for innovation and development, although this could happen sometimes', management admitted. It explained further that, in general, the company aims to become involved with the local community and 'be a contributing partner to a society wherever we operate'. InBev management considers the support of national and regional governments, both legislative and financial, is extremely important for the firm's operations in CEE.

The company works with local branch associations and business centres, as they help in developing local infrastructure. InBev also discusses common strategies for the development of the brewing sector with the local authorities. The management said they use local banks for both credits and transactions.

InBev's strategy towards suppliers depends on the price/quality ratio, logistics, tax borders, and the capacity of the supplies. The company works with its global suppliers, but also uses local ones, depending on the price and quality they offer. InBev does not cooperate with local competitors, large or small. It purchases some of them if the acquisition enhances the company's position in a particular geographical area, and if it fits in with InBev's strategy 'to become the leading industry consolidator in that market'.

As far as the CEE subsidiaries are concerned, InBev has a centralized approach. They are completely dependent on the parent company, as is the case in all CEECs. For the future, InBev plans long-term investments in the region: short-term flexible investments might occur incidentally.

The long-term strategy of the company towards its subsidiaries reveals that InBev intends to stay in the region. Yet, the embeddedness of subsidiaries in a particular local environment depends on the macro-economic environment, and it is likely that the active role of local institutions is required.

Nestlé

Nestlé SA established itself as one of the leading investors in Eastern Europe and, by the end of the 1990s, the firm owned 23 factories in the region. Despite the heavy cost of investment, this was a step in the right direction for the Swiss food producer, and the increase in sales proved this. In 2000 alone, Nestlé SA achieved sales growth of 18 per cent in Eastern Europe, a growth figure that outperformed Western Europe tenfold and by far exceeded the corporate global average sales growth of 4.4 per cent. Nestlé's strategy to become the dominant food company in Eastern Europe has been carried out through the acquisition of major local producers, their modernization, and requiring their compliance with Nestlé corporate standards. As a result of this strategy, Nestlé overtook the position of market leader in confectionery throughout Eastern Europe by storm.[20]

Nestlé is represented in every CEEC, either by imports or by a subsidiary. The company usually buys the first or second largest local manufacturer in order to establish a sufficient critical mass. According to James Gallagher, Nestlé's Director for Central and Eastern Europe, the company needs this critical mass to allow it to build the necessary transport infrastructure.[21] Nestlé also makes greenfield investments – which include, for example, a pet care factory in Hungary, a coffee factory in Russia, and so on. In most of the CEECs where Nestlé has subsidiaries, the company is involved in the confectionery business. Nestlé can only position its nutrition business in locations where it can source raw materials of an appropriate quality, and so has no nutrition businesses in this region. The company had business relations with many countries in the

CEE region before 1989; for example, the former Yugoslavia, Poland and Bulgaria. Nestlé brands also have a long history in South-East Europe. The first reported sales of infant formula were in 1874 in Serbia, and in Romania in 1875. 'And even in socialist times, the privileged few could always buy Nestlé products such as condensed milk or Nescafé', Mr Gallagher noted. In the former Yugoslavia, during the 1970s and 1980s, Nestlé built a fairly substantial business from imported products and also from products manufactured under licence, such as Thomy mayonnaise and Nestlé chocolate tablets. Only the recent wars forced Nestlé to cease this local manufacture, and the business virtually collapsed. However, despite the wars, the company always maintained some local representatives, so that it would be in a position to rebuild its business quickly when matters returned to normal. Nestlé's business is expanding rapidly and management see the CEE region as having great potential. In terms of investment in the region, excluding acquisition costs, Nestlé has invested over CHF100 million in the past 7–8 years. This investment has been in new manufacturing equipment, advertising, hiring people and staff training, and clearly shows the benefit of Nestlé to the region. Nestlé also sees this benefit. The sales are now over CHF200 million and Nestlé is profitable. One can find a full range of Nestlé products all over the region. It has market-leading positions in a few product categories, such as soluble coffee and confectionery, and the company is experiencing strong growth.

In other words, the company continues its global strategy, which is to be represented in as many countries as possible through its core brands. Management makes on-the-spot decisions as to whether and how much to invest. The interviews with the management revealed that Nestlé does not plan any complete closures of subsidiaries in the CEE region. What could happen is that, when acquiring a new factory, in line with the running process of modernization, Nestlé might close some facilities and reduce the number of employees.

Company headquarters helps its subsidiaries when they are facing difficulties, as the parent company has enormous experience in starting up and building businesses in developing markets. That does not mean, however, that the problems become easier. Management takes a pragmatic approach to solving the inevitable difficulties. As Mr Gallagher added, 'It is unrealistic to expect countries such as those in South-East Europe, after decades of communism, now to be perfect examples of market economies.' However, Nestlé expects, and already observes in most of the countries of the region, a steady reduction of the current problems. The company greatly appreciates a stable legislative framework and is happy to compete in any country, as long as the rules are the same for everyone, and are applied consistently and fairly. 'The government which can achieve this will be the winner in attracting inward investment and, believe me, this makes a big difference in Nestlé's investment decisions', Mr Gallagher admitted.

With regard to the relations of the company with local research centres and universities, Nestlé has research centres worldwide; for example, in South Africa, Germany, and Switzerland. In CEECs, there are only application centres; that is, centres that develop recipes. Concerning universities, Nestlé cooperates with them in order to recruit personnel. As Nestlé has its own research centres, it can clearly be seen that scientific partnership with the local knowledge institutions is not one of the company's global goals.

As far as retailers are concerned, Nestlé uses both multinational and local retailers, which is in line with its global distribution strategy. In Bulgaria and Romania, the company operates to a much greater extent with local retailers, simply because there are few foreign retailers. Hence, each country has its own distribution channels and the company uses this particular distributor, not because it is its global partner but because of the large size of its market share. This is a question of how the business develops. In fact, Nestlé's manager pointed out that in some CEECs, such as Hungary and the Czech Republic, 80 per cent of trade involves large Western retailers. This means that the market is highly concentrated and the local suppliers are extremely dependent on the market power of the buyers.

Nestlé's CEE subsidiaries collaborate with local food associations in order to be in line with the changing macroeconomic situation in the respective countries. Local business organizations also help Nestlé to cooperate with the better raw material suppliers.

Nestlé works with both local and foreign banks. The decision as to with whom to work is a complex matrix; it depends on the 'price of money', security issues, previous experience with the bank, and so on.

Concerning local suppliers, Nestlé's strategy is to use those that offer the lowest possible price rather than working with a particular global partner. Sometimes the company uses local suppliers, sometimes foreign. If there are high import tariffs, then the company is forced to use local suppliers. Nestlé does not cooperate with local competitors, as all the countries are under monopoly legislation and Nestlé owns the company with the biggest market share.

Nestlé's James Gallagher confirmed that regional government did not make much of an effort to keep the company in the countries. In

Romania, especially, 'it is still very difficult to work with authorities, while in Bulgaria it is a bit better', he said.

The CEE subsidiaries are completely dependent on the parent company: headquarters gives them the orders and deals with the advertising, while the subsidiaries concentrate on the production process. But, as outlined earlier, the global strategy requires centralized decision-making. The relationship that the company has with the subsidiaries varies from country to country. Nestlé headquarters has been working closely with them, as it was necessary to reduce the number of employees in many of the acquired firms in CEE, which were inefficient. Nestlé acquired about 90 per cent of its target investment in CEE, although the firm would like to buy some more companies. The investments are large and long-term.

Conclusion

This chapter analyzed the impact of global strategies on the subsidiaries of food MNEs in the CEE region. The first section presented the worldwide strategies of Unilever, InBev and Nestlé. It described the backbone of their global strategies. The major points in the global competitive plans have been the focus on core activities; the creation of global supplier and distribution networks; and, related to these global restructurings, divestments and acquisitions. The second section examined and analyzed the activities of food MNEs in CEECs through the prism of the global plans of the companies.

The following conclusions can be drawn. First, the global strategy of the company models the activities of the CEE subsidiaries; namely, they are integrated in the global production network of the company and are the object of strong centralized management.

Second, the essence of food MNEs' global strategies is to produce standardized products and sell them all over the world. This phenomenon is observed in the CEE region: apart from local brands, the subsidiaries of MNEs distribute and/or produce many global brands. Product standardization makes easy restructurings and cost optimizations possible; however, in 2004 none of the managers mentioned forthcoming closures in CEE – after EU membership, just one year later, all three MNEs closed plants.

Third, global companies organize global supply networks. CEE affiliates are integrated into the supply chain of the parent company. This means that suppliers are chosen and approved by the parent company or by the respective regional centre (it is not possible for every subsidiary to decide on inputs by itself), and all the subsidiaries use that particular supplier. However, some external factors – such as trade barriers, import tariffs, logistics and transportability of products – have an impact on MNEs' policies, and force them to source locally. Moreover, if there are high quality, competitive local suppliers, then the company might source locally and even turn those suppliers into its global partners.

Fourth, CEE affiliates cooperate loosely with local knowledge institutions. As a rule, global companies have R&D centres in Western Europe and are unwilling to internationalize R&D to new destinations. Yet, the local economy might benefit from MNEs' knowledge and best practices if there is a high domestic absorptive capacity.

Fifth, the economic and political environment is decisive for levels of investment. MNEs entered the CEE markets, attracted by the growth possibilities of the domestic markets. In addition, the purchasing power of the population, the political and business climate of the country, and the duration of partnership with a particular country have been among the variables that predetermined the level of FDI from food MNEs.

To summarize, the CEE subsidiaries of Nestlé, InBev and Unilever are integrated in the global network of the parent company. These food MNEs used market-seeking strategies to invest in the region. They rely on their global partners – some, such as Unilever, to a much greater extent than InBev or Nestlé, for example. There is a highly centralized approach to decision-making: subsidiaries are completely dependent on the parent company for strategic decision-making. As far as R&D is concerned, MNEs still prefer their home countries; however, they have demonstrated a verbal commitment to cooperate with local universities and research centres. It seems that the extent to which the subsidiaries contribute to local development depends on the protectionist measures of the national governments, the economic development of the country, and the size of the market. Hence, further efforts by national governments are needed for the development of strong domestic supply networks.

3
Privatization and Restructuring in the Agro-Food Industry

Introduction

This chapter presents the agro-food sector reforms in Hungary, the Czech Republic, Romania and Bulgaria in the 1990s. It reveals how the different restructuring policies[1] (restitution, transformation, and privatization) in the four CEECs influenced the development of the agricultural sector and the food processing companies. It also analyzes the impact of these policies on FDI. My core argument is that the preservation and effective restructuring of existing socialist production networks helped the formation of transnational linkages between local companies and multinationals, which has created the conditions for industrial upgrading.

The chapter is organized in five parts. Each of the first four sections discusses the land restitution process, state farm privatization, food industry privatization, and the recent development of the industry in Hungary, the Czech Republic, Romania and Bulgaria consecutively. The comparison of the various transformation policies, the speed and the level of privatization and restitution processes explains why the countries (for example, Hungary and the Czech Republic) that managed to keep the assets created under socialism currently enjoy good links between the MNEs in the food processing industry and the local agricultural suppliers.

Hungary

The restitution and transformation process in agriculture

The restitution process in Hungary was conducted on the basis of restitution and de-collectivization legislation since '[they] tried to apply market methods through the introduction of tradable property shares, compensation vouchers and land auctions as the major vehicles and institutions of restructuring' (Kovács, 1997: 7).

The influence of the Smallholders' Party was central to the process by which Hungary's restitution legislation emerged because the Party wanted to return land to its pre-collectivization, 1947 owners. However, this did not take place as a result of a decision by the Constitutional Court, which concluded that re-privatization and full compensation in the agricultural sector, but not other sectors of the economy, was a form of discrimination. After a number of negotiations between the Smallholder Party representatives and the government, the Restitution Bill was passed on 26 June 1991, subsequently followed by three further bills.[2] The essence of the restitution legislation, which came into force on 11 August 1991 (when the US dollar equalled 75.79 HUF), was that claims of up to HUF 200,000 were met in full; the portion between HUF 200,000 and HUF 300,000 at 50 per cent; the portion between HUF 300,000 and HUF 500,000 at 30 per cent; and the portion above HUF 500,000 at 10 per cent. Moreover, there was also an overall maximum ceiling of HUF 5 million, which in terms of land meant an upper limit of 500 hectares at the official valuation price. An important aspect of the law that deserves attention is the fact that the landowners were not restored exactly the same parcel of land they possessed before collectivization but, rather, the value of the land they had lost expressed in 'golden crown values'. Each 'golden crown value' was given the monetary equivalent of HUF 1,000 and was then converted into vouchers. Restitution vouchers could be used in nine ways, irrespective of the basis of eligibility.[3] All those eligible for vouchers were able to use them to purchase former cooperative or state land at auction from the Restitution Land Funds that each collective and state farm was obliged to set up. These land funds had to match in quality and quantity the type of land for which valid claims had been registered (Swain, 1994: 8).

In other words, the idea behind the restitution legislation was to settle the claims of the landowners, but not at any price. The logic was that everyone should receive something, but not at the expense of an excessive cost. The Hungarian process has been more focused on the future than the past. The major issue was to keep the agricultural sector in such a form that it could continue to operate successfully.

The restitution of land was very closely linked with the restructuring of the socialist cooperatives, because they possessed land. The laws defining the transformation of cooperatives were the Transitional Cooperative and Cooperative Acts.

The reform of collective farms, however, was not an easy task, as it had to deal with the existing complex ownership relationships. The problem was that, in Hungary, collective farms owned the land, rather than the members. Swain (1994) explains that phenomenon, drawing attention to how, during the socialist past, members were *encouraged* to sell their land to cooperatives, while 'outside owners', those who were no longer members (because they did not fulfil the minimum work requirements for membership), were *obliged* to sell theirs.[4] As a result, the cooperatives acquired land. In addition, the cooperatives also took over state land that they had previously been renting.

That is why the restitution and privatization were more complex in Hungary than elsewhere. Where members had always owned land, they had no need for involvement with restitution. Restitution was only for those who had lost their land and wanted it back. Collective farms were 'privatized' by valuing the assets and allocating them to members and former members who had a valid claim. The process of giving collective farm property to real owners became known as 'naming' cooperative property as, *de facto*, the property remained in the cooperative; it simply had different legal owners. Swain (1994: 3) explains, 'Cooperative privatization related to assets only; land was returned directly; and restitution only referred to land or assets confiscated from, for example, former "kulaks".'

Only in the case of Hungary, because land was owned by the cooperatives, it too was included in the privatization or 'naming' process. However, the technicalities of entitlement were determined by the restitution legislation. Those who had lost land that they or their families had given to the cooperatives, and those who had been cooperative members and employees but had never contributed land, were eligible to claim land from the cooperative under these measures. Once cooperatives had been restructured and their assets allocated to real owners, they were covered by general legislation on bankruptcy, accounting conventions, and so on as private companies (although the bankruptcy legislation has some special provisions for cooperatives and the rights of household plot holders), while private farmers were considered to be self-employed.

Despite the very well prepared legislation framework, which aimed at the preservation of cooperative assets and land, the restitution and de-collectivization processes did not happen smoothly or without losses. Katalin Kovács (1997: 6) argues:

Nobody knows exact figures about the numbers of successors and the assets they took; when the transformation losses of agriculture were mentioned in the 1997 discussions, 400 Billion Forints was estimated for the whole branch, of which about half was forever lost (was consumed, got ruined by the lack of service and proper usage), another half was reoriented and used frequently inefficiently.

However, in comparison with other CEECs, the transformation in Hungary might be considered successful, as it did not result in massive liquidations and destructions of the cooperative farms. Moreover, many of the members of the old cooperatives became members of those that were newly created. Swain (1994) reports on the results of a survey carried out by the Ministry of Agriculture at the completion of the transformation process. Out of the 176,000 members in the survey, only 1.91 per cent chose private farming; a further 1.5 per cent chose to leave the farms on a group basis; all the others that had worked in the old cooperatives continued working in the newly created cooperatives, and there was an extremely high degree of personal continuity. Put simply, the 'new' managers were actually the old ones.

State farm privatization

It is important to note that state farms are different from collective farms. The typical state farms consisted of unconnected plots of various sizes scattered over an area. The physical transformation aimed at the creation of farms with between 1000 and 2000 hectares of land, organized spatially in a more rational way (OECD, 1994).

In Hungary, there were 121 state farms and, for the purposes of privatization, they were divided into two groups. The first group was to remain under some form of state ownership, while the second group was to be totally privatized. Those farms selected to remain under state control were specialized in areas of public importance, such as seed propagation, animal stockbreeding and research. State farms had assets, excluding land, valued at HUF 93 billion.[5] The Ministry of Agriculture did not favour farms going into foreign hands, and most of the assets of the state farms went into the hands of the old employees.

Food industry privatization

In Hungary, food processing gained the highest share of total FDI in industry. International companies that have acquired stakes in the Hungarian food sector during privatization have brought with them modern practices in production, processing, marketing, and new product development. FDI has also helped many companies that were in bad financial shape and, facilitated their recovering of the export share that was lost in the early 1990s.

All 138 state-founded food companies were wholly privatized in the 1990s (OECD, 1994). The only exceptions were four plants that produced traditional Hungarian products with well-known trademarks; two salami and two paprika companies. Even in these cases, the state decided to retain only a 5 per cent share in these companies in order to be able to provide brand name protection.

Privatization of the Hungarian food industry was completed in 1997. Before transition, the industry was highly concentrated. Privatization broke the monopolies created under communism, although the national vegetable oil company was privatized in its perfect monopoly form in 1991. In the other sectors, however, privatization achieved its goal of creating competitors in industry. In the confectionery industry, the three state-owned confectionery companies were acquired with a large proportion of foreign ownership – in one case, with 100 per cent foreign participation. With regard to the sub-sector of brewing, two of the five breweries supervised by the Ministry of Agriculture were privatized with a majority private stake. A third brewery was bought by its employees and, in the case of the two remaining breweries, deals were nearing completion in May 1993. In the sugar business, seven of the 11 state-owned sugar-processing companies were privatized with foreign participation but with the state retaining majority shareholding in all cases. Unlike the oilseed industry, the monopoly here was broken, as different interests (English and French) were involved (OECD, 1994).

The biggest investors in the food industry were from the Netherlands (HUF 58 billion), Austria (HUF 24 billion), Germany (HUF 23 billion), Switzerland (HUF 18 billion), the USA (HUF 15 billion) and the UK (HUF 14 billion). In 1998, foreign ownership accounted for 49 out of the 80 largest firms in the industry. Domestic investors only controlled one out of the top 10 firms, and four out of the top 20 firms (Payne and Feher, 2002).

By 2003, the composition of shares by type of investor was as follows: 61.2 per cent foreign and 37.5 per cent domestic, while 1.3 per cent remained in state ownership. Following privatization, the number of food companies in the food processing sector increased, including a doubling of the number of small enterprises (defined as those using simplified book-keeping) up until 1996. Since then, the number of small enterprises has continually declined. However, the industrial structure appears to be quite concentrated, with the top three firms in the fish processing, vegetable oils, starch products, and tobacco sectors accounting for 100 per cent of production (DG AGRI, 2003).

Overall, the conclusion that can be drawn is that the methods of privatization, restitution, and restructuring in Hungary allowed for the preservation of the existing assets accumulated in the socialist era. The early (at the beginning of 1991) privatization of SOEs attracted a large amount of FDI. The foreign investors injected fresh money and contributed to the technological modernization of industry. Investments in the food processing industry increased the competitiveness of the sector by raising market adaptability, productivity, and the speed of concentration. In economic terms, the sector is practically integrated into the EU's food industry. EU investors provide 50 per cent of the investments in the sector, and 80 per cent of exports are to other EU countries. In other words, the sector is performing well, even against the background of strong EU competition.

The Czech Republic

The restitution and transformation process in agriculture

The basic legal framework for implementing the structural reform of the agro-food sector was established by the legislation enacted in 1991 and 1992 on the restitution of property, the privatization of SOEs, and the transformation of collective farms, as well as by the Land Law. Apart from the privatization of state farms, the process was essentially completed in 1993–94 (OECD, 1995: 16).

The basic challenge was the transformation of collective farms. The process consisted of two steps: the settlement of property rights, and the transformation of the farms into alternative corporate structures not based on collective property. Unlike Hungary, in the Czech Republic, throughout the Communist period, all land on collective farms remained the legal property of individuals, usually the members of a collective. A small amount of state land was also farmed by collectives and was dealt with as part of the privatization of state property.

In this sense, the settlement of land property rights was a direct process. In addition to land, some property was put into a cooperative at its foundation, typically livestock and machinery. These private property rights (as land property rights) also remained valid throughout the collective period. However, property rights issues only became a significant problem when an owner wished to remove them. The distribution of the assets that had been accumulated by a farm over its history was more problematic, as there was collective ownership. The Czechs solved this problem by means of an audited valuation, following which the property was converted into shares. Some of the shares were offered for sale to members and the remainder were distributed to individuals on the basis of a number of criteria. These included the amount of land and the number of years worked on a farm by members or workers.

The next step in the transformation process was the conversion of the collective farms into alternative corporate structures, such as a new free cooperative or a joint stock company. The majority of members of the original collective farms decided to adopt the new cooperative form. The number of cooperatives had increased by 40 per cent by the end of 1994 because many of them split into smaller cooperatives, and their average size fell from around 2500 hectares to about 1400 hectares (OECD, 1995: 18). Management of the farms improved somewhat and there was a decrease in employment, which contributed to increased productivity and improved the economic returns for those engaged.

State farm privatization

About half of the land and assets of state farms were effectively privatized under the restitution and compensation process. Assets remaining after restitution were privatized in the same way as any other state property, by direct sale. The most common corporate structure was the limited liability company (OECD, 1995: 18). However, it should be noted that the re-establishment of the former fragmented ownership structure did not lead to land fragmentation. At the end of 1994, about 4200 farms of at least 100 hectares occupied 85 per cent of farmland. The average size of a farm over 100 hectares was about 880 hectares. Moreover, as in the Hungarian case, the old collective farms were substituted by new cooperatives and, hence, they managed not to fragment their operations. The new farms, in whatever corporate structure, have an average size of about 1350 hectares and a strong potential to be highly productive and competitive. A large number of owners claimed only for a transfer of a part of their land (less than two hectares) from the actual user to work on it individually as part-time or hobby farmers, leaving the remaining land in use with the former occupier or with individual farmers who had decided to expand their farm size. The same phenomenon is typical of the state farms, from which farms of a few hundred hectares were created: even the group of individual farms that comprised the small farms was dominated by larger farms. Less than 2.5 per cent of agricultural land is occupied by farms of less than 10 hectares.

In short, Czech agriculture, in spite of its fragmented ownership, has kept a large-scale operation structure, which is in line with European standards. It is notable that the structure emerging in Hungary is similar, although the Hungarian voucher system of land restitution was very different from the Czech method. In Hungary, long-term leases of seven to 10 years were the most popular. Land sales were negligible, even with a subsidized interest rate of 15 per cent (OECD, 1995).

Food industry privatization

There were three main methods of privatization of the food industry in the Czech Republic:

1 Privatization of small enterprises (roughly up to 20 employees) was implemented following an extremely careful process that paid attention to their specific needs;
2 The conversion of large SOEs into stock companies, and their privatization using the voucher method;
3 Some state companies were sold directly to foreign investors (for example, the chocolate industry).

Food processing and distribution industries were mostly privatized under the voucher privatization scheme.[6]

During the privatization process, the total number of food processing companies increased from 69 large state-owned companies in 1989 to 592 smaller companies at the end of 1994. With regard to the ownership structure, the number of private firms had increased to 381 units, whereas the number of firms with mixed ownership had reached 113 by the end of 1994. Opposing these trends, the number of state companies had fallen to 121 (OECD, 1995).

In some cases, food industry privatization took place with foreign participation. However, the amount of FDI was not as significant as it was in Hungary, because the Czech approach was to privatize before looking for foreign investors. The general approach of the government was to complete the privatization process, and then leave it to the new owners to decide their attitude towards foreign investment. Only in a limited number of select cases did the government look to the direct participation of foreign capital in the process of privatization. In any case, it should be noted that putting an enterprise on the voucher privatization list did not exclude foreign investment: not all the assets had to be put on the list for voucher privatization since part could be reserved for potential foreign investors. There were no special conditions applying to foreign investment as compared with investment by Czech domestic investors;

neither were there any special conditions for investment in agro-food as compared with the other sectors.

The pre-transition industry structure was highly concentrated. After the privatization, some sectors were left concentrated, with the aim of easier privatization; for example, chocolate, and oil refining. Where large SOEs were broken up, increasing concentration could again be observed in some sectors from the mid-1990s onwards; for example, sugar processing, dairy processing, and grain milling. The privatization process in the sugar processing industry led to a reduction in the number of plants from 30 to 22 for the period 1989–94. Their sizes and the level of technology in these plants differed greatly. Four large confectionery factories were also privatized. Within the entire food processing sector, confectionery and vegetable oils sub-sectors had the highest production value per company (OECD, 1995: 103). In other sectors, there was a significant dual industry structure; for example, breweries, and meat processing. The brewing industry was dominated by nine large enterprises, some of them internationally known breweries. The breweries were in a good financial situation, and attracted both domestic and foreign investors. Beverage and tobacco manufacturing companies reported substantial American investment: about US$400 million flowed into the tobacco industry from Philip Morris, which established a joint venture with the Czech monopoly Tabak Kutna Hora, while Coca-Cola invested around US$60 million in a Czech beverage company producing Coca-Cola.[7] Other sectors, including fruit and vegetable processing, and the beverages industry (apart from breweries), remained fairly unconcentrated (DG AGRI, 2003).

By the end of 2000, FDI in the food industry accounted for about 4.8 per cent of the total FDI inflow, being the fourth largest FDI in relative terms amongst branches of the manufacturing industry (DG AGRI, 2003: 48). In general, FDI has been directed into high value-added branches (the chocolate industry, and spirits production) or branches with significant export potential (brewing) and, in addition, sugar processing. FDI contributed to the restructuring of plant – increasing plant capacity in order to concentrate production in a few plants with modern technology – and to the improvement of hygiene, quality, and environmental standards. The latter area is associated with the harmonization of Czech national food legislation with EU legislation; for example, the passing of new food quality and safety legislation in 2000 and other legislation dealing with beef standards, genetically modified organisms, and the protection of public health.

To sum up, the privatization and transformation in the agro-food chain went without any major shocks. The settlement of land and private property rights over assets in the cooperatives happened directly. The cooperatives have been legally transformed – many of them split into several – but the land has not been fragmented, despite the fragmented ownership. With regard to the food industry, it was privatized through vouchers, and this slowed down the FDI inflows for some years. However, even with vouchers, foreign participation was not excluded. Investment in the food industry was stable, increasing in 1996 in response to a short economic boom and then falling again in 1997 and 1998. It is mainly concentrated in the tobacco and confectionery industries, the vegetable oil sector, and the sugar sector. There is also strong foreign participation in the retail sector. The Czech experience is similar to that in Hungary, in the sense that both countries managed, in the main, to preserve what they had achieved during the Communist period.

Romania

The restitution and transformation process in agriculture

De-collectivization in Romania occurred mainly through the restitution of land used by agricultural production cooperatives (CAPs), which returned collectivized land to previous owners, and distributed the remainder to farm workers and other eligible Romanian citizens. There was also the privatization of state-owned land through sales, leases, and concessions.

According to Land Law 18/1991, collective farms' land was primarily restored to former owners and their heirs. The restitution of ownership rights was based on the ownership in 1945. Although the provisions of Land Law 18/1991 gave some sort of blocking rights to agricultural associations to take over the non-land assets of former collective farms instead of distributing them to individuals, the distribution of non-land assets of former farms occurred spontaneously at each farm. In most cases, the equipment previously owned by the cooperatives was distributed to individuals at a low price. Many animals bred by the former cooperatives were taken home by the peasants and either sold or killed, even before Land Law 18/1991 was issued; livestock buildings were destroyed or damaged (OECD, 2000b).

Swain (1997b: 10) brilliantly illustrates the destruction of cooperatives using the example of a Romanian village, the real identity of which is not disclosed:

> The co-operative broke up in a disorganised manner. The members simply took as many of the co-operative's 300 or so cows as they

thought that they had a right to no supervision. One of our interviewees felt that she had not been bold enough, her neighbour had laid claim to three cows. There was no suggestion of forming an association in the village to take over from the co-operative, although some reported that they would have preferred to have someone cultivate their land for them rather than have to do it themselves. Of the five stable buildings that the co-operative owned, two have remained intact and are being sold to a new mill and other new ventures, but the others were abandoned and have now been gutted, their tiles and anything else of value stolen. Although no corporate farm emerged from this chaos, B.I., the co-operative's last chairman, has done well for himself. He is respected locally as a 'good farmer' who concentrates on livestock (6 cows, 10 pigs, some horses). He has his own tractor and keeps two 'servants' or agricultural laborers, poor people without any land and any means of subsistence. The family is not without other resources. His 40-year-old daughter lives in Cluj and owns a restaurant there.

At the beginning of land privatization, new private landowners had the choice to start farming individually or to join the newly established 'associations'.[8] In 1991, there were 4.1 million family farms, accounting for 68 per cent of the agricultural area in Romania, with an average size of 2.4 hectares (OECD, 2000b). In 1999, associations cultivated about 2.3 million hectares, which was 16 per cent of the total agricultural land in Romania. Almost 70 per cent of these farms owned less than 5 hectares, and only 2 per cent more than 10 hectares. In other words, unlike Hungary and the Czech Republic, in Romania the land was fragmented into thousands of small plots belonging to different owners. By imposing a 10-hectare maximum[9] for restitution and distribution, Romania attempted to combine the considerations of historical justice and equity. In some regions in Romania, however, individual entrepreneurs tried to concentrate land use. Land fragmentation and the destruction of agricultural cooperatives turned out to be a major obstacle for technological progress in Romanian agriculture.

State farm privatization

The reform of state farms had hardly started in 1999 because of the unclear status of the land. The structure of land ownership changed radically, and different types of farming emerged. The private sector became dominant, operating on 85 per cent of agricultural land. The public sector accounted for about 2.2 million hectares of agricultural land in

Romania, 15 per cent of the total. Agricultural commercial companies cultivated about 1.7 million hectares, averaging almost 3000 hectares and scheduled for privatization. The remaining 0.5 million hectares were to remain under public ownership. By November 1999, out of the 547 agricultural commercial companies initially foreseen for privatization, only 20 were actually privatized. The remaining agricultural commercial companies were still state-owned, with the State Ownership Fund owning the majority of shares. Privatization of state farms was lagging behind, partly due to problems related to the legal status of the land and partly due to the strong political opposition to the privatization of these farms, which were considered a crucial element of Romania's food security. Many of these farms were heavily in debt and unattractive to private investors (OECD, 2000b).

Overall, privatization in agriculture was delayed by 7–8 years. The cooperatives and state farms that are the actual suppliers of the food industry were destroyed and animals killed. The land was completely fragmented and given back to millions of owners.

Food industry privatization

The speed of privatization of the Romanian food industry, as in the case of its agriculture, was very slow. In 1998, it was estimated that about 38 per cent of the sector's fixed assets were still in state hands, 44 per cent were in private hands, and only 18 per cent were foreign-owned (DG AGRI, 2002a: 21). Moreover, up until 1996, the government intervened in the agro-food system by giving subsidies to producers and consumers, and by maintaining substantial state control over the food production and distribution system. Thus, it hampered the transformation of the industry (OECD, 2000b): many medium-sized and large enterprises were characterized by a low level of productivity, outdated technologies, a lack of adaptation to demand, and a monopolistic position with regard to producers.

The progress with privatization varies by food industry branch. Privatization was the least advanced in industries such as fisheries, and canned fruits and vegetables, where only 20 per cent of enterprises were privatized (DG AGRI, 2002a).

Although many new food industry enterprises appeared, some sectors remained highly concentrated – concentration rates being between 35–65 per cent for the majority of food industry branches. These include the manufacturing of tobacco, confectionery, fish processing, fruit and vegetable processing, and wine manufacturing. In the period 1991–97, about 14–15 per cent of total FDI in Romania was invested in the food industry: the major sectors that attracted FDI were brewing, soft drinks, confectionery, and tobacco. However, FDI inflows were impeded for some considerable time due to the adverse investment climate, which included negative growth, high inflation, and high interest rates. In addition, bureaucratic obstacles and unpredictable changes in the legal framework,[10] including taxation, hindered FDI. The slow pace of privatization and deregulation in the agricultural sector also inhibited FDI development in the agro-food sector (DG AGRI, 2003).

In sum, the Romanian agro-food sector was burdened with problems of outdated equipment, absent modernization, and the lack of investment. The land market was underdeveloped. The existing small farms had high transaction costs, and it was impossible for MNEs to establish linkages with a large number of small suppliers. The levels of processing, packaging, distribution, and quality were inferior compared with those of the EU and with Central European countries.

Bulgaria

The restitution and transformation process in agriculture

The restitution of land started in February 1991 with the Law for Agricultural Land Ownership and Land Use (LAOUL). The main goals of the Law were to restore land ownership rights, and to distribute non-land assets. Later on, in 1992, the Law was amended and incorporated the goal of liquidating the old cooperative farms. As Hanisch and Boevsky (1999: 7) point out, 'The 1992 changes and amendments in the LAOUL were far-reaching. The lack of a political center allowed for a radical change in the reform strategy.' The new Bulgarian government, with the enforcement of the amendments, changed the course of land reform strategy. The co-existence of re-registered collective farms and all kinds of new legal entities, based on individual private property rights, was no longer possible. The new programme stipulated the liquidation of the former collectives through liquidation councils appointed by the local authorities. These amendments in the law accelerated the restitution process, which had only occurred slowly in the early 1990s. However, further amendments in the following years (1995–6) continued at this slow pace, and even stopped the land reform and privatization process. In August 1997, the LAOUL was changed fundamentally. Most of the amendments that had been passed between May 1995 and August 1996 were erased; instead, many of the former passages from 1992 were re-enforced. Since 1998, the process accelerated again and, by December 1999, 96.44 per cent of the agricultural land subject to restitution was returned to its legitimate owners. By December 2000, 99.79 per cent of the agricultural land subject to restitution was restored within existing or recoverable physical boundaries, or on the basis of land division plans.[11] In short, the land restitution process progressed slowly in the early 1990s due to the complexities of the privatization process. The basic factors that contributed to the slow pace of restitution were the restrictive and ambiguous laws and regulations, and poor management of the process.

The restitution process was closely linked with farm restructuring. De-collectivization in Bulgaria consisted of the restitution of land used by collective farms within the agro-industrial complexes (APKs) to previous owners or their heirs, reallocation of their non-land assets to eligible owners, and the privatization of state-owned land through sale or lease.

Swain (1997b: 10) nicely illustrates the process of de-collectivization in Bulgaria:

> The Liquidation Committee in … was established by the local administration (county and district) and was selected according to political criteria. It was made up of a railway officer, Trade Union activist, and a hairdresser. Its work was divided into three stages. First livestock was liquidated, that is to say, animals were given to members and other eligible parties on the basis of their labour share and original contribution. Since no one was prepared to receive so many animals, and members no longer had the necessary stables to keep them in, many were slaughtered.
>
> The second step was to restitute land, according to the real historic boundaries. Although they did not get back much, they even so did not have the where-with-all to cultivate it. Roughly one third of the land within the village remains uncultivated.
>
> The third stage of the liquidation process was the liquidation of machinery. Auctions were held to sell off all of the farm equipment. But before this could happen, much of the equipment was stolen or swapped for old machines; and there are enduring suspicions that all of the drivers took possession of the good tractors for themselves. Furthermore, when the auctions finally took place, the equipment went for very low prices. Finally there was the question of horticulture and the large-scale orchard that the co-operative had owned. Legally the Liquidation Committee was under an obligation to look after it, but it did not.

As this illustration demonstrates, the transformation process in Bulgaria was quite similar to the process of transformation in Romania. The land was returned to eligible owners in historical boundaries, regardless of whether they wanted it or could take care of it. The non-land assets, such as livestock, were distributed to the members of the cooperative, and many of the animals were simply slaughtered, as the new owners had no intention of taking care of them. The cooperatives' machinery was sold at very low prices and only a few benefited from the sales. In short, the cooperatives in Bulgaria, which were the main suppliers of the food industry, were destroyed.

State farm privatization

Most of the agricultural land operated by state farms was never nationalized. Therefore, individuals, municipalities, and other legal entities claimed part of the land in state farms. In 1998, there were 264 state farms, and these accounted for about 4 per cent of the arable land. The majority of state-owned farms were machinery and tractor service stations; the remainder were intensive pig and poultry units and had no agricultural land (OECD report, 2000a). State-owned land was available on a preferential basis to producers willing to cultivate vineyards and permanent crops through long-term leases (up to 35 years). With regard to a long-term lease, a four-year grant period exempts the lessee from lease payments until the young perennials reach harvesting maturity.

The fragmentation of Bulgarian farmland – the outcome of the restitution process – hampered the development of a modern and effective farming sector in Bulgaria. The land market is still evolving. In the process of its formation, the long-term lease of state-owned land was an important component. The removal of all limitations concerning leasing terms and the maximum area leased facilitated the development of the land market and the inflow of foreign investment to agriculture. On this basis, 20,000 hectares of state-owned land have been leased out, including 12,200 hectares used for growing annual crops and 7,800 hectares for vineyards and permanent crops. Put differently, the land consolidation process was facilitated using the resources available in the state and municipal land funds, as privately owned plots were substituted for parcels released from the funds. Until December 2000, nearly 1,900 transactions were registered, involving substitution of plots privately owned by individuals and legal entities for parcels released from the State Land Fund (SLF). This resulted in the transfer of 10,935.1 hectares of agricultural land from SLF to private owners in exchange for 11,135.4 hectares acquired by the Fund (Ministry of Agriculture and Forestry, Bulgaria, 2000).

In practice, there are no legal limitations for the acquisition of agricultural land by joint ventures, irrespective of the foreign share in their joint capital, if a valid registration under Bulgarian law is obtained. Data for 2003 indicate a stable market in land transactions (around 35,000 hectares per year) and a price per hectare (around €730). After the completion of the land restitution process, the major objective became the overcoming of land fragmentation. Following the adoption of the Law on the National Land Company, this autonomous, state-owned institution has been in charge of supporting transparent market mechanisms and competitive land prices to create consolidated areas (European Commission, 2004b).

Food industry privatization

The privatization of the food industry in Bulgaria included three basic methods:

1 Restitution to former owners;
2 Transformation into stock companies and their sale to foreign or local investors;
3 Voucher privatization.

Under central planning, the food industry had a strong export orientation to the CMEA[12] area. During the transition period, the industry lost a considerable proportion of its foreign markets while, at the same time, domestic demand fell. Several of the large SOEs that had been privatized were proving to be working at a low level of their capacity, and had difficulties competing with the newly established companies. The food processing sector faced many problems – such as the lack of investment, low productivity, and over-capacity, as well as obsolete plant and equipment.[13]

Under the Communist regime, the food processing industries were subordinated from the Ministry of Industry to the Ministry of Agriculture and Food Industries. With this change, the Ministry became responsible for the privatization of both agricultural and food processing enterprises. The pace of privatization accelerated in 1997 and 1998 and, by the end of 1999, most enterprises in the agro-food sector were in private hands (OECD, 2000a).

Since the beginning of the privatization process, the Ministry of Agriculture and Forestry (MAF) launched 792 individual procedures for the privatization of agricultural and agro-food entities. The number of privatization deals concluded by December 2000 totalled 508: 391 deals on whole enterprises, and 117 deals on detached parts. The payments contracted under the deals amounted to BGN240 million whereas the investment commitments alone totalled exactly the same (Ministry of Agriculture and Forestry, Bulgaria, 2000: 7). The US dollar was worth BGN1.87 in 1999.

Overall, the restructuring of the agro-food chain was a long and complicated process that led to land fragmentation, the break up of old cooperatives and their liquidation, the slow privatization of food processing companies and, related to this, the late entry of FDI and technical modernization of the sector. The inability of the country to preserve the old production networks returned the industry to a position similar to that 20 years previously, and only recently has its development begun to accelerate.

Conclusion

The common feature of the four cases is that the agro-food chain went through a process of restructuring (restitution, privatization and transformation). However, in the cases of Hungary and the Czech Republic we observe a picture quite different from that in Bulgaria and Romania. One can argue that the two groups of countries had different starting positions. In the Czech Republic, landowners kept their rights to their land even under communism and, to some extent, this was also valid for Hungary. In this context, the transformation process was easier in these cases. Yet, this is not an excuse for Bulgaria and Romania to have completely failed in their transformations. In both countries, the reforms happened with a significant delay because of political disagreements and multiple changes in legislation and regulations. Unlike the case in Hungary, where the logic behind privatization was oriented to the future – that is, based on the preservation of the cooperatives so that they could operate after the reorganization – in Bulgaria and Romania, the overwhelming emphasis of planning and strategic development concentrated on the immediate moment. As a result, land was returned to owners according to historical boundaries (Bulgaria), and this led to considerable land fragmentation (especially in the case of Romania, where, because of legal regulation, the owners received a maximum of five hectares.). This fragmentation still hampers the modernization of agriculture and the dependability of raw agricultural supplies.

With regard to privatization, different methods were adopted in each of the candidate countries. However, it is possible to identify some common features. In general, small enterprises were usually privatized by direct sale or at auction to the highest bidder, or were given back to their previous owners, as was the case in Bulgaria. Large enterprises were mostly turned into joint stock companies, with a subsequent transfer of shares to various owners. In this case, preference was often given to agricultural producers and/or to enterprise employees and managers. The former holds especially for the first-stage food processing branches, such as the dairy, milling, and meat industries. The aim of granting preferential treatment to agricultural producers was, on the one hand, to diminish the monopolistic power in the downstream sector and, on the other hand, to guarantee the supply to processors of agricultural raw materials. This was achieved in Hungary. Concerning sales to enterprise employees, they were able to acquire some of the shares free of charge or to purchase them under favourable conditions. In the Czech Republic and Bulgaria, vouchers were used to purchase shares. A special characteristic of the privatization process in Hungary was the sale of whole enterprises or shares to foreign investors. In contrast, in the Czech Republic, the direct participation of foreign capital in privatization remained limited, as, in the approach chosen, privatization preceded attempts to attract foreign investors. State-owned enterprises were converted into joint stock companies and split up into smaller entities. Privatization then took place through a voucher scheme. Privatization in Romania, which lagged behind the other candidates, advanced rapidly in the latter years with significant state ownership remaining only in fruit and vegetable processing, prepared animal feeds, and tobacco manufacturing.

Overall, the food industry has been attractive to foreign investment. The main sectors that attracted FDI are those of high-value production, often with a significant share of output being designated for export (tobacco, soft drinks, brewing, confectionery, oil refining, and certain specific dairy products). Sugar beet processing was also a popular target. In Hungary, FDI was concentrated in vegetable oil processing, as well as in the confectionery, sugar, tobacco, brewing, and distilling industries. In the Czech Republic, multinationals entered the tobacco and confectionery industries, the vegetable oil sector, and recently also the sugar sector. In Romania, the major sub-sectors to attract FDI were breweries and soft drinks manufacturers. The competitiveness of firms in these sectors has improved considerably, due to the substantial investments made. Most FDI involved the takeover of domestic firms, with subsequent restructuring including new investment, the transfer of new technologies, and marketing expertise. In some countries, privatization was a route by which foreign investment could enter the sector, and FDI flows trended downwards as privatization was completed (Bulgaria).

Factors that attracted foreign investment were local market occupation and expansion, low labour costs, cheap raw materials, and the prospects of these countries entering the EU market in the near future. However, Hungary and the Czech Republic managed to benefit to a much greater extent from the FDI inflows, as they had functioning agro-food industries. In contrast to this, Bulgaria and Romania have many small suppliers, a situation with which it is very difficult for MNEs to work.

Part III
MNEs and MNE Embeddedness in the CEEC Economies

4
MNE Strategies in Hungary

Introduction

Using the 'system' concept – that is, looking at the linkages among local companies, MNEs, public institutions, and universities as one system – this chapter addresses the level of embeddedness of MNEs in Hungary. The first section stresses the efforts of the national government to embed FDI through broad policy measures and programmes, which, on one hand, promote linkages between foreign companies and local suppliers, and, on the other hand, enforce more intensive academia–industry relationships. In this sense, a number of elements of the national innovation system are analyzed. The second section gives a recent picture of the Hungarian food industry, and underlines the challenges the industry faces following EU accession. The third section discusses the cases of Unilever, Nestlé and InBev, and constitutes the principal empirical contribution of the chapter.

Governmental policies to encourage embeddedness

Broad policy measures

One of the major actors responsible for the competitiveness and development of a country is its government. Until EU accession in 2004, the role of the Hungarian government had been very significant in the promotion of FDI through the introduction of different trade and investment policies to facilitate the linkages between multinationals and domestic suppliers. These policies related to high import tariffs; rules of origin; local content requirements; joint venture requirements (this was already a major policy aim during the 1980s and a large number of joint ventures were established); export performance requirements; and fiscal, financial and other initiatives.Trade barriers had a positive influence on local sourcing. For instance, a heavy duty was levied on importing food products into Hungary. In 1997, the rates for industrial products, and agricultural and processed food products were 8.2 per cent and 37.1 per cent, respectively. Average most favoured nation (MFN) tariffs were relatively high for imports of agricultural products and prepared food. There was no preferential access for EU and EFTA countries in these areas (WTO, 1998). This protectionist policy required foreign investors to look for domestic suppliers in order to reduce production costs and to be more competitive. In face-to-face interviews, the representatives of Nestlé, Unilever, and InBev all underlined that these measures encouraged their affiliates to cooperate with local suppliers. In short, although raw material sourcing is highly dependent on the global strategy of the parent company and the place of the foreign affiliate in the global production network, at the beginning of the 1990s, the MNEs in Hungary were 'forced' by the government to source many products locally by virtue of the high import barriers.

Fiscal measures to encourage innovations

The purchase from domestic companies, however, depends not only on the protection barriers the government introduces, but also on the product quality they offer. To increase their competitiveness, local firms have to increase efficiency by using modern production facilities, and information and communication technologies. A dynamic innovation policy can be important in this respect. Since May 2002, Hungary has followed a National Development Plan, also called the Community Support Framework (CSF) document, which sets as a priority the competitiveness of the country through innovation. One of the major challenges in this regard is to overcome the lack of finance. Tax incentives have been introduced to stimulate firms to spend more on R&D. Another step forward was the creation of the 'Research and Technology Innovation Fund', aimed at creating a stable and reliable financial ground for research, technological development and innovation activities.

The government established a Research and Technology Innovation Fund, a unique initiative for CEE, to promote demand driven innovation and knowledge based competitiveness in companies. The Fund is financed by mandatory contributions from all companies registered in Hungary, matched yearly by the government budget. The so-called 'innovation contribution' for medium-sized and large companies, based on a percentage of the (adjusted) net turnover, grew from 0.2 per cent in 2004 to 0.3 per cent by 2006.

In Hungary, the government has encouraged R&D since 1997 by means of R&D tax allowances of 20 per cent. Their rate jumped from 20 per cent in 1997 to 100 per cent in 2000, while the special 300 per cent rule (relating to location at a university or public research institute) has been applicable since 2004. Since 2004, Hungary has used several fiscal measures to stimulate R&D, the most important of which are:

- A 100 per cent Research and Technology and Development (RTD) corporate tax allowance (also available for subcontracted R&D activities if the partner is a public/non-profit research site)
- A 300 per cent RTD tax allowance if the company laboratory is located at a university or public research institute
- In the case of SMEs, there is a special intellectual property right (IPR) tax allowance. The emerging costs of obtaining and maintaining of the patents, utility model and design in Hungary can be deducted from corporate income, assuming that these costs cannot be regarded as direct costs of fundamental research, applied research, and technological development
- Others.[1]

Mr T. Balogh, Director[2] of the Innovation Department, Ministry of Economy and Transport, explained that the new fiscal measures have a considerable impact on the knowledge institutions, and local and foreign companies. The higher corporate tax allowance and the mandatory innovation contribution to the Innovation Fund motivate MNEs to cooperate with local universities and research institutes on particular projects. 'Instead of paying the Fund's contribution or carrying out their own internal R&D, many companies prefer to buy R&D services from any public or non-profit R&D institution', Mr Balogh explained. This led to an increase in company spending for R&D – the share of the business sector in financing gross expenditure on R&D (GERD) increased by 2.3 percentage points (rising to 39.4 per cent from 37.1 per cent in 2004).[3] As result of this policy development, research institutes hold much greater funds and undertake more innovative projects. Figure 4.1 illustrates the strength of linkages between MNEs and local innovative actors. One could see that there is a very strong link between the MNEs and their subsidiaries, as they are integrated in the global production network of the parent company. The mandatory payments to the Innovation Fund contributed to stronger linkages between research institutions and industry (domestic and foreign companies). In addition, the programmes that the government initiated to support SMEs through different

100

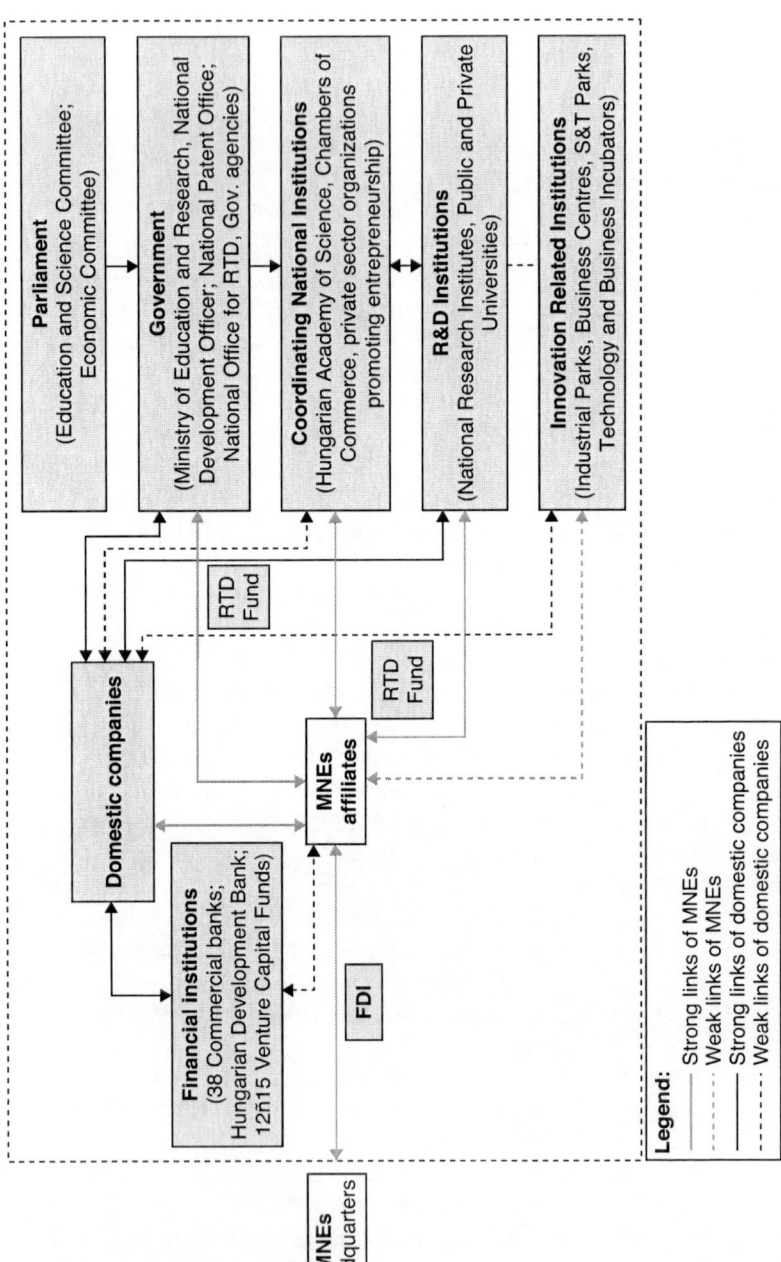

Figure 4.1 MNEs, domestic suppliers, and the linkages between the different actors of the National innovation system
Source: based on European Trend Chart Country Reports – Hungary.

financial measures turned local companies into competitive suppliers to MNEs. Hungary is the only CEE country where government, business and academia are interconnected. Although the linkages between academia and business are still very fragile, there is strong potential for development in this direction.

Apart from fiscal measures, further schemes have been designed to contribute to the enhancement of competitiveness by means of specifically targeting the relationship between academia and industry, usually by supporting the joint development of new products, services and processes. Higher education organizations, R&D institutes, and companies are jointly establishing cooperative research centres (CRCs) in order to achieve target oriented RTD cooperation for strategic purposes. One such a programme has been 'Regional Knowledge Centres at Universities', which is aimed at fostering the creation of research and technological innovation centres at universities in close cooperation with businesses.[4]

Programmes encouraging linkage creation

There are two basic approaches to promote linkages. One involves encouraging linkages between foreign and local supplier companies in general, regardless of the industries involved. The positive effects of this relationship lie in the transfer of technology, shared information, the provision of training, and the giving of financial support to supplier companies. The other approach goes further, in that it involves the establishment of a linkage promotion programme for a specific industry.

As far as the first approach is concerned, an important role in this process of linkage formation is undertaken by the supporting meso-institutions, such as chambers of commerce, business associations, or providers of business development services. 'Without this kind of institutional support, domestic firms might be unable to get the required quality certificate, training or capital needed to become competitive. Moreover, the costs incurred for foreign affiliates might simply be too high for them to become engaged in supplier development activities' (UNCTAD 2001: 173). For example, the Agricultural Marketing Centre (AMC), a public benefit company formed by the Ministry of Agriculture and Rural Development, is an important meso-institution that contributes to the promotion and upgrading of Hungarian producers. Created in 1997, this institution has launched a project to identify and protect the origins of certain Hungarian products. As result, 11 Hungarian agricultural foodstuffs have been patented with a geography-related trade name (origin labelling and geographical marking) and are on the national register of protected product origins; 10 of them have made submissions to the European Union origin protection system for the purpose of recognition and will gain a European market label (AMC CD, 2005).

Mr Jozsef Urban,[5] Project Manager, explained that the AMC also assists the marketing of Hungarian products with publications, market research, event organization, participation on international exhibitions, and markets. One only has to enter the building and talk to the people there to feel the professionalism of the AMC. The agency experts are open and provide foreign clients with a great variety of professionally prepared marketing materials. The agency focuses predominantly on promoting domestic producers. However, the AMC does not include in its priority tasks the development and strengthening of the links between MNEs and local suppliers. In general, the cooperation between local and foreign companies is not a consistent policy for any agricultural or food authority. The examples of the National Association of Food Processing Companies and the Hungarian Agricultural Chamber are striking, as they do not even communicate with MNEs.[6] As an outcome, MNEs consider the role of food meso-institutions insufficiently powerful to influence their decision as to whether or not to work with local suppliers.

The other approach applied to increase the competitiveness of local firms is the establishment of a specific linkage promotion programme, dedicated to increasing and deepening linkages between foreign affiliates and domestic firms.

In Hungary, a linkage promotion programme had already been introduced in 1997 under the name 'Supplier Target Programme'. The firms involved were representatives of the automobile industry. The programme aimed at promoting the most promising way of generating positive FDI spillover effects: the establishment of local supplier ties. However, as Laszlo Kallay[7] from the Ministry of Economy explained, the programme was ineffective. He explained that multinational companies were not interested in collaborating with local firms; their first priority was to increase efficiency, not to consider local development. In this sense, it was somewhat difficult to promote linkage creation when MNEs were not motivated to participate in this initiative. However, later on, certain basic principles of the programme were reconsidered, and it was relaunched in 2000 under the name 'Integrator Supplier Target Programme' (ISTP). The basic idea of the new programme was not to create new linkages but, rather, to develop further the already existing supplier networks in a local cluster. The development of business clusters was also supported by the Széchenyi Plan.[8] The primary purpose was to increase local suppliers' share from the current 10–20 per cent to 30–40 per cent.

In the centre of the project was the core company – the integrator. The integrator firm was the primary partner of the state agent. The chosen integrators were Suzuki, General Electric, Audi, Opel, and Rába. This time, the programme seemed to be effective. The training and advising of SMEs, and qualification and auditing of supplier members in the programme contributed to the success of the programme. In addition, long-term finance for necessary investments in supplier firms was also assured; this included participation in both loans and equity (venture capital function) (Bacskai *et al.*, 2005).

In short, since the mid-1990s Hungary has had a policy of strengthening competitiveness by means of broad policy measures, fiscal measures for R&D, and promotion programmes. Some of the institutions that promote innovation and technical development include the Hungarian Patent Office, the Hungarian Centre for Productivity, the Hungarian Innovation Association, and the National Office of Research and Technology (NORT).[9] These institutions have been responsible for the improvement of SMEs' innovation capabilities, and the promotion of the establishment and development of innovative entities among them (Bacskai *et al.*, 2002). Different support programmes for SMEs have been launched since the mid-1990s and include many incentives to encourage the creation of science and technology parks. Local governments and/or agents received payments in order to create industrial parks, industrial clusters, and incubator houses, as all these contribute to the transfer of know-how from MNEs to domestic enterprises (Szanyi, 2001). All the innovation institutions have conducted consultations and training activities, and identified possible financial resources to increase the competitivess of the local economy. The Hungarian Innovation Association, for instance, has been involved in the legislation process, and has actively participated in the elaboration of legislation, and concepts related to R&D and innovation by cooperating with other ministries, chambers, and organizations.

The question that arises now is:

Have all these governmental measures been sufficient to embed MNEs in the local economy, and to motivate them to internationalize their R&D centres in Hungary?

The next section traces the answer by presenting the development of the Hungarian food industry, and showing how deep the linkages between the MNEs and the domestic companies have become after the entry of the country into the EU.

The food industry in Hungary

Overview

This section will undertake a brief review of the Hungarian food industry in order to introduce the reader to the importance and competitiveness of the sector, and help in the understanding of the context in which MNEs operate. I also analyze the development of agriculture in order to show its potential to supply the food industry. By focusing on the consumer market, I reveal the significant contribution of MNEs for its development, and underline that MNEs have managed to become important players in the consumer market by being market leaders. Knowledge of the Hungarian food industry and consumer market will contribute to the better understanding of MNEs' strategies in the local market and in the region.

In 2005, the agriculture and food industry contributed 6.8 per cent to the gross domestic product (GDP) of Hungary, the share of the food industry being 3.5 per cent. The food processing industry is traditional in the Hungarian economy, and has a strategic role in domestic food supply and export. It occupies second place within the processing industry, which consists of 14 branches. The food industry remains one of the most important sectors in the economy, providing up to 14 per cent of industrial production, according to the Hungarian Investment and Trade Development Agency (ITDH). The industry operates with domestic raw materials, purchasing 75 per cent of the agricultural output. About one fifth of the industry's products are sold abroad. The food, drink and tobacco products group represents 6 per cent of Hungary's total exports and 3.5 per cent of imports.The trade balance has remained positive over a long period (Ministry of Agriculture and Rural Development of Hungary, 2005: 37). The food industry is a sizable employer. Although, over the years, the number of workers has decreased, it still remains significant. In 2004, it employed close to 120,000 people, which is about 4 per cent of employed Hungarians.

Hungarian products represent 1.3 per cent of the value of the products of the food and drink industry of the 25-member EU, which totals close to €670 billion. The production of the Hungarian food industry is approximately identical with that of Portugal, Sweden, Finland, the Czech Republic, and Austria. In Hungary, the share of agricultural products, which primarily end up in processing, amounts to 66 per cent (Ministry of Agriculture and Rural Development of Hungary, 2005).

Food manufacturers in Hungary are extremely diversified. There are approximately 8000 enterprises involved in the food industry,

79 per cent of which are micro-enterprises with fewer than 10 people, 19.8 per cent are SMEs, while large enterprises with more than 250 employees make up only 1.2 per cent. Considering the shares from production and export, however, the proportion is the other way around: the large companies have a share in 64 per cent of production and 72 per cent of exports. Large multinational companies are strongly represented in some branches of the industry, such as the vegetable oil and margarine industry, confectionery industry, brewing, and the tobacco industry. FDI contributed to the modernization of factories and an increase in production efficiency. The inflow of foreign capital also helped develop competition and marketing in the food processing sector, which had previously been structured in such a way that production units served their own local areas, and often the Soviet market, free from any real competition (Hastenberg, 1999). Investments in the food processing industry increased the competitiveness of the sector by raising market adaptability, productivity, and the speed of concentration. The priority has been to conform to EU standards in quality, food safety, animal protection, hygiene, and environmental protection.

The productivity of the industry, however, is still modest. A transformation of the production structure, increase of utilization of capacity, and greater specialization remain important tasks. The food processing industry depends on a well-developed agricultural production sector capable of delivering large volumes of high quality raw products. This is critical if Hungary is to compete with other nations in the EU. Small volumes of raw products supplied on an inconsistent basis will not allow for the development of a food processing industry that meets the quality and efficiency standards of EU competition.

Consumer market

The modernization of the food industry changed the trends in Hungary's consumer market. It is increasingly converging with the consumption patterns of Western European countries. Thirty-eight per cent of the population is still considered to have traditional eating habits, but there are more and more 'modern consumers'. These are Hungarians, typically between the ages of 25 and 29, who reside in urban areas and come from higher income backgrounds (Government of Canada, 2005a). As Hungarians increasingly lead busier lifestyles, the demand for processed foods that are predominantly offered by food MNEs is also growing. These include breakfast cereals, dairy products, frozen foods, ice cream and frozen yogurt, snacks, nuts, and alcoholic beverages.

In 2004, Hungarians spent about 25 per cent of their income on food and beverages. This number has decreased in recent years and is trending towards that of high-income countries, where consumers typically spend 10 per cent of their income on food. At the same time, 31 per cent of total food expenditure goes towards food for consumption outside the home.

The domestic retail food sector underwent significant changes. The key drivers for change were the demand for foreign branded goods with which Hungarian consumers had become increasingly familiar through the media and foreign travel. In addition, hypermarkets offer a great variety of products and, in some cases, at the cheapest possible price (Lidl, for example). Food MNEs also prefer working with Western retail chains, as most of them are global partners with whom they have long-term relationships. In addition, retailers stipulate a quality standard, which is very important to the work of the food processors. By introducing consumers to new varieties or products of higher quality with a longer shelf life, retail chains are increasingly shifting consumer demand towards healthier foods.

Hungary has been one of the most important expansion markets for Western retail groups since the early 1990s, and many of the continent's big names are present in the country, although a few local players are still holding their own. By the end of 2005, the competition between hypermarkets and discounters had become stronger. In 2005, Tesco was the most progressive chain, opening almost 20 new outlets, while the new discount chain Lidl had more than 50 outlets by the end of 2005. The discount channel Plus changed its strategy, and, like Lidl, offered fewer branded and more private label products (Euromonitor International, Packaged Food in Hungary 2006c).

The market leader is Metspa, a joint venture between Germany's Metro group and the Austrian Spar business, with sales of €1.6 billion in 2002, according to a recent list compiled by M+M. But Hungarian-owned CBA Kereskedelmi and Co-op Hungary are not far behind, with sales of €1.4 billion and €1.23 billion respectively, just ahead of the British market leader Tesco with €1.15 billion.[10]

In 2003, 53 per cent of the retail grocery sector in Hungary was controlled by international retail chains.[11] The changing environment of retail distribution is positively affecting food sales – hypermarkets and supermarkets enjoy substantial market power. In fact, about 35 per cent of households in Hungary already shop in hypermarkets (11 per cent of consumers buy their food from supermarkets).[12] The increasing presence of retail chains reinforces the position of hypermarkets, as families decide to carry out one large weekend shop.[13]

The Hungarian consumer groups are becoming more segmented as the income gap between the wealthy and the poor grows. Due to this difference, consumer demand for cheap food products and expensive luxury items increases. The cheapest food is offered by discounters: 21 per cent of Hungarian shoppers choose the low-price format.[14] In Hungary, Tesco's hypermarkets are the most popular, attracting 18 per cent of shoppers. Not surprisingly, the penetration of private labels is also increasing. Private labels are already well established in Hungary, with 68 per cent of shoppers saying that they buy them on a regular basis. A considerable challenge for Hungarian producers was the entrance of the Lidl chain into the discount market. This was the most important event in the Hungarian retail trade in 2004, as the chain offers prices at 20 per cent lower than the EU average. Lidl is characterized by many private label and exclusive brands in its range, and imports many of the products in its portfolio, thus generating intense competition for local manufacturers. However, the flood of cheap retailers on the Hungarian market is just one part of all the challenges that the local food industry faces.

EU impact on MNEs

In May 2004, Hungary joined the EU. This had a significant impact on the food industry, as it faced more intense competition. The relatively safe and protected Hungarian market could no longer continue. EU membership resulted in large restructurings in the local economy.

In economic terms, the sector is virtually integrated in the EU's food industry. According to ITDH, 50 per cent of the investments in the sector are from EU investors, and 80 per cent of the export goes to other EU countries. Since 2001, the trade turnover of organizations classified as belonging to the food industry has grown annually – in 2004, by 3 per cent. A decisive percentage of exports were aimed at the inner-EU market, where market expansion could be achieved as result of accession to the EU. The proportion of imported raw and processed foods from the EU member states is significant. ITDH reports that, because of accession, this proportion is growing faster than that of exports.

EU membership facilitated MNEs in following their global strategies oriented towards increased competitiveness. The accession of 10 countries to the EU on 1 May meant that export quotas, customs levies and export subsidies were lifted between existing and new member states. The null tariff barriers since 2004 allowed MNEs to import products from all over Europe. It was no longer possible to force companies to source locally; there was a global supply chain. MNEs achieve economies of scales thanks to concentration of production; that is, the different products from the global portfolio are manufactured in different countries and the products are exported to other countries. The standardized products, that is the global brands, can be imported easily from one EU country to another. To increase competitiveness, MNEs put efforts into optimizing productivity and reducing costs, often resulting in plant closures. As the government could no longer be protectionist, and the competition from EU firms was tougher, MNEs began to pull out of Hungary.

A good example is Kraft Foods, the leading manufacturer of confectionery on the Hungarian market. Its number one market share did not stop the company from relocating confectionery production to Bratislava in order to reduce costs. The company was also the third largest producer of coffee on the Hungarian market, but relocating production to Vienna, Austria seemed more efficient. The company closed down its only production facility in Hungary in the first half of 2004, with the loss of 320 jobs. Management justified the closure of the Hungarian plant as this was in accordance with its four-pillar plan for 'sustainable growth'. The plan emphasizes investment in brand development, whilst trying to reduce costs for the company's overall structure. Although Kraft Foods no longer has any production facilities in Hungary, the company confirmed that its existing lines of Kraft products would continue to be sold in the local market and that, for the most part, the products would be imported from the Vienna and Bratislava plants. Even the fact that the company was the market leader did not stop management closing the plant, and the Hungarian government could do nothing in response.

Another example is Unilever, which closed its margarine and salad dressing plant in Budapest. Unilever relocated production to plants in Katowice in Poland, Pratau in Germany, and Nelahozeves in the Czech Republic. The company dismissed 200 workers at the plant, which closed in June 2006.[15] Unilever wanted to cut operation costs, the better to serve its largest central European markets in Poland and Germany from closer locations. The company has continued to operate three other plants in Hungary, which make instant soup and ice cream.

The story of the margarine factory is interesting. It was acquired in 1992. Unilever owned the company before it was nationalized in 1948, and it produced under Unilever's licence thereafter. In short, Unilever had very strong links with this particular factory. The plant was producing the local margarine brand Delma and the global brand Rama solely for the Hungarian market. After the acquisition, the company invested heavily in new equipment in order to increase production capacity and the quality of the products. The Budapest based plant became one of Unilever's best plants (Hastenberg, 1999).

Despite this rich history of Unilever's margarine plant, Unilever closed it in mid-2006 and moved its production to other countries. This was in line with the global restructuring of the company aimed at increasing efficiency, and was facilitated by the entry of Hungary into the EU.

Before EU entry, one could certainly claim that Kraft Foods and Unilever were embedded in the local economy: they invested heavily, they were market leaders, and they sourced many products locally. In addition, as already seen, the Hungarian government had done a great deal to improve its innovation system. It was EU entry that led to the questioning of Kraft Foods' and Unilever's embeddness in the Hungarian economy.

The next section presents the activity of Unilever, InBev and Nestlé in Hungary. The interviews with the management staff of these companies reveal the strategies that dictate their operations. Business managers were asked directly about their relations with local suppliers, research institutes and universities, and retailers.

Firm case analysis

Unilever (Hungary)

Unilever started its expansion into the CEE marketplace in the early 1990s. Unilever Magyarország Kft was established in 1991, and entered into the ice cream, margarine, and detergent businesses through acquisitions, rapidly becoming a dominant player in the Hungarian consumer marketplace.[16] In addition to its well-known international brands, Unilever acquired a wide range of domestic brands, which have subsequently been integrated into its portfolio. Unilever (Hungary) boasts several manufacturing facilities in Hungary, as well as a research and development centre in Nyírbátor, Eastern Hungary.

The former Vice-Chairman[17] of Unilever (Hungary and East Central Europe) Mr A was contacted to discuss Unilever's policies. The manager had been directly involved in the negotiations for CEE acquisitions, and he mentioned that Unilever had been interested in CEE markets since 1988. The first negotiation regarding a joint venture with a Hungarian company took place in February 1988. In mid-1991, Unilever started to build the Hungarian business in foods, ice cream, frozen products, detergents, and personal care. The company introduced its global brands; however, it kept strong local brands – for example, Delma, Biopon, Amodent, and Baba. It produces or distributes margarines (Rama, Delma,

Flora), dehydrated stocks (Knorr), mustards, ketchups, mayonnaises, teas (Lipton), ice creams (Carte D'or, Magnum, Vienetta, Cornetto), cleaning supplies (Biopon, Domestos, CIF), soaps, shampoos, and body care products (Baba, Dove, Sunsilk, Signal, Amodent). Since 1992, Unilever has been a market leader in fast moving consumer goods in Hungary – margarines, tea-based drinks, ice creams, domestic cleaning products, and tooth-care products. Since 1996, Unilever (Hungary) developed the former Yugoslavia, Bulgaria and Albania.

According to Mr A, the major factors that explain the higher level of embeddedness of Unilever subsidiaries in Hungary and the Czech Republic, compared with Bulgaria and Romania, are:

• The stage of economic development
• The legislative framework of the country
• Transparency in the privatization schemes in the early 1990s.

By comparison, in Bulgaria and Romania the move to the market economy came later; the privatization schemes were not clear and the legislative framework was not developed. In these circumstances, the risks of investing in these countries were rather high. 'If you are not sure that you will get your money back when you invest, you simply do not go for this', the manager said. 'We were in a negotiation process for acquisition of some Bulgarian and Romanian factories; however, there was great uncertainty.' Subsequently, Unilever bought a detergent company in Romania and, in Bulgaria, the margarine company Kaliakra. The Bulgarian subsidiary is relatively small and is governed by Unilever (Romania). In 1997, because of the political and financial crisis in Bulgaria, Unilever closed its operation and returned to Bulgaria in 1998.

How did Unilever decide which local companies to acquire?

Mr A explained that the company has a very clearly defined strategy concerning which markets to enter.

• First, their strategy is to pick up the best companies, no matter how big or small.
• Second, speed dictates their approach, as the competitive advantage of being the first mover is crucial.
• Third, Unilever's idea is to buy local well-known products that might become strong brands.

Unilever has one operation in each of the countries in CEE, but in some countries, there could be more than one factory; for example, Unilever (Hungary) runs four factories[18] with approximately 1500 employees.

Unilever's strategy is not to produce all brands in each country; that is why they specialize in different products in each country, depending on that country's facilities (in Bulgaria: margarine; in Romania: the detergent business; in the Czech republic: mainly the food business, in Hungary: food, ice cream, detergents, and personal care products). All countries enhance their portfolios with global brands by importing them from their place of manufacture.

With regard to the backward integration of Unilever, this is a permanently changing process. In 1992, Unilever had very strong backward integration with local suppliers. More than 90 per cent of the raw materials – for example, sunflower and rape – were locally sourced. The rationale was that governments limited imports into each country by means of high import regimes, and Unilever was under considerable pressure to work locally. Packing suppliers were also local firms, although many of them were later purchased by Unilever's Western packaging suppliers, which had come to Hungary together with Unilever. In any case, local packaging suppliers benefited because they acquired Unilever's know-how in packaging and Western quality standards. When Unilever acquired a factory, there was a network of suppliers in existence and the company made use of it; however, they also developed new suppliers themselves, and many Western suppliers also came to the area. Unilever's aim is to globalize its sourcing networks. All CEE countries are fully integrated in Unilever's global networks.

Unilever worked closely with a number of Hungarian universities and business schools for the recruitment of young trainees and qualified staff. The student organizations AIESEC and IAESTE undertook a survey to discover who was the most preferred employer; the results showed that Unilever was placed at the top of the list for several years in the mid-1990s. Unilever's strategy was to train its managers, the best of them being trained abroad. In Hungary, the Czech Republic and Romania, Unilever has internal R&D centres responsible for certain categories of products; the company also has its own network of R&D centres. It undertakes market research worldwide, while only basic research is done in home countries with personnel from other parts of the world. Unilever also contributed to local development by introducing standards to consumer goods. However, management development is considered to be Unilever's strongest contribution to the Hungarian economy – much more so than helping suppliers to upgrade. Unilever came with an 'army' of experts to train youngsters, and to help in the creation of an integrated Unilever identity. Of course, technological investments were also an important benefit for Hungary.

At the beginning of the 1990s, Unilever used predominantly local retailers; as there were no others. In addition, local retailers were unfamiliar with the integrated supply chain. They had no capital and limited know-how, and Unilever tried to develop these. As from 1994, Western retail chains began to enter the Hungarian market, which changed the situation.

Unilever distributes in two ways: in part, directly – mainly to large retailers; and, in part, through its concessionary distributors, to small retailers. Distributors sell two thirds of the overall production of the company. Unilever itself is also engaged in a form of retailing. Under the name Algida Express, ice creams and other deep-frozen products are distributed directly to consumers by vans in regular, scheduled journeys.[19]

Concerning Hungarian competitors, it transpires that most of them disappeared in the transition years or occupy the low-market niches in Hungary. Unilever works with the local branch associations and governmental institutions. Mainly, their cooperation is aimed at creating a favourable legislative framework. The associations of particular importance for Hungary and Unilever have been the Branded Association and the Food and Detergent Association.

Mr B – who had been in charge of the subsidiaries in Hungary, Croatia and Slovenia[20] until 2005 – elaborated on the picture relating to Unilever's strategy in Hungary. When asked whether Unilever had a regional investment strategy plan that pre-determined the level of investment in a particular country, he confirmed that there was such a plan. However, he explained that the level of development of the country influenced this plan. The manager explained that, in general, the more developed countries attract greater investment. This helps us to understand why Unilever invested to a greater degree in Hungary than in Bulgaria and Romania.

The duration of the partnership is also relevant. Unilever had had a good relationship with Hungary since the 1970s (different brands of Unilever products were produced under brand licences – Rama margarine, for example). Otherwise, Unilever invested heavily in Hungary at the beginning of the 1990s.

First and foremost, the reason for investment in Hungary was the strong opportunities the company saw in the local market. Second, the company was attracted by the proximity of the Western and Central

European markets. The stable political and economic situation also had an impact on the decision; the legal context of the country was significant. Next, Unilever's strategic decisions were influenced by the production performance of the sector, the low labour costs, and so on.

Unilever mainly produces for the local market, but also for export: it exports ice cream and detergents to Eastern and Western Europe. In 2004, when Mr B was asked whether there was a likelihood of closing a plant in Hungary, his response was that a distinction should be made between two situations: (1) the complete shut-down of all the activities of the subsidiary; and (2) the closure of a product line, or a reduction in production in general. In relation to the option (1), he pointed out that this was quite difficult to achieve. It would only be possible under circumstances of *force majeur*, such as war (as in the case of the former Yugoslavia) or political instability, and so on. Concerning option (2) closure of a plant might occur at some point as Unilever had a global supply chain strategy, and any particular product could be imported instead of being produced in Hungary. Two years later, it became clear that the moment had arrived, as Unilever closed its Hungarian margarine plant.

As far as retailers are concerned, it became clear that it is essential that Unilever work with both local and foreign retailers. In Hungary, for example, Co-op is an extremely mobile and strong local retail chain with which Unilever has a good relationship. The subsidiary tries to find a good balance between both local and foreign retailers.

Unilever cooperates with universities and professional schools, as it needs a qualified labour force and does not wish to experience a vacuum in labour supply.

> Does Unilever receive help from the local branch associations, business centres or agencies for regional development?

Unilever is, on the one hand, an MNE, but, on the other hand, it is also a local company. Hence, the company works within the national legacy and with the local authorities. No specific support or relations were underlined.

Unilever (Hungary) uses a mix of local and Western banks, but the company does not use them for credit purposes: this is a decision taken at parent company level. Unilever's strategy towards suppliers is a balance of global and local suppliers, according to the best interests of the company. Global suppliers are related to logistic services, telecommunications, and packaging. Local suppliers are used to provide them with raw materials, packaging, and particular services.

Unilever's strategy towards local competitors in the region is to compete with them in different ways. There is no such a thing as a 'small' competitor. Local competitors deserve considerable attention. Unilever has distribution agreements with some of its competitors in Croatia and Slovenia. The Hungarian subsidiary is independent from the parent company in its everyday decisions, but is dependent for global decisions.

InBev (Hungary)

In Hungary, only a few local brewers owned by large international holdings are active. There are four big beer producers on the Hungarian market: Borsodi Brewery (InBev), Brau Union Hungarian Breweries (Heineken Group), Dreher Breweries (SAB), and Pecs Brewery (Ottakringer Group, Vienna). In addition to introducing new products, brewers create innovative forms of packaging for their traditional beer products from year to year. Beer produced in Hungary is traditionally of excellent quality (Association of Hungarian Brewers, 2004).

InBev's Communications Director[21] explained that beer is an expensive product to transport, as it contains water and is heavy. Therefore, it is clear that, if brewers want a particular market, they have to buy an enterprise there. When Interbrew (since 2004, InBev) was in the process of negotiating the purchase of a Hungarian brewery, a spontaneous privatization was undertaken – there was still no privatization agency at the beginning of the 1990s. Heineken was also negotiating for Borsodi but, while Interbrew was interested in buying good local brands, Heineken only sought good facilities. This contributed to Interbrew attaining ownership of Borsodi in 1991, as its strategy included the retention of local brands. This acquisition led to significant changes in the life of the brewery, as privatization gave new momentum to the procedures targeted at the improvement of quality, technologies and products. Yet, Inbev's management admitted that buying a local brand is a risky business, as the brewery might face market difficulties if there were economic or political changes.

The success of InBev in Hungary motivated the parent company to start a process of acquisitions on a broader scale in CEE. Since 1991, InBev has bought companies in Romania, the Czech Republic, Poland and Russia. In Bulgaria, following the same strategy of keeping local brands, Interbrew bought several breweries, as they were quite cheap; however, they could not maintain the brand portfolio and lost market share.

In Hungary, InBev owns one factory – Borsodi Sörgyár Rt., with 550 employees and an office in Budapest, where the sales managers are situated. InBev also had a malt plant, which was sold in 2004. Borsodi is one of Hungary's largest breweries, having begun producing beer and malt in 1973 in the suburbs of Bőcs, a settlement located in the vicinity of Miskolc.

Hungary and the Czech Republic are somewhat mature markets. Borsodi is a market leader in Hungary; however, it only has a 2–3 per cent advantage over the second ranked company. In socialist times, all breweries had well-defined operation regions in Hungary. There was no competition among the breweries with regard to regional markets. Borsodi was responsible for the Eastern part of Hungary. After the privatization process in the early 1990s, all breweries became competitors, as they were fighting for the largest possible share of the Hungarian market. Borsodi Sörgyár Rt. managed to remain one of the biggest players in the market, and further strengthened its position on the Hungarian beer market by offering a wide choice of brands to beer drinkers. The principal brand of the brewery is 'Borsodi Sör', the biggest selling beer brand in Hungary. In order to maintain and improve the market position of this best-known and most popular brand, Borsodi, the factory pursues intense marketing communication activities. The brewery regularly participates in the organizing and sponsoring of various sports events (both mass events and professional competitions) and music events. In addition to Borsodi Sör, other members of the Borsodi family are Borsodi Barna (a brown beer); Borsodi Póló (an alcohol free beer); and Borsodi Bivaly (The Buffalo of Borsodi), introduced to the market in 2003. Borsodi Bivaly, the result of domestic research and development, is a lager with an alcohol content of 6.5 per cent ABV and created a new segment in the Hungarian sales market.

Borsodi cooperates with Miskols University for market research projects. The University also has a post-graduate programme where Borsodi's personnel are trained. The other university with which Borsodi cooperates is Kerteszeti Egyetem (the Food and Agricultural University), Budapest, which produces food engineers.

During the spring of 2003, Borsodi Sörgyár introduced an innovative product – a new Hungarian premium brand called Borostyán ('Amber'). In the wide range of products offered by the brewery, there is another popular premium brand in the Hungarian market – this is the global brand Stella Artois and Stella Artois NA, an alcohol free beer. This is one of the dynamically developing brands in the premium segment of the Hungarian beer market that has significantly expanded its position during recent years. Among the brewery's products are Holsten, the 'light'

American Rolling Rock, the traditional Kinizsi beer, and the favourites of connoisseur beer drinkers – the imported Staropramen, Leffe, and Hoegaarden beers.

In Hungary, there is a strong Czech beer culture, and that is why Borsodi decided to import Staropramen. In addition, there is a strong Czech film culture; every year there is a festival of Czech cinema and Czech companies have subsidized the marketing of Staropramen. InBev headquarters agreed to import Staropramen into Hungary, but they were sceptical about importing the beer into the CEE region as a whole, as this might have been unprofitable. InBev also offers the global brands Brahma and Beck's; the latter is brewed in Hungary. The key factors of the company's success are long-term strategic planning, consequent brand construction, consistently excellent quality, the European level of productiveness, outstanding cost efficiency, and the company's innovation practices (Association of Hungarian Brewers, 2003). InBev's results are due to its preparedness to be quick to respond; the flexibility with which it reacts to consumer and market demands; and its product and packaging innovations, which enable it to act as a trend setter in the Hungarian beer market.

At the beginning of the 1990s, when Interbrew bought the Borsodi plant, the beer was low quality and very cheap. The main consumers were low-class people working in heavy industry. When they were laid off, the consumption of beer decreased considerably. At the same time, the price of beer also went up, and this additionally shrank the beer market. Hungarians used to consume over 100 litres of beer per capita; however, the average beer consumption per capita decreased and, in 2006, is around 72 litres. InBev's management said that approaching the beer consumption that characterized the 1970s and 1980s (over 100 litres per capita) no longer seemed to be a realistic target. There are very high levels of competition from wine producers. Wine consumption became popular in Hungary and took a progressively larger market share. There are many good private wineries and many people prefer drinking high quality wine, which is considered very healthy. In addition, many members of parliament have wineries, and the excise on wine is very low (for years, there was no excise duty on wine production at all). As many of the beer consumers are mainly low-income people, a strong factor contributing to the decrease of beer consumption is the so-called 'junk wine' – a very cheap beverage made of chemicals and containing 12 per cent alcohol. It is a beverage that has been produced illegally and has attracted clients with low incomes. Put differently, 30 per cent of the beer market has disappeared, and there is no prospect of its being recovered. Borsodi has a productive capacity of 3 million hectolitres but only sold 2.26

million hectoliters of beer in 2004 – 1.3 per cent less than in 2003. The company's net sales returns decreased by 4.6 per cent compared with 2003 because of a strong competition from low-cost imported beer. In contrast to earlier years, the company's pre-tax profit underwent a drastic fall of 45 per cent, decreasing to HUF 4 billion in 2004, accounted for by a flood of cheap, imported beers (Association of Hungarian Brewers, 2004).

In response to customer demand, and following international trends, brewers in Hungary have successfully increased the market share of beer sold in aluminum cans (Association of Hungarian Brewers, 2004). As a somewhat adverse development in the years before 2004, the gradual saturation of the consumer market was coupled with a significant, if not dramatic, increase in the level of the most important taxes in the sector: consumer tax and excise tax. Since the 1990s, excise duty has increased gradually. In 2006, for example, excise duty on a 0.5 litre bottle was HUF 25; VAT in 2006 was 20 per cent (having been 25 per cent in 2004). Although VAT decreased, the excise duty increased, and so the price of the beer did not go down. Put differently, there is around a 50 per cent tax burden on beer.

Until 2004, the Hungarian beer market had been closed. Hungary's accession to the EU brought about fundamental changes in the situation of brewers in the Hungarian market. As of May 2004, all import restrictions and levies on beer produced in other EU member states were lifted, and even import duties to non-EU members decreased significantly (Hungary faces competition from Croatia). This resulted in an excessive volume of cheap canned beer being dumped on the Hungarian market, which had a significant negative impact on the local brewers' positions. Another reason for the flood of canned beer into Hungary was that, in January 2004, the German Bundestag introduced environmental legislation according to which producers had to pay a deposit fee of 0.25 cents on each beer can in a drive to reduce littering. The legislation, in one sense, proved to be dramatically successful; the German beer market had to switch from cans to recyclable packaging. However, this left German brewers with underused canning lines and desperate for new markets. In Hungary, beer was at good prices and canned beers were considered to be premium. This motivated German beer producers to move their can production facilities to Hungary, in order to dispose of the stock they had. 'In Hungary, multinational retailers are very strong and a German producer can easily sell its production because retailers were interested in selling cheap products', Mr A of InBev explained. 'Moreover, beer is one of the so-called attractive products as it invites customers to enter the supermarket. This additionally motivated retail chains to have cheap beers.' By June 2004, the Hungarian market was flooded with cans. It was physically impossible for InBev (Borsodi) to produce a beer in a can at an equivalent price. However, the company reacted to this market challenge and the situation changed. Borsodi worked with the government over new environmental legislation promoting recyclable packaging. The legislation has been in effect since January 2005 and limits the production of cans. If a particular producer exceeds its quota, then that company has to pay a penalty tax. This is also valid for retailers. In this way, producers and retail chains are no longer motivated to sell unlimited quantities of cheap beer in cans. However, it should be taken into consideration that, for the beer business, price has become a progressively more crucial factor. Retailers introduce their own private label beers to satisfy the low-income market niche. And, even though the beer that they distribute is often of a lower quality, it still attracts a great deal of custom.

As far as governance of the company is concerned, Borsodi has always been overseen by local managers. During the early years of investment, there were two or three foreign managers but, as the operation process was going smoothly, governance was transferred to local management. However, since 2005 InBev's policies have changed and, from January 2006, Borsodi has once again had a foreigner as an executive director. This was as a result of global strategic reorganization by InBev since December 2005. In the past, the parent company did not intervene locally as long as the market share was growing. This situation has changed and the parent company uses a more centralized approach. In any case, marketing activities for Borsodi beers are local; for Stella Artois, they are global.

Borsodi also receives centralized orders, which suppliers use to determine at what price and under what conditions to work with them. Purchasing of malt has also been centralized following the sale of the malt plant to InBev's global suppliers and, hence, the parent company negotiates with them. Packaging activities are centralized. IT issues are also centrally negotiated. The energy supply is local. Some years ago, in 2001, for example, Hungarian brewers (including Interbrew) paid special attention to purchasing input materials locally (agricultural materials, packaging materials, chemicals, fuels, and electricity), and were thus considered to be major drivers of raw material and energy demand in Hungary (Association of Hungarian Brewers, 2001).

Since 2004, following two major events – Interbrew became the global world leader; InBev, and Hungary entered the EU – the picture is a little different. Borsodi turned into a highly centralized subsidiary, completely integrated into the global supply chain of the parent company. The suppliers are centrally approved, the executive director is a foreigner, every activity is reported to the parent company, and all decisions are concentrated at a regional or global level (the only exception being sales issues).

Nestlé (Hungary)

Nestlé Hungary runs five factories in Hungary, in Szerencs, Diósgyôr, Bük, Kékkút and Törökbálint. Nestlé entered the Hungarian market in 1991, acquiring two chocolate factories in Szerencs and Diósgyôr. Initially, there were three confectionery companies in Hungary: the Budapest Chocolate Company, Gyôri biscuits (privatized by Danone), and the Szerencs company: Nestlé bought the Szerencs company. Since 1992, Nestlé has consistently improved its businesses. In 1998, Nestlé Group acquired the pet food company Jupiter in Bük, close to the Austrian border. Moreover, Nestlé has chosen Budapest as a location for its CEE pet food headquarters. The reasons were that:

- The company had a good history in Hungary
- The production of pet-food in Hungary was relatively cheap compared with Western Europe
- Before 2004, there was a 'custom curtain' between CEE and Western Europe, and therefore many products had to be produced locally.

In 2000, Nestlé acquired a water business in Kékkút and, in 2003, further extended its activities into the ice cream business in Törökbálint. The Group has between 1500 and 2000 employees, as they mainly use seasonal workers in the ice cream and water businesses.

In Hungary, the company is present in the market with instant coffee, chocolate and confectionery, culinary products, cocoa powders, breakfast cereals, infant nutrition, pet food, mineral water, ice cream, and frozen foods.

Nestlé's Human Resources Managing Director[22], Mr Istvan Kapus explained that Nestlé (Hungary) improves its portfolio with imports of products from neighbouring countries, such as confectionery products from the Czech Republic, Kit-Kat from Bulgaria, and chocolate waffles from Romania. Hungary normally exports beverages to the other CEE markets. In short, in line with the global restructuring of Nestlé, each country is specialized in the production of particular products.

Nestlé's high volume of investment in Hungary is justified by the early opening of the Hungarian economy. Entrepreneurship in Hungary has been encouraged since the 1980s, when many foreign companies started to collaborate with local companies, either by creating co-packing agreements with them or with licensing agreements. Nestlé had a licensing agreement with the Szerencs plant and the Group subsequently acquired that company, as they already had good business partnership relations. In short, Nestlé bought plants that had previously produced Nestlé products and, at the same time, these products were a core priority for Nestlé. In any case, in the early 1990s Hungary had a competitive advantage over all countries from the region, as it had skilled workers and semi-skilled workers who were willing to work and management cadres who spoke foreign languages. In addition, Nestlé had a relatively advanced financial system and a feasible infrastructure. Hungarian customers were used to Western products; they probably purchased the highest quantity of 'Western' goods out of all the CEE countries. The Nestlé Group is the biggest food company in the world, and its products were well known in Hungary even before the company decided to be among the first foreign investors.

In the early 1990s, customs barriers were very high, so MNEs had to buy local companies if they wanted to be present in a particular market. After the Central European Free Trade Agreement (CEFTA), the circumstances changed and so did Nestlé. It introduced a regional strategy, the essence of which was a specialization of different countries in different products and the importation of all other products from the portfolio from neighbouring CEE countries.

In the late 1990s, Nestlé closed one plant, Zamat, that had been manufacturing ground roasted coffee. The rationale behind the closure was that this was not a core business; some of Zamat's activities, such as the production of Nesquick, were transferred to Szerencs. In the early years of investment, Nestlé had had to restructure the newly acquired plants, as they had very low efficiency levels and very wide product ranges. In Szerencs, for example, 1600 people worked, producing less than 10,000 tonnes of products. In 2006, there were 350 people producing 25,000 tonnes. This change could be attributed to the replacement of the handmade production of chocolate and sugar products with automated beverage production.

Nestlé's supply is organized on global scale. There is the so-called 'Euro purchasing team', which is responsible for the whole of Europe; for example, purchasing different types of packaging materials, such as boxes, bottles, and so on. The Hungarian Purchasing Manager is responsible for the purchases for the Czech Republic and Poland. There is a global trend towards standardizing packaging materials.

To better illustrate Nestlé's global supply chain, let us take, for example, the production of beverages. The raw materials are cocoa or coffees, which are imported from Germany or Spain. The jars come from Poland, the filling is made in Hungary, and the production uses only the best suppliers in the region.

The production of Nesquick presents another example of the production chain. The raw materials are sugar and cocoa powder. Cocoa powder is imported from the Czech Republic. The sugar is imported from abroad, as the sugar company in the immediate vicinity does not meet Nestlé's criteria – the highest quality at the lowest possible price. It is according to this principle that Nestlé chooses suppliers, no matter whether local or global. The foreign supplier charges lower prices and carries better quality products. These lower prices abroad are the result of long-term contracts for worldwide supplies in large quantities. This enables the Nestlé Group to buy raw materials and semi-manufactured articles at very favourable prices. Nestlé makes use of such networks of approved suppliers for worldwide supplies. Besides this, Hungarian local suppliers generally cannot offer the large quantities involved, so they have little chance of becoming an approved supplier.

Nestlé distributes its products through local and foreign retail chains. The company works with the local retailers such as Co-op and CBA, and multinational chains such as Tesco or Auchan and Metro. The foreign chains have a greater market share and so they sell most of Nestlé's products. Nestlé pursues a 'wherever, whenever, however' distribution strategy, specifically designed to find alternative distribution channels to the food retailers for products such as pet food, ice cream, and bottled water. There is a special team in Nestlé (Hungary) that is responsible for alternative channels of distribution, such as corner shops or petrol stations.

Nestlé collaborates with the Technical University in Budapest and the Budapest University of Economics. However, the company does not have any special contracts with them as the company employs very few of the graduates from these universities. However, the company stays in touch with the younger generation, as it is the basic consumer of Nestlé's products.

Nestlé management is convinced that different governments have different attitudes to the company. The previous government, which was conservative, preferred to support the local small and medium-sized entrepreneurs, while the social-liberal government in place in 2006 is better able to recognize the role of the MNEs.

EU membership further increased competition. Salaries grew by up to 3–4 per cent, and energy prices went up. However, the prices of food products could not grow by more than 0.5–1 per cent, which meant that Nestlé had to be increasingly more efficient. Improvement in efficiency is crucial for Nestlé's success in the Hungarian market. However, Nestlé Hungária Kft. posted record sales growth in 2004, achieving exceptional progress. The company made more than HUF 70 billion in net sales, a 20.5 per cent increase compared with 2003. This growth, achieved in a competitive environment, shows the success of the company's business policy and its growing role in supplying CEE with its products.

Conclusion

This chapter presented the efforts of the Hungarian government to increase the competitiveness of domestic enterprises and embed multi-national companies in the local economy. In order to root foreign companies, the government applied broad policy measures such as high tariffs and customs duties, rules of origin, joint venture requirements, and so on. From 1997, it began to introduce programmes to encourage the creation of linkages in general, and programmes that encourage the further development of the already existing links between suppliers and foreign companies. Moreover, since the mid-1990s Hungary has been working to improve its innovation system. The greatest effort undertaken following Hungary's entry into the EU in 2004 was the introduction of R&D tax allowances. This measure serves as a tool to motivate foreign and domestic companies to cooperate with the research institutes and uni-versities for R&D services: they have either to pay contributions to the Innovation Fund or to invest in R&D, receiving HUF 2 in return for every HUF 1 invested. Despite all these government efforts, it seems that food multinationals are not 'locked' into the host economy. When Hungary entered the EU in 2004 and all the protectionist measures were removed, food multinationals commenced intense processes of restructuring in line with their global growth strategies. The strong competition forced them to choose regional optimization plans. MNEs relocated activities all over CEE and Western Europe, and fully integrated their CEE subsidiaries into their global supply chains.

The chapter revealed that food MNEs did not collaborate with the local institutes and research centres. None of the three companies had a research centre in Hungary and had no plans to open any. MNEs cooperated with universities only to recruit personnel, but did not have any other projects related to common scientific projects, the training of students, PhDs, and so on. Therefore, further governmental efforts are needed to strengthen the partnerships between food companies and local knowledge institutions, so that the local economy benefits further from the knowledge and know-how of the foreign investors.

The next chapter shows how these conclusions are similarly applicable to the case of the Czech Republic, following an analysis of MNEs in the Czech Republic and their behaviour following EU membership.

5
MNE Strategies in the Czech Republic

Introduction

Of all the new member states, the economy of the Czech Republic is the most advanced. It was among those CEECs that attracted the most FDI in the region, thanks to its liberal trade rules (WTO, 1996a) and generally open direct investment regime. The introduction of investment incentives in 1998 stimulated a massive inflow of FDI into both greenfield and brownfield projects, and, since 1993, more than €46 billion in FDI has been recorded. The food and tobacco industries occupy fourth place, taking 11 per cent of all FDI (1993–2004). The first place was occupied by the manufacturing sector – 41 per cent of FDI; the second by the metallurgy sector – 15 per cent of FDI; and the third by the refined petroleum and chemicals sector with 14 per cent of FDI. The Czech food sector is considered the best placed out of the new member states (CzechInvest, 2007). Yet, the accession has been the Czech food industry's biggest challenge since the fall of the Communist regime in 1989, as the food industry faces increased competition and regulation.

The following chapter analyzes the role of government with regard to the competitiveness of the Czech food industry. It is divided into four sections. The first section analyzes the national innovation system of the country by explicitly stressing the different governmental measures that aim at embedding FDI in the local economy. The second section discusses the Czech food sector and its development. It observes the gradual changes in consumer tastes and preferences since the opening of the Czech economy at the beginning of the 1990s, and underlines the important role of Western retail chains for progress in the food industry. This section also draws the reader's attention to the role EU membership had with regard to MNEs' policies in the Czech Republic. The third section examines the linkages of Nestlé, Unilever, and InBev with the local firms and organizations from the 1990s until recently.

Linkage creation in the Czech Republic – the role of government

Broad policy measures

Before accession in 2004, the Czech government had the power and capability to protect the local economy using a variety of measures, including trade measures. Food and beverages, and textile and clothing were the most protected sectors. The Czech Republic applied high import tariffs, tariff escalation, tariff rate quotas, and export subsidies to protect the agricultural sector. The reason for this was that agricultural goods were very sensitive. In addition, the local agri-food sector underwent a radical and painful process of restructuring at the beginning of the 1990s. In 1996, the Czech Republics most favoured nation (MFN)[1] tariffs were particularly high for food products and beverages, which had tariffs averaging 19 per cent – nearly triple the level elsewhere in the economy. Tariff escalation with the level of processing was also very noticeable in food processing. Tariff quotas and seasonal tariffs were applied to agricultural imports. Export subsidies were granted in 1995. The state was also involved, through setting intervention prices for some commodities and by providing concessionary loans and credit guarantees (WTO, 1996a).

During the period 1997–9, trade was further liberalized. Most agricultural goods, however, were still protected by relatively high tariffs. The simple MFN tariff average for agriculture products in 2001 was 13.4 per cent, compared with an average rate of 4.3 per cent for non-agricultural goods. There was no preferential access for EU and EFTA countries in this area. Before accession, most rates of customs duties ranged from 0 to 5 per cent and from 5 to 10 per cent. The remaining duties, particularly on agricultural products, were above 10 per cent (WTO, 1996a).

This high tariff protection was the basic factor in the stimulation of multinationals to use local agricultural producers, as the other option – importing the raw materials – was much more costly. Since May 2004, the Czech Republic has adopted the EU's common external trade policy and measures and, consequently, Czech import tariffs have aligned with EU tariff rates, which were generally lower than the original Czech rates.[2] As will be illustrated further later in the chapter, the null import tariffs within the EU made it easy for MNEs to follow their global supplier strategies, which resulted in a decrease in the level of local sourcing.

Programmes encouraging linkage creation

By 2003, the Czech Republic did not have a precisely formulated innovation policy strategy. However, a variety of programmes and initiatives stimulated the development of SMEs, and the improvement of links between SMEs and MNEs, and R&D institutes and universities (Figure 5.1). As can be noted in Figure 5.1, the strongest linkages are between domestic companies and the government, and between domestic companies and MNEs. Overall, the government's innovation policy has been predominantly oriented towards supporting the development industry and SMEs.

In 2000, the Ministry of Trade and Industry prepared a sector operational programme (SOP) for 2001–6, which prioritized structurally affected regions, supported structural changes in enterprises and SMEs, human resource development in industry, and the use of new technologies and the development of trade.

To improve links between SMEs and industry, and R&D institutes and universities, the Ministry of Industry and Trade initiated two specialized support programmes for SMEs. They were aimed at research, development and innovative business (Transfer Programme CZ 01), and Science and Technology Centres – formerly Park II (CZ 12). Support programmes for SME industrial research and development, such as the Konsorcia programme, were launched to stimulate the establishment of teams formed by research institutions and industry sectors. The government approved several R&D programmes that started operating in 2004. One of them – POKROK (CZ 15) – has been designed to foster cooperation with foreign research organizations and firms. That is just one of the programmes through which the Czech Republic acts as a part of the European Research Area (ERA) (EC, Country Report Czech Republic 2003). Another one is TANDEM (CZ 16), a programme designed to orient research towards the industrial sector. IMPULS (CZ 17) is a programme for industrial research, which was launched in 2005 and will operate until 2010.

The government has also elaborated a medium-term policy to support SMEs by simplifying their market access, and thus increasing the adaptability of the Czech economy to the European market. These programmes complemented the regional development policies and grasped the particular problems in each region.

The Czech and Moravian Guarantee and Development Bank and the Grant Agency of the Czech Republic played a very important role in the process of the promotion of SMEs. Support measures include contribution to payment of interest, credit at a low interest rate, returnable financial assistance and subsidies, credit guarantees, and guarantees to

128

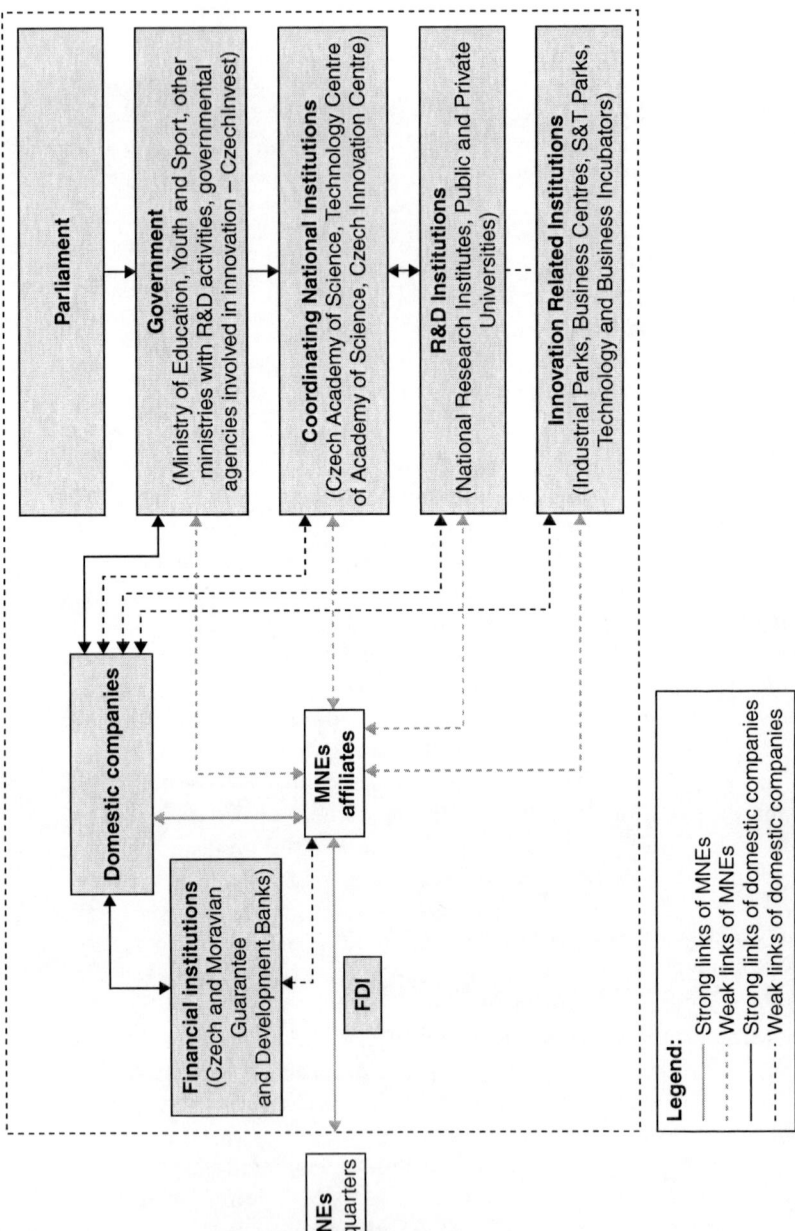

Figure 5.1 MNEs, domestic suppliers, and the linkages between the different actors of the Czech innovation system
Source: based on European Trend Chart Country Reports - Czech Republic.

the investors of development and risk capital (EC, Country Report Czech Republic 2003: 8).

In short, the efforts of the Czech government were highly oriented towards the upgrading and innovativeness of domestic companies. Among the priorities of the Czech government was the creation of linkages between MNEs and SMEs. The government tried to embed FDI through a variety of measures. One good example is the Supplier Development Programme, which was designed to boost the number of foreign investors collaborating with Czech based suppliers. The Czech Republic is the only country in CEE that has such a programme. The agency responsible for the supplier programme was CzechInvest – a national development agency attracting FDI and improving the Czech investment climate.[3] In an interview with the author, Vít Švajcr, Director, Supplier Development Department at CzechInvest, underlined that the Supplier Development Programme helped the creation of a rich Czech supplier database, which is one of the country's major competitive advantages.

The Supplier Development Programme[4] was launched in May 1999 for a period of three years, and was to identify good Czech suppliers and link them up with multinational companies. First, CzechInvest collected data from nearly 1000 Czech manufacturers and created profiles that were then made available on its website. Next, in 2000, the agency began matching selected major foreign manufacturers with suppliers. Meanwhile, domestic companies from various sectors (automotive, engineering, health care, biotech, and aerospace) had the opportunity to join the EU's training programme to improve their financial strategies, human resource management, and material resources. The selected firms were involved in an upgrading plan that reflected their individual capacities and requirements. The upgrading process included consultancy and training support in such areas as the utilization of technology, general management operations, quality control, and organizational change. Švajcr summarized the outcome of all these efforts as follows: 'Czech companies are often able to prevail, even against Western competitors'. The Supplier Development Programme led to a sharp rise in interest in both Czech and foreign companies.

When the Supplier Development Programme finished, the Twinning Programme was launched as its continuation. It started operating in 2001 and its second phase ended in October 2004. In 2002, the initial results of the Twinning Programme showed that companies that joined the project were much more likely to be accepted by multinational companies as suppliers.

Apart from linkage promotion programmes, the Czech government also encouraged linkage creation by supporting joint ventures and long-term cooperation between Czech and foreign firms. Again, CzechInvest was the major actor in the process. It promoted the development of joint ventures between foreign and Czech firms through its database of Czech suppliers. In addition, the agency tried to embed FDI by offering full tax relief for 10 years for newly established companies, and partial tax relief for 10 years for expanding companies. Moreover, the government would cover 35 per cent of the costs of training in regions where the unemployment rate was higher than the country average. However, the total amount of the investment incentives (with the exception of training and re-training) could not exceed 50 per cent of the investment (65 per cent, in the case of SMEs) made in long-term tangible and intangible assets.[5]

To summarize, CzechInvest's initiatives to stimulate linkage creation between multinational companies and Czech suppliers have been very successful. 'It raised the overall standard of domestic suppliers and assisted selected companies in becoming suppliers for multinational companies', said Vít Švajcr, Director of Supplier Support at CzechInvest. The programme had a focus on the priority sectors of the Czech Republic – the electro-technical and electronics industries – and, as Mr Švajcr said, 'It did not have too much impact on agro-food industry.' Yet, the interests of the Czech food processing sector were defended. The Federation of the Food and Drink Industries (FFDI)[6] in the Czech Republic, which represents the sector at both national and European level, contributed heavily to this process. The membership in the FFDI is voluntary, and its members are the branch unions and associations; individual firms, from SMEs up to big multinational companies; universities; research institutes; and others related to the food industry. The basic priorities for the association were to help the companies present their view to government bodies with regard to the Czech Republic's future accession to the EU; to increase export opportunities for local industry, and to handle Czech relations with CEFTA countries. In addition, the FFDI role is to facilitate the contacts between the Czech food companies and their suppliers, and between the Czech and EU food processing businesses. As Mr Miroslav Koberna,[7] Director of FFDI, said, the main priority of the Association is 'to provide specialized food and technology counselling in the area of processing of agricultural production, drinks, and food production, including comment on proceedings of legislative amendments and support programmes'. FFDI is a member of the Confederation of the Food and Drink Industries (CIAA) of the EU and a member of the Chamber of Commerce of the Czech Republic, which helped a great deal in the preparation for EU entry. FFDI has also been active in negotiations concerning funds with the Ministry of Agriculture and EU authorities, as it has good contacts in Brussels. Between 2002 and 2003, the Ministry of Agriculture invested around CZK 0.5 bn (€17 m) in business incentives, and this support, in turn, generated €3 bn in investments. FFDI lobbied to have the transitional period for new labelling laws extended. Mr Koberna underlined that FFDI actively works to create a partnership with the other links in the food chain, from the agricultural sector to retailers at European and international levels. He mentioned that, together with the Agricultural Chamber, they play a crucial role in reinforcing the links throughout the agri-food chain, and supporting the development of the sector through concrete programmes and marketing activities. In view of the importance of the food industry in the Czech Republic, and the need to increase its performance and competitiveness, FFDI, together with the Ministry of Agriculture, the Research Institute of Agricultural Economics, and other organizations and experts, prepared a strategy for this sector for the period following accession, 2004–13. The strategy underlines the good prospects for the food industry, and stresses its relatively considerable potential for further development.

Food multinationals in the Czech Republic are members of the Federation, and they played an extremely important role in the process of the harmonization of the Czech Republic with EU legislation. As the MNEs have large and very powerful legal departments, the Food Federation could rely on companies' experts for advice, consultation, and assistance while working on legislation related to food. Mr Koberna admitted that the Federation has very good relations with its members, and food and beverage multinationals; however, it could not really intervene on their decisions regarding which suppliers to use – local or global. 'It depends on their strategies', Mr Koberna said. According to him, none of the branch associations could influence MNE policies towards suppliers. If local producers offered a sufficient supply of good quality raw materials at competitive prices, they would be chosen as suppliers. Koberna considers that the preparations of the agri-food sector were sufficient to compete at EU level. The Czech government has spent a great deal of money on investment, particularly to fulfil all EU requirements, especially the hygiene and veterinary standards. The Czech Republic was the only country among the candidate countries that has used all the funding from the support programmes, money that was intended especially to improve hygiene conditions and standards. All the Czech companies that did not fulfil EU requirements by the time of accession were closed. There are only about 20 companies that have asked for a transition period. Mr Josef Sajdl, Head of the Federation of the Food and Drink Industries of the Czech Republic's Legislation Department, said: 'We are at the top [among Hungarian, Polish and Slovakian counterparts], because many of these sectors still have problems implementing EU regulations. For example, one country recently completed a project after which 50 per cent of food companies were HAACP compliant.[8] In the Czech Republic, every firm was compliant prior to accession, or they were closed down.[9]

Mr Koberna said that many multinationals work with local suppliers; that is, there are backward linkages between foreign and domestic companies. Moreover, in a relatively large number of cases the MNEs helped locals to improve their performance. Companies such as Nestlé, Unilever and Danone, which entered to the Czech market in 1992, introduced all the EU hygiene and veterinary standards to their suppliers. The rationale is that they could not buy raw materials that do not fulfil their quality criteria. Or, put differently, these are examples of indirect spillovers of FDI on the local food industry.

In short, the Czech food industry was the best prepared for EU accession among all the new member states. Czech manufacturers invested more than CZK 30 billion to raise standards. All food processing companies had complied with EU requirements before accession. The result of this preparation meant that the Czech food industry was placed in a strong position. This happened thanks to the FFDI, which successfully represents the food industry and, by following the Food Law Act, is able to negotiate in the name of the food sector. It has been a long process of linkage creation between local companies and multinationals, during which the latter helped domestic firms to upgrade. These linkages were stimulated by the protectionist Czech trade regime and reinforced by the good work of the FFDI.

The food industry in the Czech Republic

Overview

This section will briefly touch on the agricultural sector as the basic supplier of raw materials to the food industry. It will also give an overview of the domestic food industry so that the reader may have a greater understanding of the importance of the sector to the local economy, its preparedness for EU membership, the potential for linkages between MNEs and domestic suppliers, and the role of FDI in helping Czech companies to catch up with Western companies. The significance of the input of food MNEs and Western retailers to the introduction of healthier lifestyles of the population is best revealed by focusing on the consumer market and trends. MNEs transferred their marketing strategies, production standards, and management practices to their Czech subsidiaries, thus contributing to the progress of the domestic agricultural and food sector.

The agricultural sector, which is the supplier to the food industry, constitutes only 3.4 per cent of the Czech Republic's GDP, and employs 4 per cent of the population. The sector is expected to achieve slow growth by 2013. Arable land comprises over 70 per cent of total agricultural land. The country is famous for its meat exports, and possesses self-sufficiency in wheat, barley, vegetables, potatoes and fruit. Approximately half of the Czech Republic's cattle are bred on arable land, and 0.3 per cent of land is unused. There are 240 square kilometres of irrigated land. The Czech government finalized its 10-year agricultural strategy in 2004, which ensured the successful restructuring of the farming sector and an extension of the country's grassland area. The Czech Republic's farms are expected to grow in size and, primarily, become cooperatives by 2013 (Government of Canada, 2005b). In other words, the Czech agricultural sector is not large, but its efficiency can be seen by virtue of its high level of productivity, especially when compared with Eastern European standards. This is a good prerequisite for food and beverage MNEs to source locally and link with the domestic suppliers.

The food industry in the Czech Republic belongs to the key sector of the manufacturing industry. Since the mid-1990s, the sector had gone through immense transformation – restructurings, liquidations, and bankruptcies – so that, by 2004, it was considered to be the best prepared sector for EU accession out of all the CEE countries. In 2003, the food industry accounted for 12.4 per cent of sales in the processing industry, 11.2 per cent of accounting value-added, and 10.3 per cent of employment (Ministry of Agriculture of the Czech Republic, 2003).

Multinational companies play a major role in the development of the sector. They dominate both domestic food processing and food trade. Nestlé, Danone, SABMiller, Masterfoods, Unilever, Kraft Foods and Groupe Bongrain successfully penetrated the country at the beginning of the 1990s. Multinationals dominate high value-added segments of the industry; namely, the sweets, soft drinks, vegetable oil, and tobacco industries. Processors of meat, poultry, dairy products, and alcohol, and the canning industry are, for the most part, Czech companies. The Czech Republic has two large dairy companies – Madeta and Olma, two large meat suppliers – MasoKombinat Schneider and Kostelecke Uzeniny, and a large canned and ready-meals producer – Hame. The country is famous for its breweries – being the ancestral home of Pilsner – and is characterized by the highest annual per-capita consumption of beer in Europe. The privatization of the food processing sector was completed by 1997–8, and government ownership accounts for only a few per cent of production – it still owns the famous Budejovicky Budvar (Budweiser) brewery.[10]

Czech membership in the EU has been a great challenge for the agro-food sector, as the businesses face open competition from other member countries. The competition is particularly strong for primary commodities producers. It is hard, for example, for Czech potato growers to compete in the EU market. For Czech processing companies, the situation is much better; for them, EU competition is manageable, as they were well prepared before accession. However, there are also firms that went bankrupt because of increased imports. This is especially notable in dairy products, as the price of raw milk has risen due to a higher level of exports. Madeta, the largest distributor of dairy products in the Czech Republic, has gradually been cutting staff due to a decreasing delivery of milk from Czech farmers, who have started to export some of their milk production to Germany at higher prices. Madeta management dismissed about 300–350 employees in 2005. Czech dairies have to absorb this price increase and maintain a stable price for products due to price competition caused by stronger retailers and competition from foreign players. Bakeries face a similar problem: high production costs due to more expensive energy and gas prices, and, at the same time, the inability to increase the prices of final goods because of strong retailers. However, the general trend is that most companies implemented changes prior to accession. Yet, in order to survive in the EU market they need strong marketing support. As Mr Sajdl stressed, 'There is nearly no assistance in this matter. Most help goes to the agrarian sector, so manufacturers are stuck' (GAIN, 2002). The advantage of the Czech food industry is its high quality, typically Czech products (such as beer and bakery goods, for example), which, once adequately supported, can find their niche in the EU market.

Consumer market

The changes in eating habits and consumer preferences play a crucial role in the work of food processing companies and retailers. Food distribution has been increasing through non-traditional convenience outlets such as petrol stations, kiosks, video shops, and leisure centres, and through vending machines. This is important in attempts to gain market share in the fast-growing convenience food market. Online shopping for food also seems likely to grow (Eurofound, 2004).[11]

Presently, Czechs allocate approximately 18 per cent of household expenditure for the purchase of food and beverages. Since the 1990s, there have been a number of trends and changes in the Czech Republic's consumer market. The demand for traditional Czech dishes has decreased, and healthier foods have become popular. For instance, between 1998 and 2003 Czech consumption of red meat fell by almost 10 per cent, while that of chicken increased by 37 per cent. Czechs are increasingly using vegetable oil and margarine in place of butter. Moreover, healthy ingredients began to be introduced in food that is traditionally seen as unhealthy. In the confectionery industry, for example, artificial flavours have been replaced with healthier natural variants. Healthier confectionery has been introduced that is enriched with vitamins and minerals. Nestlé (Cesko) launched the boiled confectionery Boon Pari Vita Zele with added vitamin C and minerals Mg and Ca.

Consumer demand for convenience products, frozen foods, and ready-made meals – mainly manufactured by MNEs – are also on the rise, as the number of single and childless households is growing. Sales of unprocessed fresh meat are declining as a result of this trend towards ready-prepared food. Many consumers do not want to spend much time preparing food. Snacking and spread out meal times are also more frequent with changing work and family patterns. According to *Food Manufacture* (2005), the savoury snacks sector had been growing by 6.6 per cent annually, and it predicted that the market would grow by nearly 50 per cent in 2008.[12] Soft drinks consumption increased by 42 per cent between 1998 and 2003. In the case of bottled water, this increase was even more dramatic – 63 per cent over the five-year period. Major factors contributing to this shift in consumer behaviour included price sensitivity and healthier eating habits. The busy lifestyle of the country's active female workforce also plays a critical role.[13] Women do not have the time to cook, so convenience foods are definitely preferred.

Organic products have strong market potential and are of serious interest to many consumers. Many retailers are familiar with this demand and try to provide the highest possible quality goods, keeping their stores free of genetically modified products. Moreover, Czech farmers have converted more than 5 per cent of agricultural land to organic management, which is the highest percentage of organic agricultural land in Europe. The increase of consumer purchasing power in the near future is expected to reinforce the demand for organic health products.[14]

The retail sector is the most developed segment of the agro-food sector; chains offer a great variety of high quality products. Retailers have a stronger position in the Czech Republic than suppliers or wholesalers, as they are concentrated. As a result, most suppliers have to pay a great deal of money to have their products placed on the store shelves. The smaller producers who sell brands that are less well known or products that are less essential are in the most disadvantageous position, as they have to pay higher listing fees. The sector has been penetrated by foreign capital to a huge extent and enjoys a rapid growth of hypermarkets, supermarkets, and discounters. The market share of the large players on the Czech retail market continues to grow year-on-year (the top retailers own 70 per cent of the market); however, the pace of their growth is slowing down. Supermarkets are stagnating and are looking for new concepts to attract customers (for example, the retail chain Delvita opened supermarkets in the small cities). Since EU entry in 2004, many new discount stores have emerged. Delvita, Tesco, Lidl, and Spar are among the MNEs that fulfilled their ambitious plans to expand their discount stores. The entrance and expansion of the discount stores became possible following EU accession, as retailers could purchase some products directly from their central office in the EU in order to save costs. The discount shops are a threat to local producers, as these are pushed to decrease their prices – even to levels below the production costs.

According to the GFK marketing agency, Prague, Czechs mostly prefer to shop at hypermarkets (36 per cent), followed by discount stores (19 per cent) and supermarkets (19 per cent), and small self-service grocery stores (18 per cent).[15] The major retailers in the Czech Republic are Ahold, the Union of Czech and Moravian Consumer Cooperatives, Rewe, Kaufland, Tesco, Globus, Delvita, Carrefour, and so on. The popularity of hypermarkets is growing due to their wide range of products, low prices, the high quality of fresh food products, large parking areas, and the variety of services offered. The average store size is 253 square metres per 1000 inhabitants (in Germany, it is 330 square metres). There is a highly competitive environment in the Czech retail sector: supply is higher than demand, and retail chains fight for customers by keeping prices low, introducing cheap private labels (some offer more luxurious private labels), bonus/loyalty cards, and advertisements in the press.[16] More and more retail chains are distributing private label products. In some cases (for example, Ahold) the private label range is up to 20 per cent cheaper than branded products. Hence, it is not surprising that Czechs are increasingly buying private label products. However, some producers remain critical of the private label phenomenon, as they fear possible loss of share for their brands. Not all the players are willing to produce private label products for retailers. However, many Czech manu-facturers see private label production as an opportunity to increase sales, thanks to the higher exports of private label goods.[17]

EU impact on MNEs

EU impact is discussed in a separate sub-section, as the liberal EU trade regime proved to be one of the major factors that influenced MNEs' behaviour. As the last section of this chapter will reveal, Nestlé, Unilever, and InBev – which, as a result of the size of their investments and govern-ment measures, aimed to keep themselves in the local economy as well as the dynamic and growing consumer market – seemed to be locked into the country, but nevertheless started to reorganize and relocate.

EU membership led to an increase of both imports to and exports from the Czech Republic. The rationale for this was that new member states no longer applied trade protection policies on a national basis. All pro-tection measures used by the new member states to other EU members were removed, and vice versa. Equally, measures between the new mem-ber states also ceased. Jitka Findejsova, a Nestlé Project Manager based in Prague, emphasized that EU accession had a positive impact on inter-national business. She said, 'It is better now because we have fewer taxes.'[18] The free trade regime was beneficial not only for companies, but also for the consumers, who enjoyed a greater choice of products and lower prices. Moreover, the price of food dropped due to cheaper products being imported, mainly from Poland.[19] The tougher competi-tion coming from the cheaper imported goods and the removal of the trade measures pushed MNEs to fulfil their global plans for product opti-mization and restructuring in order to keep their leading positions in the market.

In October 2004, for example, Nestlé (Cesko) closed down the fac-tory where the oldest Czech chocolate, Orion, was produced because of divestment from the cocoa business. The size of the cocoa processing fac-tory in Modřany was not suitable for the company's European project. Nestlé's global European project was to 'strengthen globally its focus on branded higher value-added foodstuffs and gradually move out of simple processing of agricultural raw materials. On a European scale a project is therefore under way to sell Nestlé cocoa processing activities to Cargill'.[20] In other words, Nestlé was no longer interested in the processing of raw materials and, hence, in the cocoa factory in Modřany.

The next example is Unilever. It closed a plant in Zábreh in 2005, which resulted in 250 job losses from a total of 280 employees. As revealed in

Chapter 4, Unilever has a strategy of global competitiveness. CEE countries are part of Unilever's European business, especially the supply chain; manufacturing is organized on an optimal European basis. The closure of the plant was part of this optimization process. The production of mayonnaise, tartare sauce, and dehydrated food was relocated to the plant in Nelahozeves and other European manufacturing centres. The plant in Nelahozeves produces vegetable oils and spreads and, thus, Unilever concentrated its food production in one place. In line with the optimization process, production of soaps and cosmetics has been transferred from Nelahozeves to plants elsewhere in Europe. After the closure in 2005, one year later Unilever (Czech Republic) expanded once more. The reason for this was that part of the margarine production from the Budapest plant moved to the Czech Republic.

The third company, InBev, has also undertaken major restructurings in CEE and Western Europe within its European strategy. The company closed two breweries in Belgium. In the Czech Republic, in the first quarter of 2007, InBev shut down the Branik brewery (which dated back to 1899). The move led to 80 job cuts. The plant had to be closed because the Branik brewery has reached its maximum capacity and further modernization of the facility was not possible, given its location and the fact that the building is a national cultural monument. Jan Veselý, Executive Director of the Czech Beer and Malt Association (ČSPAS) was unable to comment on the closure; he merely stated that 'such strategic decisions are outside the scope of the association's influence'.[21] The production of the Branik unit was transferred to Staropramen, which took over the production technologies from Branik and was to be modernized with investment exceeding €20 million.[22] InBev's plan for its European restructuring operation included the creation of 295 new jobs in the Czech Republic and Hungary, and cancellation of 360 jobs in Western Europe. The company's plan was to concentrate support services in the Czech Republic, and financial operations in Hungary.

To summarize, since 2004 the Czech Republic has removed all trade protection measures. This has led to improved logistics for goods. Economy imports entered the country and producers faced fierce competition. The strong retail sector did not allow for the dramatic increase of food prices and, hence, producers had to invest a great deal in order to optimize their production processes. A number of local companies went bankrupt, and others had to be restructured. Food MNEs implemented their global restructuring plans in order to keep their leading positions in the market (locally and regionally). Their optimization plans meant plant closures, employee lay-offs, and redirection to global suppliers instead of local ones. EU enlargement proved that MNEs are not 'embedded' in any country from the Union. The following section presents a detailed overview of Unilever, Nestlé and InBev in the Czech Republic. It aims to give deeper coverage of these companies' strategies, and to explain why 'rooting' MNEs in the local economy is challenging.

Firm case analysis

Unilever (Czech Republic)

In an interview in Prague in 2005, the Corporate Communications Manager of Unilever, Mr C[23] (Czech Republic), discussed the company's activities. There are two Unilever production facilities in the Czech Republic: Nelahozeves and Zábřeh na Moravě. Nelahozeves was acquired in 1992, immediately after Unilever entered the local market. The original name of Nelahozeves was PTZ (Povltavské tukové závody), and this name was kept both internally and externally for the sake of tradition. The Zábřeh plant was acquired as a result of the global merger of Unilever with Bestfoods in 2001, as this plant had belonged to Bestfoods between the early 1990s and 2001. In 2005, the company employed a total of 850 people in the Czech Republic (600 in Nelahozeves; 250 in Zábřeh).

Compared with Hungary, Bulgaria and Romania, the Czech subsidiary has the largest product mix. Thus, this book seeks to identify reasons for this growth. Specifically it asks:

Are there particular local factors that contributed to Unilever's development, or was it mainly the result of parent company decisions?

By 2005, Unilever Czech Republic had a wide product mix. It produced both food (margarines, dairy spreads, mayonnaise, tartare sauce, and mustards) and home and personal care articles (soaps, deodorants, and creams). However, the Communications Manager explained that this portfolio would be modified after 2005. In fact, in 2006 Unilever changed the mix of products produced in the Czech Republic. Non-food products were transferred to other Unilever locations – primarily, in Europe. In line with this, Unilever (Czech Republic) further developed its PTZ site by investing in the area of food product innovations: dairy spreads, salad dressings, and so on. The Communications Manager explained that this decision came from the parent company and had little to do with local capabilities; rather, it was based on the results of a European/regional supply chain restructuring study (which Unilever had undertaken in connection with EU expansion) and the then existing status of the markets in which the company was operating. Unilever's strategy is to focus on those products/categories that have strong growth potential and a sufficiently large volume to satisfy the local market. All other products/categories that do not have a sufficiently large production volume and growth potential (for example, the soap bars market in Europe is continuously declining because consumers prefer shower gels) will be moved to locations where they do have such potential.

Does Unilever (Czech Republic) establish backward linkages with local supplier companies?

As far as raw material and service suppliers were concerned, Unilever relies mostly on local companies. However, he underscored that Unilever's supply chain is interconnected and harmonized within Europe, which means that, if it were practical and more effective, the company might simply have one regional partner.

Does the company use the same suppliers as its sites used before the privatization?

'Where there is a business logic we kept them, otherwise we changed them', replied the Communications Manager. Actually, this phenomenon is in line with the company's global strategy and has already been noticed in Hungary.

The Unilever CEO for the Czech subsidiary, Mrs D,[24] talked about Unilever's investment strategy in CEE and, in particular, the factors that influenced their decision to invest in the Czech Republic. The CEO underlined the role of the traditional location advantages, such as the growth opportunities of the market, and the profit maximization that can be reached in a particular place. The educated labour force also attracted Unilever. Following this statement, the Manager was asked whether Unilever was likely to close its subsidiaries in some CEECs if the market situation changed. The response was that, in general, it is a painful and very radical decision to close a subsidiary; however, this could happen in any CEEC if the purchasing power of the population decreased drastically.

During the conversation, it became clear that Unilever (Czech Republic) prefers to work with multinational retailers because, normally, they have long-term strategies on which Unilever can build long-term business for sustainable growth. However, the company also uses small local retailers and large local retailers, as it aims to achieve deep penetration in the local market. Czech and Polish retailers have a stronger influence on Unilever's policies than the other CEE retailers. The reason for this is that there are approximately 20 international chains fighting for the market share, and this generates high complexity and price wars. As a result, the retail chains push Unilever to decrease its prices. After EU accession, cheaper Polish imports made competition even fiercer. The Executive Director admitted that it is not easy to make money from food in the Czech Republic.

The strategy of the company is to work with international and local suppliers. However, their choice depends on the quality, cost, and services offered. Ultimately, efficiency is the most important criterion for the company, so it therefore chooses the supplier that makes the best offer.

Unilever's strategy towards competitors is to cooperate with the largest. As far as the role of the government is concerned, the Executive Director explained that, normally, the government invites company experts to participate in the national strategy for the development of the food industry. But the government does not have a strong role in company activities.

The Czech subsidiary is dependent on the parent company for its strategic decisions. In line with the global strategy, the subsidiaries are subordinated to company headquarters.

To sum up, Unilever (Czech Republic) is completely integrated in Unilever's global production chain. Strategic decisions are taken at headquarters level and implemented by the subsidiary. In the Czech Republic, Unilever sources locally and regionally. Although there have been initiatives from the FFDI to promote linkages between foreign and domestic companies, it seems that the parent company's strategies predetermine the level of embeddedness of the company and, in this sense, local authorities such as the Food Association or the government are not strong actors. It is important to recall the point of the Director of the FFDI; namely, that the Association has little influence over MNEs as far as suppliers or any other strategic decisions are concerned. In other words, Unilever follows its three pillar growth strategy illustrated earlier, and all decisions are subordinated to the major goals. The Executive Director of Unilever herself could not clearly indicate any government policies that were crucial to Unilever's work in the Czech Republic. Additionally, EU membership weakened government's power to have any impact on foreign companies. Pushed by tough global and local competition, Unilever had undergone a process of restructuring, thus closing the plant that produced home and personal care products in the Czech Republic. EU accession allowed the company to improve its efficiency through the reallocation of firms' activities, and thus improve its economies of scale and scope.

Nestlé (Cesko)

Nestlé entered the Czech Republic in 1992; together with Danone, they created a joint venture named Copart in which they were 50:50 shareholders. The reason for this joint holding company was that the Czech government did not want to split the one-time monopolistic conglomerate Cokoladovny but, rather, wished to privatize it as a package. This was Central Europe's largest producer of biscuits, chocolate and confectionery.[25] In 1992, the European Bank for Reconstruction and Development (EBRD) was among the investors; the EBRD later on sold its shares to Copart. Noreen Doyle,[26] EBRD's Deputy Vice-President, Finance, and a member of Cokoladovny's Board of Directors, stated:

> Cokoladovny has successfully restructured and rationalized its production operations, distribution, and sales organization. Its brand portfolio has been an important focus of time and investment, and is now one of the company's core strengths. Its traditionally Czech brands are highly regarded and well recognized among the country's consumers – in a very competitive market. The overall transformation of Cokoladovny was achieved by the company's strong management team with the close assistance and helpful cooperation of its industrial partners Nestlé and Danone.

Later on, in 1999, 'Group Danone and Nestlé SA agreed through Copart to split Cokoladovny into two companies'.[27] Nestlé assumed chocolate and sugar confectionery operations and formed Nestlé-Cokoladovny, while Danone specialized in biscuit manufacturing, creating Danone-Cokoladovny. This formed two focused companies, which became better integrated within Danone and Nestlé European networks, and gave Czech products easier access to their export markets. The split of Cokoladovny allowed Nestlé to find international synergies within the Nestlé group, in particular in the fields of purchasing and information technology, and especially in exporting and importing Nestlé products to and from other European Nestlé companies.

During the early years of investment, in the early 1990s, Nestlé had to cope with the expected difficulties linked to the overall restructuring and reform as part of building the market economy. In order to challenge increasing competition, Nestlé had to restructure the acquired plants, build and promote its brands, improve customer services, introduce innovative sales and marketing techniques, and train its people. In general, there were no surprises that were unique to the Czech Republic. The macroeconomic situation was stable and the legislative framework clear.

In 2006, Nestlé had two factories in the Czech republic: the Zora factory situated in Olomouc and the Sfinx factory in Holesov. Overall, the company employed 2000 people – factories, sales and marketing departments, and management staff. Sfinx, whose origins go back to 1863, was converted into a modern international production centre for sugar confectionery and the Zora Olomouc factory, founded in 1898, was modernized into a highly competitive international producer of high quality chocolate products. The former General Manager of Nestlé (Cesko), Mr Bruno Le Ciclé, explained:[28]

> Our restructuring project aimed at creating two high performance Nestlé confectionery production centres in the Czech Republic – ZORA Olomouc and SFINX Holešov – was successfully completed. The ORION brand with its tradition dating back to 1896 will remain our strongest local chocolate confectionery brand based on production of ZORA factory in Olomouc. The legend of ORION chocolate continues in ZORA.

Nestlé (Cesko) has a large product portfolio – not only local products, but also many imported goods that are part of the company's global portfolio. Each country specializes in producing different products. Goods that are not manufactured locally are imported from other Nestlé subsidiaries. For example, the Czech Republic imports coffee from Hungary, Switzerland, and France; culinary products such as bouillons, soups, and pasta ready-meals from Slovakia; baby biscuits from Italy; Maggi seasonings from Poland; and Kit-Kat from Bulgaria and Germany.

Mr Walter, Corporate Affairs Manager, Nestlé (Cesko), said that it was quite difficult to say exactly what percentage of foreign–local suppliers Nestlé (Cesko) uses. They source locally dried milk, starch syrup, sugar and, to some extent, packaging. For example, the sugar supplier is the local Eastern Sugar Company owned by Tate & Lyle from Great Britain and Saint Louis Sucre from France, and the milk supplier is the local producer Madeta. Some special materials in much smaller quantities are acquired by importing. Also, cocoa, one of the main raw materials for chocolate production, is imported. In these cases, Nestlé (Cesko) relies on synergies of purchasing, as Nestlé negotiates for more than one market. The company functions as one mechanism – each and every subsidiary is an integral part of it. Nestlé, for example, has a Europe-wide agreement to buy cocoa from Cargill (as mentioned earlier, Nestlé divested from the cocoa processing business and sold it to Cargill). Local managers take responsibility for negotiations with local suppliers, whereas negotiations with European suppliers are handled by European lead buyers (for example, cocoa). Nestlé (Cesko) sources some raw materials locally, as this leads to lower transport and other related costs, and also tries to benefit from tariff-free imports from other EU markets, since tariffs have to be paid when products are imported from non-EU countries. Nestlé (Cesko) does not have backward linkages with suppliers, as the company does not use agricultural supplies from farmers. Nestlé supports suppliers on a global level in countries where it sources raw materials directly from agricultural farmers, such as Ghana, Vietnam, and Costa Rica. In the Czech Republic, for example, Nestlé buys dried milk from processors, not fresh milk from farmers, and purchases processed sugar from sugar mills, not sugar beet from farmers. Mr Walter said, 'There is no commercial reason to source raw materials directly. Moreover, the global priority of Nestlé is to concentrate on higher value-added foodstuffs and to move out of simple processing of agricultural raw materials.'

Some of the suppliers with whom Nestlé works are the same suppliers of the old Cokoladovny enterprise, but they have been restructured – for instance, the milk producer Madeta. Many other suppliers have been privatized by foreigners. When the company develops a new product and needs, say, high-clarity glucose syrup, it prefers to purchase from those suppliers that have more advanced technologies. For example, a Slovakian supplier of cornstarch is among those preferred over Czech suppliers of syrup based on potato or wheat starch, because of the higher level of technology their product entails. In short, the company's choice of suppliers depends on the portfolio of products the company has and on the conditions (price, quality, and reliability) the suppliers are able to meet.

Nestlé (Cesko) has one regional brand: Orion. It has many local brands, and also global brands, such as Maggi and Nescafé, for example. The product portfolio is very broad, with brands that have a long history. Such an example is Orion (dating back to 1896), which was the strongest local brand, even before the Second World War, and which Nestlé chose to retain. In the Czech Republic, Orion is synonymous with tablet chocolate. Another famous local brand is Granko, the origins of which go back to 1978; this is a soluble cocoa drink diluted in hot or cooled milk. This was the only available cocoa drink before 1990; Nestlé converted it into a brand name by providing the necessary development of brand support and promotion. Nestlé produces many other products but, given the need to focus on key priorities, many of these brands do not receive brand support in the form of advertising. Mr Walter underlined that Nestlé (Cesko) has been completely integrated into Nestlé's global network since 1999.

The Czech Republic has a strong network of suppliers. Nestlé (Cesko) uses many of them, but also sources from abroad if it can find better prices and quality. However, the company purchases locally; not only raw materials, but also finished products that it sells under the Nestlé logo. One example is a local producer of ice cream (Tipa), whose product's quality is of such an exceptional standard that Nestlé collaborates with the firm. In short, Nestlé management believes that, as a strong, long-term investor, their company is completely integrated in the local food industry. They use many local sources and actively participate in the local media and advertising market. The company collaborates with local universities. It recruits management staff and food engineers. The management cadres are from the Prague School of Economics, and the engineer specialists from the VSCHT Prague University of Chemistry and Technology, and the Prague Agricultural University. Nestlé cooperates with the student organizations AIESEC and IAESTA, and participates in their job fairs and Euro manager project.

The Czech retail market consists of local and international retail chains. International chains have 60 per cent of the market. However, as 40 per cent of the market remains in the hands of local retail chains, Nestlé (Cesko) must work with both. Mr Walter said that the role of imported goods and private labels is growing. However, in the confectionery market, for example, as well as in soluble coffee, Nestlé holds the position of market leader.

Interestingly, local management is not empowered to identify factors that might encourage the parent company to internationalize its R&D centres in the Czech Republic. The parent company considers this is a strategic decision. A Nestlé (Cesko) application group participates in the development of some products with the product technology centre in York in the UK.

Nestlé (Cesko) does not consider the government to be of direct help to investors who are already in operation. Corporate tax is set at 24 per cent, and is being gradually decreased by the Cabinet. VAT is 5 per cent for essential foodstuffs and 19 per cent for non-essential food products (confectionery, and coffee), which Nestlé's products mainly are. In other words, in terms of VAT, there is discrimination between food items, resulting in increased in prices for non-essential food products.

EU membership in 2004 did not result in any dramatic changes. Before EU membership, the whole legislative framework was harmonized with that of the EU. Even before 2004, the level of liberalization of customs rates was high and, hence, there were almost no tariffs. Double profit agreement was reached with the EU before EU entry. A positive outcome of EU membership was the dismantling of customs controls and the subsequent increased speed of transport, specifically as a result of time not being wasted waiting at borders – in itself, an improvement in efficiency. Immediately following accession, import customs duties with some non-EU countries, such as Bulgaria and Romania, temporarily increased, but subsequently they were returned to a zero rate as a result of 'Double profit' agreements with these countries. Competition increased following EU membership and, to a large extent, this was more as a result of improved logistics. Mr Walter explained that the retail chain Lidl entered the market and is a serious competitor because of the low prices of its products. In addition, many retail chains offer higher discounts on confectionery goods; private label goods are also a serious threat. In other words, to remain competitive Nestlé (Cesko) has to follow the global growth strategy of the company and be highly efficient.

InBev (Czech Republic)

The beer industry has a long tradition in the Czech Republic. Czech malting and brewing are among the oldest crafts and are among the most respected industrial activities. Following the end of Communism, the Czech brewing industry experienced dramatic changes. The number of breweries has fallen sharply, and global giants now own most of the leading producers. The largest producer of beer is the Plzeňský Prazdroj Group, owned by SABMiller.[29] Second is the Staropramen brewery, which was first bought by Bass and then, as a result of Interbrew's purchase of Bass, the shares of the company were transferred to Interbrew (now InBev). Its share on the domestic beer market represents 14.4 per cent. Budvar from České Budějovice[30] holds third position.

There are 38 companies brewing beer in the Czech Republic in 48 industrial breweries. There are also 36 restaurant micro-breweries still functioning, the oldest of which was established in 1499. In 2003, the total output of beer from these breweries reached 18,548,314 hectolitres, with almost 12 per cent of that earmarked for export. Beer exports have increased significantly, while the Czechs per capita consumption of beer has remained very strong (around 160 litres per annum). At present, the Czech Republic enjoys more than 300 kinds of beer.

Bearing in mind that the beer industry occupies an important place in the culture and traditions of the Czech Republic, it is logical for one to presuppose that companies that invest in this business could be considered 'rooted' in the local economy. In a country where each brewery has many years of tradition, it is not an easy issue for a plant to be closed. However, we witnessed such a phenomenon in the closure of the old Branik brand by InBev. This happened within the global process of reorganization, which InBev started in the second half of 2006.

InBev is present in the Czech market with premium, low-price, and non-alcoholic beers under a variety of brand names. Its flagship brand is the local emblematic beer Staropramen.[31] Some of the newer brands it brews include Velvet, Kelt and Rallye. It also imports beers from its core portfolio, such as Stella Artois, Hoegaarden White, Beck's, Belle-Vue Kriek, and Leffe Bruin. By 13 October 2003, Pivovary Staropramen was operating under the name Pražské Pivovary.

InBev currently operates three production units in the Czech Republic and employs 1020 people. Two of the breweries are located in Prague. These breweries include the Smíchov brewery, which manufactures Staropramen, and the Branik brewery. The company's third brewery is called the Ostravar brewery and is located in Ostrava. In terms of the different types of beer brewed, no other Czech company can compete with Staropramen. Management[32] explained that InBev invested a great deal in the modernization of the Prague brewery. The process of upgrading started in 1996, when one of the largest and the most modern brewhouses in Central Europe was built, and the power block was modernized. By launching the trial operation of CK tanks, the second stage of the upgrade of the Staropramen Brewery was completed in Smíchov at the end of 2004. Production of beer in CK tanks enables the company to reduce energy consumption and significantly improve the working conditions for employees.

Pivovary Staropramen is the third largest exporter of beer in the Czech Republic; its beers are exported to 36 countries worldwide. The most important export markets include Germany, Slovakia, Russia, Sweden, the UK, and the USA. One factor helping to strengthen Staropramen's position in foreign markets is the fact that by 2002 Interbrew had already made its most famous beer, Staropramen, part of its global premium brands portfolio, as one of only six brands with this status.[33] InBev established overseas subsidiaries located in Germany and Slovakia in order to have direct control over sales of Staropramen beer in those countries.

In order to keep its strong competitive position as a world leader, InBev began reorganization on a global level, including within CEE. InBev focused on a strong supply chain structure. In order to achieve the perfect functioning of this structure, cost-cutting initiatives were required across all of InBev's operations. This meant that the individual subsidiaries would become progressively more dependant on the decisions of the parent company and the regional centres. Before the merger of Interbrew and AmBev in August 2004, Interbrew followed a multi-domestic strategy. The Czech subsidiary (similar to the one in Hungary) used to be independent with regard to the basic decision-making process. Moreover, the members of the board of directors and the supervisory board were all Czechs – except the Executive Director Mr Vincent Lefere, who was Belgian. Yet, once InBev had become a global leader, it decided to further consolidate its activities; namely, to concentrate support services in one place, the Czech Republic, and all financial operations in another, Hungary.[34] The European Export and Shared Services Centre located in the Czech Republic is intended to deal with exports, finance, and procurement activities for InBev breweries in 12 European countries; the Hungarian based financial centre serves 10 countries. Part of InBev's global strategy includes the outsourcing of its European business systems and application services divisions to an external supplier, with the aim of providing a more consistent approach at an optimal cost.[35]

Pivovary Staropramen uses both local and foreign retailers. Foreign retailers have about 70 per cent of the market and the company distributes its production mainly through foreign retailers. In addition, the brewery franchises 18 Staropramen branded restaurants and pubs. These are modelled around several different concepts, but offer a wide variety of beers from the company's portfolio and are also important distributors.

As far as suppliers are concerned, the company uses a local malt supplier and a combination of foreign and local packaging suppliers. Some of the suppliers are imposed by the parent company, as it negotiates with suppliers at the European level to achieve better price conditions.

In short, InBev possesses the famous Staropramen brand, which has been turned into a regional product and is distributed around CEE. The Staropramen Brewery offers the greatest variety of beers in the Czech market, as it is the largest and most modern brewhouse in Central Europe. These points imply that the subsidiary has taken a strategic role in InBev's global chain. Moreover, as result of global reorganization since 2006, the Czech subsidiary will accomplish the functions of the European Export and Shared Services Centre. Yet, it is difficult to talk about the 'embeddedness' of InBev in the Czech Republic. The local subsidiary is strategically dependant on the parent company; the main suppliers are negotiated regionally; and InBev has already closed the Branik plant, relocating activities to Staropramen. It is difficult to predict whether the parent company will keep the key role of the Czech subsidiary in its global portfolio of subsidiaries or will, again, relocate activities to another CEE country – for example, Romania.

Conclusion

This chapter tracked the developments of the Czech food industry since the 1990s. Special attention was given to the impact of EU member-ship, as this proved to be the major factor that unlocked the processes of restructuring and reorganization all over Europe. The chapter was organ-ized in three sections. The first section stressed different governmental policies that aimed at embedding FDI in the local economy. The second section discussed the Czech food sector and its development. The third section examined the courses of Nestlé, Unilever, and InBev from the 1990s until recently.

It became clear that, of all the new member states, the Czech food industry was the best prepared for EU accession; that is, it was character-ized by a strong supplier network. The government invested in the sector, and so did domestic firms in order to comply with all EU regulations. It has been a long process of linkage creation between local companies and multinationals. The government played a crucial role through the introduction of protectionist trade regimes (tariff and non-tariff barriers, sector subsidies, and so on), thus forcing MNEs to source locally. In add-ition, the FFDI was also a main actor in the process of linkage creation through the introduction of different programmes and initiatives that encouraged partnership between foreign and domestic companies. The FFDI also had very good links in Brussels, and was able to lobby strongly for the Czech food industry.

Since 2004, there have no longer been trade protection measures in the Czech Republic. In addition, logistics with regard to goods improved and cheap food goods entered the country, making the competition tougher. The strong retail sector did not allow for a dramatic increase in food prices; however, producers had to invest and reorganize their activities in order to keep their market shares.

Unilever, Nestlé, and InBev initiated optimization plans that led to plant closures, employee lay-offs, and the redirection of activities to global suppliers. Unilever shut down its plant in Zábreh in 2005; Nestlé (Cesko) closed down the factory where the oldest Czech chocolate, Orion was produced; and InBev closed down one of the oldest Czech breweries, Branik. Therefore, the question that requires attention is:

Can we consider these companies locked into the host economies?

We have seen that the three food giants have a very centralized approach to their Czech subsidiaries, leaving them very limited space for management decisions. None of the three companies has located R&D centres in the Czech Republic and, at the time of writing, there are no plans for their creation. The reason does not lie in the scarcity of highly qualified personnel to operate them, or the absence of effective protection of intellectual property rights; it is simply a question of strategic need. Company headquarters do not perceive any such needs at present and, hence, do not think about the likelihood of creating such centres in CEE and, in particular, in the Czech Republic. At the same time, the observed multinationals are major players on the Czech market, and possess the most modern plants within their sub-sectors. Yet, economic integration led to higher efficiency in operations and the related process of restructuring. This showed that domestic actors could not intervene and prevent plant closures.

The next two chapters are devoted to Bulgaria and Romania; two countries that had not yet become EU members while I was undertaking the field research in 2005 and 2006. They are second-wave EU accession countries, lagging behind Hungary and the Czech Republic in terms of economic development. Nestlé, Unilever, and InBev entered these markets in the mid- and late 1990s, much later than was the case in Hungary and the Czech Republic. The level of investment was also lower than in Central Europe. In addition, the local authorities and the national government did not undertake programmes and measures to embed FDI on a scale comparable to that of the CEE countries. The consequences of EU membership remain to be seen. If MNEs have been able to relocate within Central European countries, and even leave some of them, one might foresee the same events happening in Bulgaria and Romania.

6
MNE Strategies in Bulgaria

Introduction

The objective of this chapter is to address the level of embeddedness of MNEs in Bulgaria. It is organized in three sections. The first section provides a brief overview of the Bulgarian innovation system. It analyzes the government's investment promotion policies and looks at the policies that encourage the creation of linkages between MNEs and domestic firms in general: there is no information available for the food industry in particular. This section also discusses the degree of interaction between foreign companies and host organizations and institutions. The second section focuses on FDI in the food industry in Bulgaria. It draws attention to the gradual change of consumer behaviour in Bulgaria, and the role retail chains and MNEs play in the promotion of Western lifestyles. Consumer trends and the purchasing power of the population have a considerable impact on the strategies of food MNEs, as busier lifestyles lead to higher consumption of frozen and semi-prepared products, which are mainly manufactured by large MNEs. The third section discusses the policies and indirect spillovers of Unilever, Nestlé and InBev in Bulgaria.

Firm embeddedness in Bulgaria

The innovation system of Bulgaria

This section explores the Bulgarian innovation system in order to understand MNEs' propensity to lock in. It pays special attention to the main actors in the system, and looks at the government's investment promotion policies. Figure 6.1 presents the links between these actors.

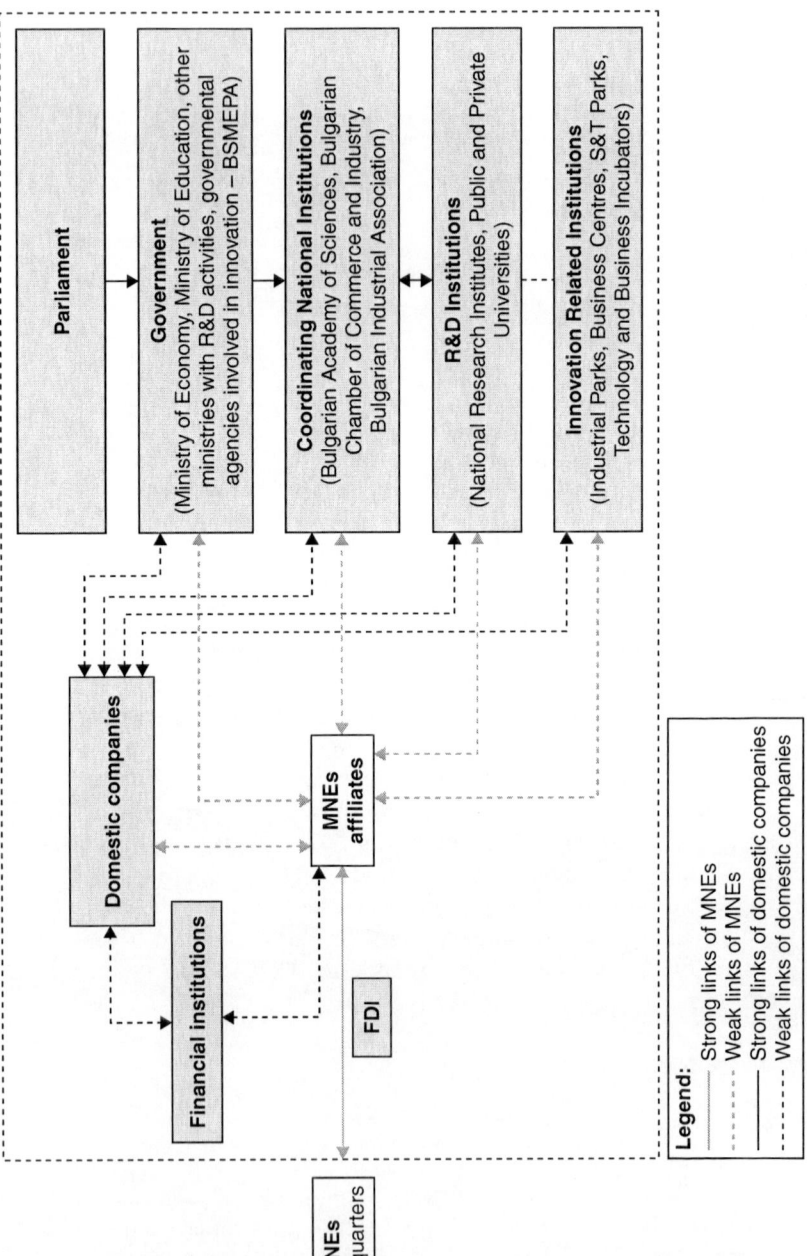

Figure 6.1 MNEs, domestic suppliers, and the linkages between the different actors of the Bulgarian innovation system
Source: based on European Trend Chart Country Reports – Bulgaria.

As shown in Figure 6.1, there are very weak linkages between MNEs, local companies and knowledge institutions. The only strong links that exist are between subsidiaries and their parent companies. It is difficult to discuss the embeddedness of FDI in Bulgaria and linkage creation between MNEs and local companies, as this goal was not a governmental priority. Rather, the government's focus was towards achieving macroeconomic stability, which presented a serious problem until the late 1990s. Due to lack of financial sources for innovative projects, the state had already withdrawn from an active role in research and innovation by the beginning of the 1990s. From 1996 to 2004, the R&D:GDP ratio fluctuated at around 0.5 per cent; private R&D expenditure was at a very low level of around 20 per cent of the total R&D expenditures.[1] The enterprise sector was the only innovative actor; however, it started to play a declining role in the development of science in Bulgaria, as the government did not support it. Put differently, in Bulgaria we cannot detect any focused policies in the early and mid-1990s that aimed at the embedding of FDI. In fact, there was nothing to be embedded, as the level of FDI was very low. The massive privatization that occurred in Bulgaria began in the mid-1990s, when most MNEs entered the market, and, even then, the privatization schemes were unclear, the political environment was not stable, and the legislative framework was constantly changing. Hence, as I cannot talk about concrete programmes and initiatives for linkage creation in the 1990s, I will focus on government measures taken recently to attract FDI and link it with the national innovation actors. It should be noted, however, that the majority of these measures have only recently been launched or are at project level, and the outcomes remain to be seen.

The Bulgarian government, pushed by EU accession conditionality and the Lisbon strategy adopted by the European Community, recognized the need for a national innovation system, and accepted its role in the management of the process of knowledge-creation. The Global Information Technology Report 2005[2] ranked Bulgaria 64th out of 114 countries, using a Networked Readiness Index.[3] This position meant that Bulgaria needed to develop close connection between ICT policies and effective investment in social and educational improvement in order to enjoy sustainable growth. The first steps in this direction were undertaken in 2004, when a national innovation strategy (NIS) was put in place. The strategy targets an increase in GDP, in productivity and in value-added by Bulgarian industry, and a higher level of foreign investment.[4] Among the main policy objectives are the encouragement of the employment of young specialists in SMEs, cluster development, attracting FDI in R&D activities, and setting up and encouraging existing technology parks.[5] The financial realization of innovation priorities has been ensured by the creation of the National Innovation Fund (NIF), promoted and administrated by the Bulgarian SME Agency (BSMEPA). The National Innovation Fund is the first proactive, purely innovation-related enhancement policy measure in the transitional history of Bulgaria. The main functions of the Fund are 'to increase the competitiveness of the Bulgarian economy through the encouragement of market-oriented applied research for the needs of industry, as well to create the necessary background for public investments in innovations according to the Innovation Strategy of Bulgaria'.[6] Although the NIF budget is very modest (€2.5 million) compared with the economic need to boost innovation, it is expected to result in fruitful cooperation between business entities and research institutions.

The second significant event to promote innovation has been the formation of a business association involving the most influential branch associations in the ICT sector. The goal of this newly established organization is to serve as an ICT cluster in the country. The ICT cluster aims at creating an opportunity for the Bulgarian economy to be the IT centre for the Balkans. However, so far the government has not been very active in pursuing this goal.

The third significant step that aims at promoting innovation was the establishment of a National Registry of Scientific Research.

The agro-food sector also finds a place in the NIS and the NIF. There is a strong interest in research in this area. The creation of agro-food clusters has been suggested as a priority and, therefore, a pilot project including research, extension of services, food production, and food processing will be supported.

Outcomes of the National Innovation Strategy policy measures

Attracting FDI: A law on investment promotion was adopted in 2004, in line with the National Innovation Strategy. The positive results of this legislation were immediately felt. In 2004, Bulgaria attracted its greatest amount of FDI since the 1990s (Figure A.2 in the Appendix, p. 237). The legislation on investment promotion predominantly favours large investors, offering them faster administrative procedures, personal assistance throughout the administrative process, voluntary transfer of a property right of real estate – private state or municipal property, and even some infrastructure construction for the largest investment projects (above €50 million).[7] However, reducing the administrative burden for companies and improving the environment for SMEs remain significant challenges that still need to be addressed. At present, large investors are better supported by the state than SMEs.

As far as property protection is regarded, (in 2007) there are no restrictions to foreign-owned companies acquiring land and real estate, neither are there any restrictions limiting individual land ownership. The Constitution was amended in February 2005 to allow foreigners to acquire land. Guarantees against expropriation of property are well respected. Fair compensation is enshrined in legislation. Intellectual property rights (IPR) legislation now complies with international standards. A Memorandum of Understanding on enhanced measures for the protection of IPR was signed in June 2005.

The agency Invest Bulgaria plays a crucial role in the process of investment promotion. The agency possesses a high level of expertise in investment promotion, recognized advocacy and a policy advice role, and budget resources. It is becoming increasingly effective in supporting potential and existing investors with after-care services, a 'one-stop-shop', and specific programmes. Services are well segmented according to three categories of investors, depending on the amount invested. Invest Bulgaria is an equal competitor to the other investment promotion agencies from CEE (FDI inflow in 2004 was one of the highest in South-Eastern Europe (SEE) at approximately €257 per capita).

Bulgaria has a tax policy that is very attractive to foreign investors. The corporate income tax rate of 15 per cent is in line with other SEE countries and is lower than the average in Central Europe.[8] There is also a low rate withholding tax on dividends to non-residents. However, the range of tax incentives that support large capital investments and job creation in deprived regions are limited. Those tax incentives norms in place now do not discriminate between foreign and domestic investors. Losses in Bulgaria can be carried forward for up to five years, in line with the SEE average. All large companies, banks, and insurance companies apply International Accounting Standards, while SMEs apply national Financial Reporting Standards.

Although government policy has addressed some of the innovation performance challenges, there are many more that have been ignored. In order to improve its business climate, Bulgaria needs efficiency in tax administration and reduction in the level of corruption in the tax revenue sector. The VAT tax refund process is still quite slow – an average of 56 days. The need to boost business R&D expenditure is underestimated by policy-makers. There are no tax incentives for innovative enterprises, for example. The implementation of the e-government project has been seriously delayed and the mandatory e-signature subscription is still widely unaffordable because of the low supply of e-government services. Some institutional innovations are only developing slowly, as result of policy demands. For example, increases of internal company funds for innovation (by introducing mechanisms for reducing mutual company debt) were left until 2006; alternative mechanisms for boosting the state financing of innovative and export-oriented activities (such as setting up a fund using privatization revenues) are discussed only at expert meetings and are unlikely to be accepted by policy-makers, although such alternative mechanisms have to be introduced to stop many European Innovation Scoreboard (EIS) indicators for Bulgaria from falling further behind the EU-25 average. In addition, the good measures for improving the business climate introduced in 2003 and 2004 are either not known in the enterprise sector, or are poorly implemented by the officials. This mainly refers to the legislation for reducing administrative regulation and administrative control over economic activity.

To summarize, Bulgaria's weak economic performance did not allow the government to concentrate on the development of a strong innovation system. The main factors that have constantly been hindering enterprises' innovative performance are low-tech product specialization and the export structure of the economy, which offer predominantly low-tech employment; enterprises' short-term planning horizon; poor human resources management systems within enterprises; the lack of venture capital schemes; and the absence of policy incentives for high-tech employment.[9] The funds deficit for R&D did not stimulate enterprises to invest in innovation activities, and the links between business and academia deteriorated. Considerable progress has been made since 2004, when innovation strategy and investment promotion legislation was adopted. However, it is difficult talk about embeddness of FDI in Bulgaria. The government and regional authorities have been very passive with regard to the creation of linkages between domestic and foreign companies. In the case of local authorities, they face a shortage of adequate skills and a limited local budget. Therefore, if any linkages exist, they were the result of the companies' own initiatives and not because of a focused national innovation policy. Actually, the government indirectly forced foreign companies to cooperate with local suppliers; this is particularly true for food companies. The protectionist trade policy for agricultural products pushes foreign companies to link with local suppliers and help them upgrade.

Trade policy

The transition process affects all sectors of the Bulgarian economy. Agriculture and food processing were most the severely disrupted because of a chaotic process of land reform and restitution. The trade regime affecting agriculture has also undergone considerable transformation. After the fall of the highly controlled central planning system, trade policy was initially used for short-term interventions aimed at micro-managing domestic supplies and prices. Instruments for the implementation of these policies included automatic and non-automatic licences on both imports and exports; export quotas, taxes, and bans; minimum import and export prices; and duty-free import quotas. For instance, basic regulations governing licensing exemptions were changed no fewer than 25 times prior to 1997 (WTO, 2003: 83). In this earlier period, in order to prevent or relieve critical shortages of foodstuffs and other essential products, export taxes were applied to products such as sunflower seeds and oil, hides and skins, timber, firewood, wood in the rough, wool, and grain flour, (WTO, 1996b). Since 1996, when Bulgaria joined the WTO, considerable progress has been made towards the liberalization of the agricultural trading regime. Since 1997, licensing requirements for the import and export of agricultural products have been removed; as of 2006 there are no automatic or non-automatic licensing provisions or export taxes on agricultural products and livestock. The only import protection on agricultural goods is through tariffs.

Bulgaria is moving towards the full adoption of EU trade policy and gradually liberalizing its trade regime. Since the beginning of 2005, more than 1000 tariff rates have been changed to close the gap between Bulgarian and EU tariff rates. Imports and exports are free of quantitative restrictions, except for some agricultural goods. EC standards are applicable for all export products and for most domestically traded products. It has signed Free Trade Agreements (FTAs) with all SEE countries, and signed the Accession Agreement in April 2005. However, Bulgaria applies customs duties that are still significantly higher than the EU average.[10] In short, Bulgaria's agricultural trade regime is characterized by high MFN tariffs and preferential agreements with EU and CEFTA. For this reason, until 2005 Bulgaria had a constantly positive trade balance for food and live animals (Figure 6.2).

There is a strong drive for technical standards to comply with EU and international norms. Some progress was made in applying EU food safety, veterinary and phytosanitary standards. A special project in 2004 by the Ministry of Economy supports SMEs in the introduction of the Hazard Analysis and Critical Control Point System (HACCP) and production for the EU market (meat and milk processing industries). Since September 2005, HACCP and ISO 22000:2005 have been compulsory standards for all organizations in the food chain. However, only 10 per cent of enterprises are EU certified (as of March 2006, for example, 1722

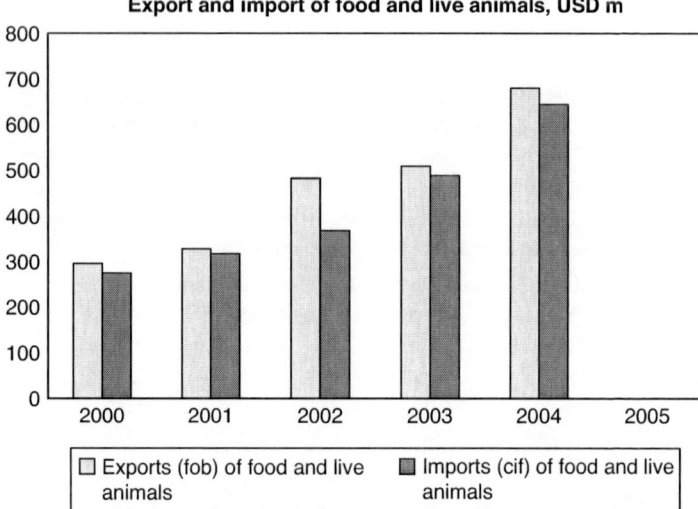

Figure 6.2   Export and import of food and live animals, Bulgaria, 2000–5
Source: UN Trade Statistics, Euromonitor Plc (2006).

companies have been certified under ISO 9001). There are no important trade restrictions for capital goods – no customs duty on them and VAT reimbursement is in 45 days, even more rapid for large investments. Finally, customs and administrative procedures are still complex and time intensive. The private sector perceives that levels of corruption in customs administration remain high.

To sum up, by 2007 Bulgaria had continued to enjoy high import tariffs, which, in a way, stimulated foreign investors to source locally (in particular, food companies).

The food industry in Bulgaria

Overview and FDI

This section briefly presents the agricultural and food sectors in Bulgaria, underlining the very important place they occupy in the Bulgarian economy. It analyzes the FDI that the food sector attracted, and its impact on the development and upgrading of the industry. It also observes the change in consumer lifestyles and the expansion of the retail market, as these have impacted MNE strategies in Bulgaria.

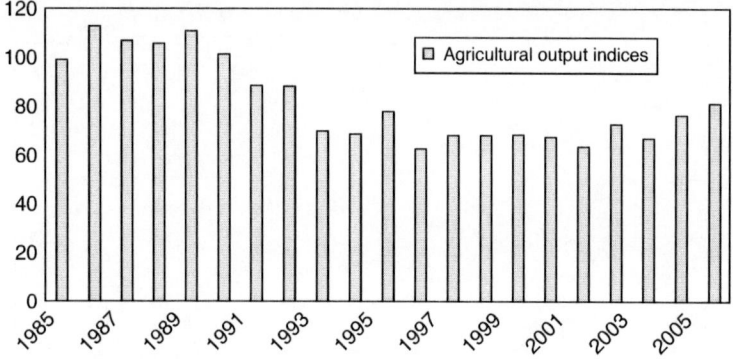

Figure 6.3 Agricultural output indices, Bulgaria, 1985–2006
Source: UN Food and Agriculture Organization, FAOSTAT.

Agriculture

Almost 56 per cent of Bulgaria's land is agricultural; a further 35 per cent is covered by forest, and about 5 per cent by water. Of the agricultural land, 69 per cent is arable, 27 per cent permanent pastures and meadows, and about 4 per cent is vineyards and orchards (OECD, 2000a). Agriculture accounted for 9.4 per cent of GDP in 2004[11] and employed 11 per cent of the employed population (see Table A.1 in the Appendix). Before 1990, Bulgaria was a major exporter of food and agricultural products[12] to the CMEA market. Food and agriculture have historically been major components of Bulgaria's foreign trade, contributing up to a quarter of total exports. During the transition years, the rural economy suffered considerable decline because of the loss of the CMEA market and the severe reduction of the domestic market, particularly up until 1997. For example, between 1992 and 2005, cereal production reduced by nearly 20 per cent, cattle stocks declined by 55 per cent, sheep by 66 per cent and pig numbers by 70 per cent (see Tables A.2 and A.3 in the Appendix). Overall, production levels remain well below those of the early 1990s (Figure 6.3).

Since 1998, when around €7.8 million was invested in agriculture, the second large wave of FDI occurred in 2004 (Figure 6.4). The change in the constitution that allows foreign citizens to buy Bulgarian land will further increase investment in agriculture and farming.

Agriculture, the backbone of the food industry, has come through a very difficult phase due to uncertainties arising from the privatization process, trade reforms and macroeconomic instability. The main policy

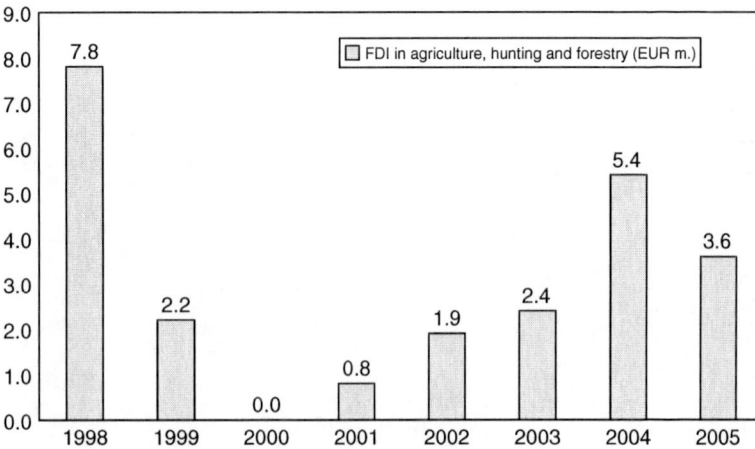

Figure 6.4   FDI in agriculture, hunting, and forestry, Bulgaria
Source: Bulgarian National Bank.

focus was on deeper restructuring and productivity improvement in the agri-food system. Land was given back to its owners in 'real boundaries', and this resulted in high ownership fragmentation and difficulties in land cultivation. Large state cooperatives were destroyed and livestock sold or killed. All this led to a dramatic fall in output, and contributed to the destruction of the networks between the agricultural suppliers and food processors.

The food industry

The food and beverages industry is traditional in Bulgaria and provides 16.2 per cent of total industrial production (2004).[13] It employs 3.6 per cent of the total workforce.[14] Since 2000, the export of food, beverages, and tobacco products has been growing steadily, reaching US$905 million in 2004 (Table 6.1) – about 10 per cent of the total export of the country.

The food and beverages industry has been of particular interest to large MNEs. Among the major foreign investors are InBev, Carlsberg, Kraft Foods, Nestlé, Coca-Cola, Brewinvest, Klarina Holdings, Luxcraft, Delta, and Chipita. In 2003, FDI in food processing registered its highest inflows – US$87.6 million (see Figure A.3 in the Appendix). Investments in the food sector concentrated on a narrow range of products including tobacco, beverages, sugar, confectionery products, and vegetable oils.

Table 6.1   Exports of food, beverages, tobacco, live animals, Bulgaria, 2000–4

Bulgaria **Exports of food, beverages, tobacco, live animals; historic – US\$ m.**	*2000*	*2001*	*2002*	*2003*	*2004*
Exports (fob) of food and live animals	289	320	476	502	671.9
Exports (fob) of beverages and tobacco	154	128	134	158	233.1

Source: UN Trade Statistics, Euromonitor International (electronic database).

In comparison with the Czech Republic and Hungary, which welcomed FDI in the early 1990s, large foreign investors entered the Bulgarian market no earlier than 1994. The majority came in 1997, following the launch of mass privatization. Hence, the potential benefits offered by foreign capital were delayed for seven years. FDI was impeded by various factors, including unclear privatization schemes, the lack of profitability in the sector, and the uncertain legal framework, as well as labour and other social restrictions placed on investors and management. In addition, the macroeconomic situation was not very stable in 1997 and foreign investors were careful with regard to large investments. These are some of the explanations why most MNEs invested much less in Bulgaria than they did in Central Europe. Moreover, as well as the volatile business environment, the purchasing power of the population was the other crucial factor affecting MNEs' investment strategies. The annual disposable income of Bulgarians was much less than that of CEE (see Figure A.4 in the Appendix).

Consumer market and retail market

In 2005, Bulgaria's population was 7.68 million, and had been steadily decreasing since the 1990s because of low birth rates, an increase in deaths, and an increase in emigration – especially that of young people. Bulgaria is a small market.

The average age of the population is 40 years (see Table A.4 in the Appendix). About 70 per cent of the population is urban and 30 per cent is rural. The rural population has no access to modern Western-type products, as foreign chains do not invest in the small cities and villages, where people have low purchasing power and the infrastructure is still poorly developed. Moreover, Bulgarians in the small cities and villages do not shop a great deal; they still largely rely on their farms for the

Table 6.2   Consumer expenditure, BGN per capita

Consumer expenditure BGN per capita – current	2000	2001	2002	2003	2004	2005
Bulgaria						
Consumer expenditure	2355.30	2612.10	2893.40	3011.40	3326.30	3628.70
Consumer expenditure on food and non-alcoholic beverages	860.58	945.84	1064.10	1109.00	1232.20	1353.90
Consumer expenditure on alcoholic beverages and tobacco	192.26	214.46	241.77	246.04	268.51	293.18

Sources: National Statistical Institute, OECD, Eurostat, Euromonitor International (electronic database).

supply of many food goods. These goods are usually meat (mainly pork, as well as some chicken and beef), fresh milk, yoghurt, fresh vegetables and fruit, pickled food, and so on (Euromonitor International, 2003). The urban population is increasingly choosing to shop in supermarkets and hypermarkets.

Disposable income is the most important factor, as it pre-determines the shopping behaviour of the population. Average spending on a shopping trip in 2004 was around BGN10 (€5). It remains one of the lowest spending rates in Eastern Europe. In 2005, 37 per cent of consumer expenditure went on food and non-alcoholic beverages. (See Table 6.2)

Bulgarian households are used to shopping for their food every day, and they do so from independent groceries or specialized shops. Bulgarians visit the local bakeries for fresh bread, butchers or the meat market for meat, and prefer going to the market for fresh fruit and vegetables. The reason for the dominance of groceries is that small local shops proved to be the most flexible during the uncertain economic period, while, at the same time, large foreign retailers did not enter the market because of the economic instability. As illustrated in Figure 6.5, in 2005 independent groceries still dominated the retail structure in Bulgaria, where 75 per cent of all types of retailers were independent groceries.

Until 1998, the development of Western retailing had been impeded by unfavourable economic conditions in the country and low levels of FDI on the whole. Foreign investors entered the Bulgarian market quite late in comparison with their entry into Central Europe, when Metro Cash & Carry and Billa opened their first outlets in 1999 and 2000. In 2000, independent grocers made up 67 per cent of all food retail sales nationally; however, the emergence of supermarkets and cash-and-carry

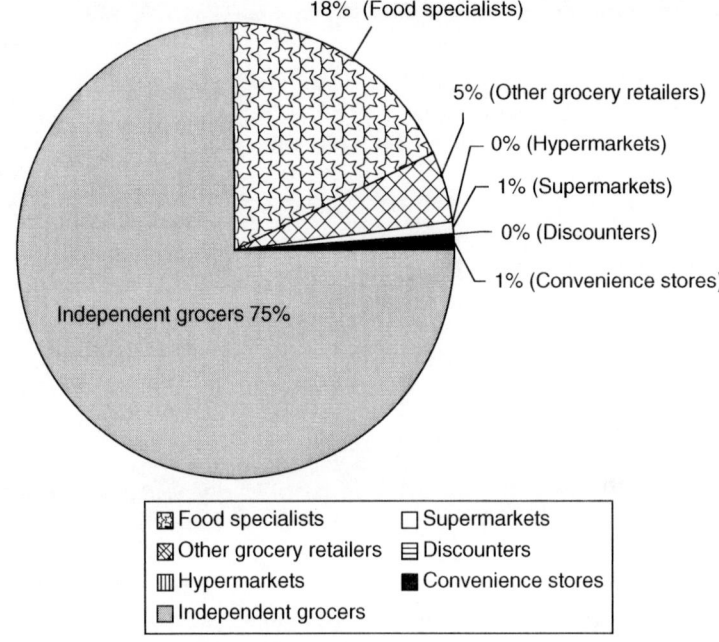

Figure 6.5   Grocery retailing outlets/sites, Bulgaria, 2005
Source: National Statistical Institute, Bulgaria.

outlets decreased their share to 54 per cent in 2005 (see Figures A.5 and A.6 in the Appendix).

Supermarkets in Bulgaria contributed to the improvement of product quality and food safety in the domestic market. The difference in quality between products destined for local and export markets is narrowing (GAIN, 2005). Retailers use private standards to standardize product requirements from suppliers. There are two types of private label products: products using the name of the supermarket chain, so-called 'store brands'; and products whose brand was especially created for the supermarket chain. Private label products are important to retailers, as they increase their business, and enhance their image and competitive edge. Metro, Billa, and Fantastico offer more than 100 products with private labels (GAIN, 2005). They choose the best quality and price offered by producers for different products specified by the management of the chains. Large companies that are well situated in the market usually win in the competition for the best offer, which guarantees high quality standards. Such companies have the potential for the future expansion of products in line with new brands and higher prices.

The growth of supermarkets and the increase in the incomes of the population has been reflected in consumer shopping habits. The busier lifestyle of the population in urban areas means they shop less often, mainly in the late hours of the day or at the weekends (Euromonitor International, 2003). This change is significantly more noticeable in young professional people. Multinational companies and Western brand products have become increasingly visible. Consumers are growing more sophisticated, and have a greater demand for products offering health benefits and convenience. The busy lifestyles of young professionals have accounted for increases in the demand for labour-saving breakfast cereals, snack foods, and ready-to-eat meals. One of the most dynamic growth sectors has been in the sales of products as ready-meals – frozen pizza, dehydrated soups, dried food products, and pasta and other noodles. Foreign investments in private label product development have helped drive the demand for high-value processed foods.

Older people (who rely mainly on pensions for their income) and low-paid workers stick to traditional independent grocery shopping. These consumers go shopping in supermarkets if they are located close to their homes. In general, they are not loyal to particular brands and are inclined to purchase the cheapest products without considering quality. In addition, they go for traditional Bulgarian products and are unwilling to experiment with a new variety of food or with an imported food. In most cases, they buy only what they have decided on in advance; impulse purchasing is uncommon. Food MNEs are challenged to offer their products at the lowest possible price while still retaining their quality standards.

Since 2000, the Bulgarian retail market has developed rapidly. Five large foreign retailers began operations in Bulgaria in 2004: the German hypermarket chains Kaufland and Lidl, the supermarket chain HIT, and the DIY chains Prakiker AG and OBI. The Schwarz Group, with its Kaufland hypermarket chain, planned to invest €300 million to build 40 outlets in Bulgaria. The first ten opened their doors in 2005 but did not enter the Bulgarian market (for discount stores). The hard discount stores were expected to make an entrance soon after (Euromonitor International, 2004a) but have not yet done so. Domestic retail chains are competing successfully with foreign chains: there are 46 chains with 445 stores around the country.

To summarize, the agro-food sector is an important sector of the Bulgarian economy, employing about 15 per cent of the workforce: 9.4 per cent of GDP consists of agriculture, and the food industry provides 16.2 per cent of all industrial production and 8.8 per cent of total exports. The turbulent political and economic environment delayed the entry of foreign capital into the country; most of the large companies invested in 1997–8, approximately seven years later than they did in Central Europe. The risky business climate was also an obstacle for investment for large Western retailers. The retail market started dynamic development at the beginning of 2000 and, thus, initiated a change in consumer behaviour towards foods offered by MNEs – frozen foods, snacks, dried soups, and so on. Young professionals have a Western shopping mentality: because of their intense lifestyle they go shopping once a week, they are willing to experiment with new brands of foods, prefer healthier foods and semi-prepared food. Older consumers still prefer traditional Bulgarian foods, opt for cheap products and are unwilling to buy unfamiliar brands.

The next section analyzes Unilever, Nestlé, and InBev in Bulgaria, and tries to achieve a deeper understanding of their policies in the country and the factors that have been crucial to their strategic decisions.

Firm case analysis

Unilever (Bulgaria)

Unilever invested in Bulgaria in 1999 and, at the beginning of 2000, Unilever (Bulgaria) was integrated into the framework of Unilever South and Central Europe, whose headquarters are in Romania.

Unilever (South and Central Europe) produces and distributes goods for seven countries: Albania, Bosnia and Herzegovina, Bulgaria, Macedonia, Moldova, Romania, and Serbia-Montenegro. It is one of the largest producers of household care products, detergents, frozen food, margarine and spreads, ice cream, cooking products, tea, and personal care products (such as shampoo, toothpaste, soap, deodorant and fragrances).

In Bulgaria, Unilever is most famous for its detergents (Omo and Dero); fabric softener (Coccolino); household cleaning products (Domestos and Cif); soaps (Lux and Dove); deodorants (Rexona and Axe); toothpaste (Signal); Knorr instant soups, savouries and seasonings (Knorr); and Lipton tea. Worldwide, Unilever is the producer of Calvin Klein fragrances.

Since its creation in 1999, Unilever (Bulgaria) has marked a 30 per cent annual growth. In 2003, Unilever (Bulgaria) purchased the plant for the processing of vegetable oils and production of Kaliakra margarine in Dobrich. The plant employs 400 people (Invest Bulgaria Agency, 2006). Kaliakra is one of the largest local producers of margarine and sunflower seed oil. It has the leading market share in the Bulgarian market. The plant accounts for 80 per cent of domestic consumption, and its total turnover for 2001 was BGN 33 million. With an investment of

US$11 million, Unilever (Bulgaria) modernized the plant and brought it into line with EU standards. However, the Bulgarian office is entirely dependent on the Romanian office for all decisions.

The Managing Director, Foods, Unilever South Central Europe, Mr E,[15] explained that the main factors that pre-determine Unilever's investments in each country, including Bulgaria, are the growth potential of the market, the size of the market, and political and economic stability. A sudden hyperinflation or a political turmoil could even result in the closure of Unilever's subsidiary. Actually, something similar has already happened in Bulgaria: Unilever left in 1997 when there was a financial crisis in the country, and returned in 1999 when the economic situation had stabilized. However, the company's withdrawal reflected the amount of investment and Unilever's long-term strategic decisions. It is important to remember that the level of Unilever's investment in Bulgaria is lower than the amount invested in Romania, the Czech Republic, and Hungary. The initial redistribution of investments among these four countries has had a long-term impact. For the future, Unilever management has planned further large investments in Romania; in Bulgaria, flexible short-term investments are to be expected – those necessary to upgrade the acquired production facilities.

As shown earlier, the retail market in Bulgaria developed relatively late. Unilever was forced to work with local retailers in order to increase its market share. The ratio of local to foreign retailers is 70 per cent to 30 per cent. Normally, Unilever prefers to work with global retail partners, as this increases the opportunity to negotiate greater discounts on a Europe-wide basis. However, there were few retailers present in Bulgaria by 2004. Metro and Billa were relatively large, but not yet significant players. The Manager underscored that the advantages of multinational retailers are a more clear trade terms structure, professional store management, and greater opportunity for branded products to demonstrate strength and quality. However, local retailers also have their advantages. In particular, they are very flexible in negotiations regarding the terms of trade.

Unilever cooperates with Bulgarian universities to recruit top-level graduates. Yet, for fundamental research, the company relies on Unilever's Central Research Divisions in Western Europe. The lack of collaboration with Bulgarian research institutes reveals that Unilever's linkages with the local knowledge institutions are very weak and, hence, there are fewer chances for the local innovation system to benefit from the company's expertise.

The role of the local authorities is similar to that of government. Mr E pointed out that local business and regional development centres invite

Unilever representatives to different seminars and conferences; however, he could not explain how decisive their role was to the company's work.

As far as suppliers are concerned, Unilever has Europe-wide contracts with guaranteed quality level suppliers and at good prices. Yet, local suppliers are used for many local products, and all of them are up to Unilever's strict quality standards. Import tariffs also matter in the choice of suppliers; the higher import tariffs stimulate the company to source locally. The Unilever Group Vice-President, Mr F,[16] added that IT suppliers, for example, are global; packaging suppliers are local, sometimes global. Packaging suppliers are global when there are high taxes on packaging, when Unilever prefers to import. The Vice-President (Central and Eastern Europe) said that Bulgaria is still lagging behind in its efforts to develop strong supply networks.

In short, Unilever (Bulgaria) is a subsidiary that is completely dependent on Unilever's Romanian subsidiary. The unstable political and economic climate presented serious obstacles to the initial investment Unilever made in Bulgaria. The most pertinent example of the impact of the political climate is found in the temporary pullout during the 1997 financial crisis. The company returned in 1999 and, even then, did not find it easy to buy an appropriate plant. The former director of the Hungarian subsidiary of Unilever, Mr A,[17] mentioned that the process of finding an appropriate factory was a long one, and that this explains why they bought a plant as late as 2003. Unilever was willing to invest in more plants in Bulgaria; however, the company did not find any support from the national government and only bought one plant. To conclude, taking into consideration all of the points made concerning Unilever's experience in the country, it is very difficult to draw any conclusion other than that the company can hardly be said to be embedded in Bulgaria.

InBev (Bulgaria)

In contrast to Unilever, InBev entered Bulgaria's market much earlier, in 1995, when the Belgian firm Interbrew bought the Kamenitza brewery in Plovdiv, which was followed by more acquisitions of breweries in Haskovo (Astika AD), Burgas (Burgasko Pivo AD, purchased in January 1999) and the north-western city of Pleven (Plevensko Pivo AD), along with several mergers (for example, Kamenitza and Plevensko Pivo merged in 2002).[18] In June 2005, Kamenitza started producing InBev's Staropramen beer at its Haskovo brewery. The company also produces Bulgaria's only alcohol-free beer, Kamenitza Zero Percent. InBev (Bulgaria) brews Stella Artois, Beck's, and Staropramen under licence, while its local brands include Astika, Burgasko, Kamenitza, Pleven and Slavena. Other global InBev brands sold in Bulgaria include Hoegaarden and Leffe. InBev (Bulgaria) exports some of its brands to the USA, the UK, and other nations with significant Bulgarian emigrant communities. In May 2005, InBev (Bulgaria) began testing the market in the former Yugoslav Republic of Macedonia (FYROM) by exporting its Kamenitza and Slavena brands there.

The company's General Manager, Mr B,[19] mentioned the brand Kamenitza, explaining that it had an 18 per cent share of the Bulgarian beer market in 2005, according to data from the world's leading marketing information company, AC Nielsen. After privatization in 1995 by Interbrew, Kamenitza has become the main player on the local market, and, since 1998, has consistently been the best-selling beer brand in Bulgaria. In fact, the multinational companies Heineken, InBev, and Carlsberg produce over 80 per cent of the beer sold on the domestic market.

Since 1995, InBev has developed the beer market as a whole, and has introduced a series of innovations and varieties of beer entirely new to Bulgaria. Kamenitza has spent more than BGN 86 million (€43 million) on production facilities, advertising, trademarks, information systems, and personnel training. Currently, the brewery – based in Bulgaria's second-largest city of Plovdiv – employs 650 people. InBev invested heavily in the country.

In 2005, InBev closed its Pleven brewery in order to optimize its production activities. Production was transferred to the remaining two breweries, Plovdiv and Haskovo: 98 employees were affected by the closure. The decision to transfer brewing and packaging operations to the two other sites was based on excess capacity, and on the disadvantages that this creates. The Pleven site will continue its production of malt, and sales and distribution activities, as well as logistics operations. The concentration of production was in line with the global reorganization plans InBev had formulated in 2005.

The company's management staff confirmed the statement that the Czech and Hungarian subsidiaries are more advanced than the Bulgarian and Romanian subsidiaries because the business environment in Central Europe is better developed. In addition, Central European countries – and, in particular, the Czech Republic – have a very strong beer culture. This has impacted InBev's strategic decisions in terms of investment and management responsibilities.

The basic reason for investing in Bulgaria was the market. Interbrew's first years of investment were not easy. The volatility of the business climate and the constant changes in legislation had an impact on the profitability of Interbrew business. Moreover, the environment of the beer industry was unpredictable.

As far as suppliers are concerned, 60 per cent of the suppliers that InBev uses are foreign (raw materials and packaging suppliers); its marketing supplier is a local company. And again, as already proved by Nestlé and Unilever, the reason for sourcing abroad is that there are no strong local suppliers that can satisfy InBev's quality criteria. Import tariffs are high, but this has not lead to a sourcing of supplies locally, as the company was constrained by their inability to find local suppliers able to provide goods of a sufficiently high quality.

To the extent that InBev works with local suppliers, it has backward linkages with them and tries to guarantee long-term engagements. InBev established predominantly new suppliers, as there were no existing supply networks.

Retail sales through local retail chains represent about 80 per cent of the total sales volume. There are few international chains and, hence, InBev works mainly with local retailers. The company believes that the situation will progressively improve with Bulgarian EU membership.

InBev (Bulgaria) is completely integrated into InBev's global network system and enjoys the parent company's knowledge, know-how, and its negotiation of agreements on a Europe-wide basis.

InBev collaborates with many local universities to recruit personnel. In terms of the search for executives, Bulgaria is considered to be a smaller market. In this respect the management shares the opinion that it is difficult to find qualified staff as the base from which to choose is small. The company faces a serious challenge finding the right people to expand its business.

Management staff admitted there is no research collaboration between the company and the universities/research centres.

According to InBev management, Bulgaria's accession to the EU is a considerable challenge: the up-side is that borders are open for imports and exports to the EU, but the down-side is possible product dumping on the local market. The Country Director recalled that, after Hungary opened its borders to the EU, it was flooded with cheap German beer.

In sum, InBev entered the Bulgarian market in 1995, when Interbrew bought the Kamenitza brewery. Since then, the company has acquired several more breweries. After mergers and restructurings, two breweries are left – in Plovdiv and in Haskovo. InBev invested largely in Bulgaria and, hence, by this criterion, it can be considered as locked into the local economy. However, the company is not part of the country's innovation system; it does not cooperate scientifically with research centres and universities, and does not have an R&D unit in Bulgaria. It sources locally but only to a limited extent, as there are no good supplier networks. Hence, local suppliers cannot benefit from the know-how the company could offer. The retail market still needs further development and that is why, for the moment, the company uses local retail chains.

Nestlé (Bulgaria)

Nestlé entered the Bulgarian market very early, in 1994, after the purchase of the largest confectionery plant in the country, located on the outskirts of the capital, Sofia. The company produces tablets, boxed chocolates, and wafers and biscuits. Its brands – Nestlé Classic, Mura, Adventure, LZ, Taralejki, Jiten Dar – are well known on the Bulgarian market, and are highly valued by Bulgarian consumers. For the last 10 years, Nestlé has invested more than US$33 million in Bulgaria (excluding acquisitions), renovating its manufacturing process, innovating its products, elaborating efficient marketing, establishing distribution controlling systems, and developing effective experts and managers. Special attention has been paid to the research and development process, as well as to quality, environmental protection, and safety issues (OECD, 2005c). Utilizing the experienced local organization, from 2000, Nestlé (Sofia) started to import international Nestlé products: Nescafé, Nesquik, Maggi, breakfast cereals, infant nutrition, and so on.

The company's microbiological laboratory in Bulgaria was certified as the Nestlé laboratory that ensured the most precise analyses worldwide. Operating in the changing business environment in Bulgaria, the company has lived through all the difficulties of the transition period. In 2004, it had already experienced dramatic business growth, and foresees that this trend will be profitable and sustainable. The company recorded a 25 per cent year-on-year sales increase in 2004. Nestlé has two enterprises in Bulgaria with approximately 1700 employees: Nestlé Bulgaria AD and Delta Ice Cream Bulgaria.

Mr James Gallagher, Director for South-East Europe, was approached to explain the lessons that the company had learnt and the difficulties that had been met in the Bulgarian market. He said:

> We are learning lessons all the time in developing countries, and unfortunately even sometimes repeating mistakes. But, as in all countries, the most important issue is putting in the right people. Nearly always, our problems have stemmed from getting this wrong. Obviously, the wrong choice of Director can set you back years; for

example, someone who isn't sensitive to local culture, or who can't build a balanced management team or create an appropriate business model. Less obvious is the problem of building your company culture from scratch, installing values and ways of working, which we often take for granted in long established businesses. It's often surprising how things can go wrong when a group of managers just don't operate under the same values and company culture.

As clearly indicated, getting the balance of expatriate and local people is very important. Local employees must not feel that they are second-class employees, blocked from the best jobs.

'Understanding local consumers is also of fundamental importance, and getting this wrong results in serious mistakes', Mr Gallagher said. For example, Nestlé bought the leading chocolate company in Bulgaria, but the quality of its products was poor, which the management thought was in accordance with the local taste. That company put the Nestlé logo on these products, expecting that this endorsement would improve sales. In fact, sales dropped by more than 50 per cent in a couple of years, as Bulgarian consumers simply could not accept that such poor quality could come from Nestlé. 'It wasn't until we improved quality, better than the competition, that we managed to completely reverse this trend', said Mr Gallagher. According to him, Bulgaria is also a good example of where a series of personnel oriented mistakes drove the company into losses; a significant improvement in profitability only resulted when Nestlé got the management basics right, including installing the Nestlé culture and sales tactics.

Nestlé faced serious challenges with the high import duties on Nescafé in Bulgaria. According to company headquarters, this only led to smuggling, higher consumer prices, and counterfeit products. 'So not only Nestlé and the Bulgarian government, but also the consumer was cheated', Mr Gallagher noted.

'In Bulgaria, only the elite could buy our products until the fall of Communism, and it wasn't until we acquired the largest confectionery business in this country in 1994 that our business gained critical size', the Executive Director said, proudly. At present, a full range of Nestlé products are sold in Bulgaria, which have either been imported or manufactured locally, and the MNE has a fast-growing, profitable business.

Mr Yannis Lazaridis,[20] Country Manager, was interviewed in order to explore the local perspective of Nestlé's strategy. He admitted that Hungarian and Czech Republic subsidiaries attracted more investments

Table 6.3   Nestlé's European supply network

	Local %	Foreign %
Ratio of local to foreign suppliers		
Total raw and packing (R&P) materials	30	70
Raw materials only	25	75
Packing materials only	85	15
Services and indirect materials (S&IM)	90	10
Nestlé Top 10 suppliers		
Cocoa	Foreign	
Flexible packaging	Foreign	
Paper/cardboard packaging	Local	
Sugar	Local/foreign	
Milk powder	Foreign/local (trader)	
Vegetable fats	Foreign	

Note: All calculations are based on value-turnover with suppliers but not on the number of materials or volumes purchased. The data are provided by Nestlé Bulgaria.

than those in Bulgaria and Romania. Mr Lazaridis explained the reason: 'These are more advanced markets in terms of modern trade, closer to the Western European countries and with higher incomes.'

When Nestlé invested in Bulgaria, they were looking for a combination of strong brands, and a variety of products and prices. And, as Mr Gallagher, the CEE Director at Vevey explained, 'Nestlé always targets the companies that are market leaders.' He said that, taking into consideration the prevailing conditions back in 1994, the privatization scheme of the factory was quite clear. In the process of restructuring and modernization, Nestlé closed the production of sugar confectioneries.

As far as the company's supply network is concerned, Nestlé has both local and foreign suppliers, the share of foreign suppliers being much higher. The reason is that local suppliers cannot reach the quality standards Nestlé demands. The supply networks that existed under socialism were destroyed and never re-built. 'Local supply networks need further improvement to gradually align their quality of products, and technical, commercial and service levels to reach those of the leading European suppliers Nestlé works with', said Mr Lazaridis, before presenting in much greater detail the suppliers that they use (see Table 6.3).

Nestlé works very closely with its local suppliers, providing technical assistance and support. An integrated programme for supplier assessment through defined Supplier Service Process Performance Indicators and on-the-spot audits with Nestlé quality assurance (QA) involvement has been put in place. 'The ongoing process of suppliers continuous improvement is supported by Nestlé recommendations concerning the suppliers' QA system and systems of working; technical and commercial level', Mr Lazaridis said.

In 2006, Nestlé (Bulgaria) only produces local brands, and there are no plans for the transformation of those brands into regional ones. However, Nestlé (Bulgaria) is also the producer of some international brands that are sold throughout the world; for example, Nestlé Kit-Kat. The Bulgarian subsidiary is completely integrated into Nestlé's global network.

Nestlé contributes to local development by being a socially responsible employer. When the company came to Bulgaria, it offered employment to a considerable number of people. The working conditions in Nestlé are far better than those in many companies. The high levels of safety and quality control Nestlé has in place worldwide allows the Bulgarian consumer to enjoy the high standard of quality products that Nestlé offers. 'We are often used as an example that Bulgaria is a good place to invest in – demonstrating that the investment climate is good and that other foreign companies may follow our suit', said Mr Lazaridis.

Nestlé uses 85 per cent local retailers and distributors, and 15 per cent international retailers. As already mentioned, the retail market only expanded from about 2004 and the greatest share of the market remains in the hands of local retailers. The retailers that Nestlé uses to a greater extent are: Metro Cash and Carry, Rewe (Billa), Fantastico, Picadilly, and Familia.

Nestlé collaborates with many Bulgarian universities to recruit personnel, including faculties at the St Kliment Ohridski University, Sofia; the University of Food and Technology, Plovdiv; the University of National and World Economy; the Medical University, Sofia; and the Technical Universities in Sofia, Varna, Ruse, Gabrovo, and Plovdiv, as well as many others.

Nestlé's Director considers the government of Simeon Saxe-Coburg-Gotha (2001–5) to be very helpful, as it has passed numerous changes in the law that have helped the smooth operation of the business, and has established legislation that has fostered the business's performance in the free-economy framework and legal competition.

To sum up, Nestlé is the largest food company in Bulgaria to invest heavily in local plant in order to modernize and upgrade it. A strategic rule of the MNE is always to buy the largest company in a particular country, and this has been the leading idea in Bulgaria. The economic and political uncertainties did not stop the parent company from investing considerably in the country (but, then again, the amount invested is less than that invested in Hungary and the Czech Republic). Yet, judging by the amount of investment, we can consider the company to be embedded in the local economy. As far as its links to local suppliers and retailers are concerned, the situation is the same as has already been observed with Unilever. Bulgaria does not have well-developed supply networks, and Nestlé sources regionally. The import barriers do not present an obstacle to the company; guaranteed quality is a more important factor. Nestlé's products are predominantly distributed by local retailers, as there are still only a few foreign chains in the country. The company cooperates with local universities to recruit personnel; however, there are no deep linkages with the research institutions for scientic projects. R&D activities are concentrated in Western Europe. The previous government was very helpful to the company by improving the legislative framework of the country. Apart from the large amount of investment, there are no other criteria according to which the company is embedded in the local economy: local actors cannot offer very much to the MNE.

Conclusion

This chapter discussed the level of embeddedness of MNEs in Bulgaria from the innovation system perspective. The first section analyzed the innovation system in Bulgaria. The conclusions drawn are that macro-economic instability was the government's major obstacle to focusing on the establishment of innovation and competition policy, the development of human capital, and investment in R&D. The lack of funds for R&D did not encourage enterprises to invest in innovation activities, and links between business and academia subsequently deteriorated. Considerable progress has been made since 2004, when innovation strategy and the investment promotion legislation were adopted. However, there is not much to say on the embeddness of FDI in Bulgaria. The government and regional authorities are very passive with regard to linkage creation between domestic and foreign companies. In the case of local authorities, they face a shortage of adequate skills and a limited local budget. Furthermore, high import barriers have become a tool that has forced MNEs to source locally. However, as was shown in the last section, this measure has been effective only to a certain extent. Neither Nestlé, nor InBev or Unilever sourced locally, pushed by the high import tariffs. Even if they wished to do so, they could not, as there were weak supply networks that could not satisfy their high quality and quantity standards.

The second section emphasized FDI in the food industry in Bulgaria. It tracked the gradual change of consumer behaviour and the role of retail chains in the promotion of Western lifestyles. Consumer trends and the purchasing power of the population are highly influential factors that determined the company's initial investment, and subsequently influenced all the consecutive investments made in a particular country.

The third section completed a deep micro-level analysis. It presented in detail the policies of Unilever, Nestlé, and InBev in Bulgaria, trying to illustrate the factors that influenced the investment decisions of these three large MNEs. This section concluded that food MNEs could be considered as embedded in the local economy only by virtue of the size of the investments they undertook and, hence, it would be difficult for them to shut down their subsidiaries completely and leave the country. It should be noted that the investments in Bulgaria, although large, are actually much smaller in comparison with those undertaken in Hungary and the Czech Republic. Some of the main reasons for this were the volatile business climate in Bulgaria and the low disposable incomes of the population.

It became clear that Bulgaria does not have well-developed supply networks, and all MNEs source regionally. Import barriers do not present an obstacle to the company, as the most important factor is guaranteed quality. Products are distributed predominantly by local retailers, as there are still only a few international retail chains in the country. All companies cooperate with local universities to recruit personnel but, however, there are no deep linkages with research institutions for scientific projects. R&D activities are concentrated in Western Europe. In short, local actors cannot offer very much to the MNEs to embed them in the local economy.

7
MNE Strategies in Romania

Introduction

This chapter explores the complex and multifaceted linkages existing between the different actors of the national innovation system of Romania and business. Special focus is given to the development of the national innovation system from the Communist period until 2006. The government's role in increasing the competitiveness of the local economy is also examined. MNEs as basic drivers of innovation are analyzed with regard to other actors in the innovation system.

In this chapter, the first section looks at the innovation system in Romania. It analyzes the government's innovation policies, and examines the strength of the links existing between MNEs, domestic firms, and innovation actors. The second section presents the food industry in Romania. This examination of the framework within which the companies operate allows a greater understanding of their strategies and, hence, their greater willingness to embed in the local economy. This section also touches on the role of retail chains in the development of the consumer market and distribution of MNE products. Consumer trends and the purchasing power of the population are examined, as they have a considerable impact on the investment strategies of food MNEs. The third section, through in-depth interviews, empirically presents the level of embeddedness of the three MNEs Unilever, Nestlé and InBev in the Romanian economy, and shows the ability (or inability) of the government to link them into the national system of innovation.

Firm embeddness in Romania

The innovation system of Romania

This section explores the Romanian innovation system in order to understand MNEs' propensity to lock in. Romania is characterized by one of the most difficult transition periods of all countries in the region, and this has had a huge impact on the innovation performance of the country. The dramatic economic decline of the 1990s led to major financial constraints that did not allow significant resource allocation for R&D. The level of business R&D declined from 0.38 per cent of GDP in 1998 to 0.24 per cent in 2003; public R&D funding reached its lowest level of 0.19 per cent of GDP in 1999 and slightly increased from 2000 onwards, but it is still far below the level at which R&D could effectively act as a driver of the country's socio-economic development. The lack of funds led to an outdated scientific infrastructure, and this created a huge gap between EU countries and Romania. Many researchers migrated to other economic sectors in the country or to other countries. The country takes the second to last position on the Summary Innovation Index (SII)[1] out of 33 countries. Its worst performance is for intellectual property rights (IPRs), with almost no USPTO patents and zero Triad patents. It performs very poorly on innovation drivers and knowledge creation, and poorly on innovation and entrepreneurship, and applications. Only two indicators are above the EU average: the percentage of SMEs that have introduced non-technical changes; and the new-to-market product sales. The success of these two indicators is probably due to very poor initial conditions.[2] The business sector predominantly imports equipment and technology, and then invests it in its own innovative products. To summarize, the main trend in the Romanian economy since 1989 has been to depend on the competitiveness offered by Romania as a location with low-cost labour and low value-added exports rather than high innovation performance.

According to the European Commission (2004a), only about 17 per cent of firms are innovators (Figure 7.1).[3] On innovation modes, 83 per cent of Romanian firms do not innovate, which is the highest percentage out of 19 EU and 4 non-EU countries. The National Institute of Statistics, following the methodology of the Community Innovation Survey (CIS), found that 17 per cent of the enterprises developed product or process innovations, as compared with 44 per cent in the EU. Another interesting fact is that 70 per cent of Romanian researchers working in the business sector are employed by companies with more than 250 employees. The business expenditures on innovation, of which one quarter are on R&D,

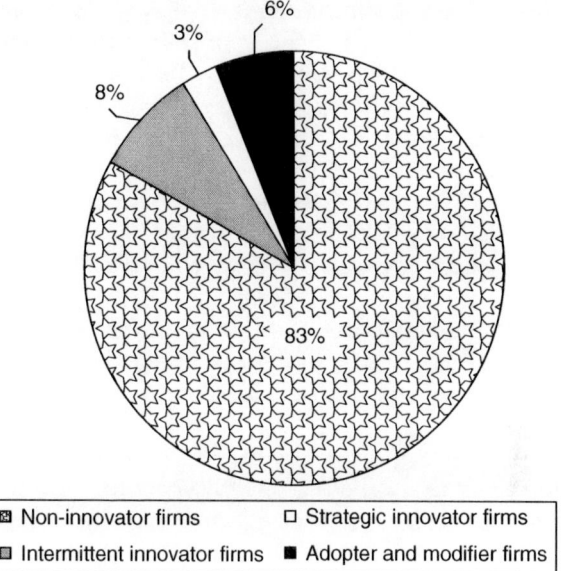

Figure 7.1   Innovative firms in Romania
Source: European Innovation Scoreboard (2004).

represent about 3 per cent of the total turnover. It can be concluded that in 2004 in-house R&D was low and not a major source of innovation in Romania (NASR, 2005a).

In order to understand the strengths and weaknesses of Romanian R&D and the innovation system, it is necessary to analyze the structure of R&D activities before 1990. During the late 1960s and early 1970s, Romania had no R&D activities concentrated in universities or industry. All the research was conducted by state-owned research institutes specialized in certain industry branches; for example, the Institute of Biochemistry, the Institute of Food Bioresources, the National Institute in Marine Research and Development, and the Geological Institute, and so on.

After the collapse of the Communist system, public funding for R&D decreased dramatically and the demand for R&D diminished. Some institutes were shut down, others fragmented, and many of them lost large numbers of staff because of the minimal wages paid. The state institutes readjusted to the needs of the new market economy. Some remained as public institutions affiliated to different ministries, while others operated as private companies (though still associated with certain ministries, in some instances). The structure in 2004 therefore was one in which there were over 600 research organizations, including 264 public institutions associated with various ministries (of which 37 are designated as National R&D Institutes in 19 specific fields, and a further 65 fall under the auspices of the Romanian Academy); 270 state or privately-owned companies that have R&D as their primary activity; and 74 universities which, in reality, undertake only a modest amount of research.[4] In addition, it is estimated that as few as 5 per cent of firms in the Romanian manufacturing sector undertake R&D activities (Vass, 2005). Therefore, it is not surprising that there is no cooperation between the universities and industry; this type of cooperation has simply never existed. The linkages that had existed were between state enterprises and state research institutes, not universities, but they were destroyed during the economic transition.

Since 2005, the main actors of the innovation system have been parliament, government, co-coordinating national institutions, R&D institutions, technology transfer and innovation related institutions, R&D personnel, and financial institutions. The most important player of all is the Ministry of Education, Research and Youth (MER).[5] MER was responsible for the implementation of the most important programmes that deal with the improvement of the innovation system: the National Plan for R&D and Innovation,[6] the programme 'Research of Excellence',[7] EU Framework Programmes, Sectoral R&D plans and the INFRATEH programme.[8] MER collaborated with nine ministries and nine government subordinated agencies for the implementation of national research, development and innovation (RDI) objectives. MER, in cooperation with the Ministry of Economy and Commerce (MEC), prepared the National Development Plan for 2007–13, the main focus of which is to increase the country's innovation performance. In 2005, the state budget for R&D increased by approximately 20 per cent over that of 2004 (from 0.55 per cent of GDP in 2004 to 0.70 per cent of GDP in 2005).

Apart from MER, the other very important actor in the innovation system is the National Council for Science and Technology Policy, whose major role is to establish the legislative framework for the implementation of the National Strategy on Scientific Research and Technological Development. In this respect, the Council coordinates RDI policies with other social and economic policies at governmental level. Founded in 2002, the Council is headed by the Romanian Prime Minister and comprises eight ministers and the President of the Romanian Academy. In order to apply the National Strategy successfully, the Council aims to create and strengthen linkages between local and central public administration bodies, the Romanian Academy, higher education organizations, R&D institutes, business entities, employers' federations and labour unions. Although the goals of the Council are very ambitious, there is no evidence that its work is efficient. An in-depth look at the Romanian innovation system reveals that the links between research institutions and domestic and foreign companies are very vague (see Figure 7.2). The only strong link that foreign companies have is with the parent company. The subsidiaries are completely integrated in the global production network of the parent company and benefit from its capital, know-how, and management and organizational skills. This cannot be said for domestic companies; they rarely enjoy a transfer of knowledge or financial support from MNEs. Foreign companies work with domestic suppliers, but there are only a few cases where a strong partnership exists. The reason is that no strong supply networks have developed in Romania and, hence, the MNEs cannot find inputs of the quality they desire. As domestic firms do not have the minimum level of technological capacity, they cannot take advantage of the knowledge that the foreign companies possess.

When observing the innovation system in Romania, it becomes clear that MNEs do not work closely with the local financial institutions either.

MNEs arrange their funds globally and, hence, use their global financial partner, which is normally the major financial institution situated in the home country of the MNE. The logic here is that the banks in Western Europe offer better financial conditions than those in Romania, where the business climate is more risky. Access to finance is also one of the crucial problems for SMEs with regard to upgrading, development, and being sufficiently competitive to become suppliers to the MNEs.

To sum up, innovation is a concept that remains a rather abstract notion in Romania. The public funds for research activities are scarce, and there are almost no financial or fiscal measures offered by the government to stimulate innovation. Research institutions and business do not cooperate. The low absorptive capacity of the domestic firms leads to brittle linkages between local firms and foreign enterprises. In other words, the country performs very poorly not only on innovation creation indicators, but also, what is more serious, it performs poorly in innovation diffusion. In short, Romania faces serious challenges in building a functioning national innovation system. Compared to other EU countries in terms of innovative capacity and competitiveness, Romania is ranked 67th (out of 117 countries examined) in the Growth Competitiveness Index, which is a medium ranking in general, but is the lowest among Bulgaria, the Czech Republic, and Hungary.[9] This means that additional

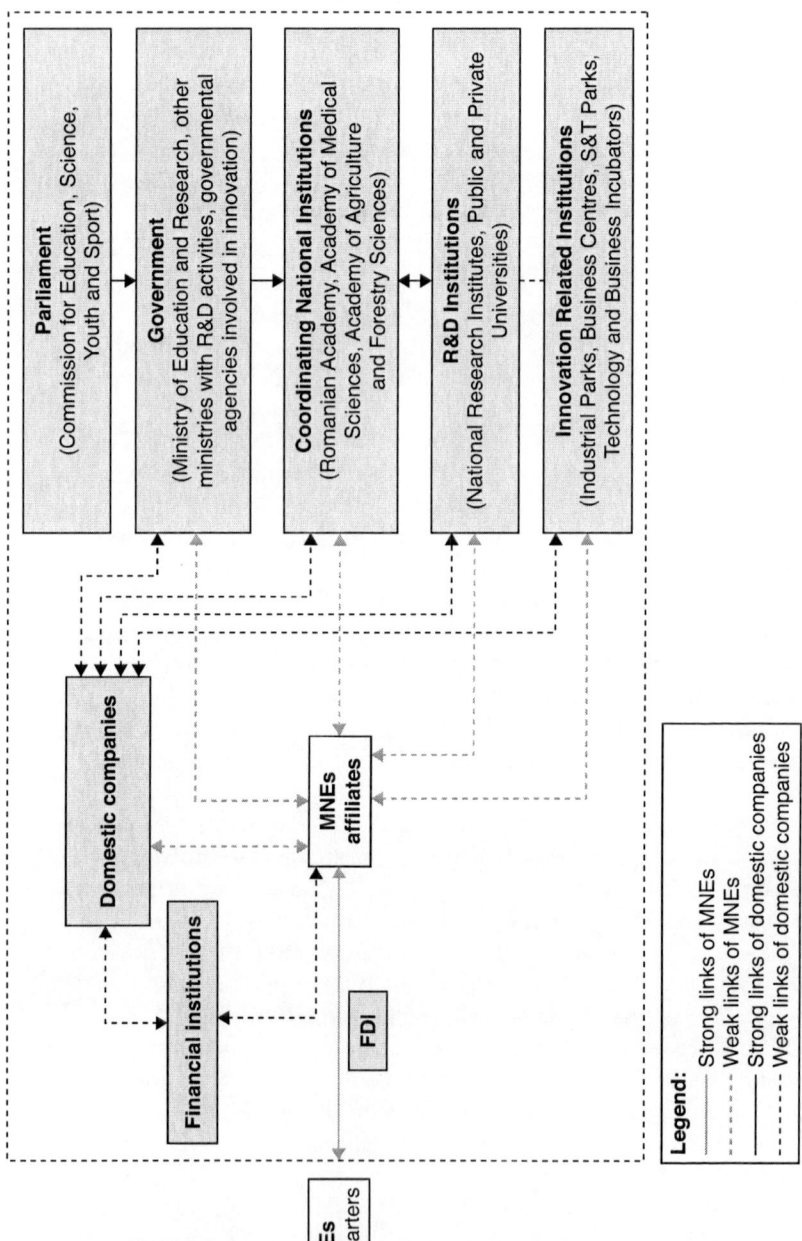

Figure 7.2 MNEs, domestic suppliers, and the linkages between the different actors of the Romanian innovation system.
Source: based on European Trend Chart Country Reports – Romania.

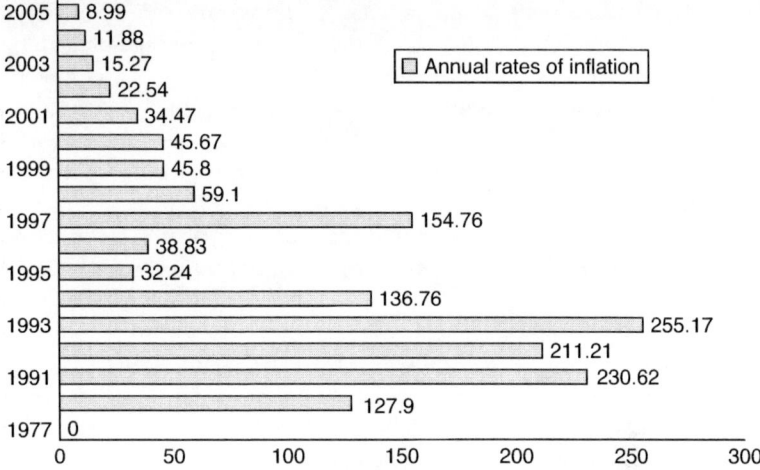

Figure 7.3   Annual rates of inflation, Romania
Source: Euromonitor International (electronic database).

efforts are needed to improve the country's macroeconomic performance and to increase the efficiency of public institutions and the technological capacity of the country.

The explanation for the weak performance of the Romanian innovation system is hidden in the 'economic disaster of the first ten years without Communism'.[10] The country was distinguished by the highest inflation rates among the transition countries: in the 1990s, inflation was 230 per cent and, until 2000, it remained very high, approximately 46 per cent (Figure 7.3). In 2004 the situation was under control through the steady pressure of interest rates (averaging over 21 per cent for 2003 and 2004) and fiscal tightening, all closely observed by the World Bank, the IMF, and the European Union (WTO, 2005: 4).

By 2000, there were no properly functioning financial, labour, and goods markets. In fact, the country still suffers from a lack of resources, relatively limited use of high technologies, and a predominance of low-cost labour, incomplete economic restructuring, and poor implementation of government innovation policies.[11] The Comprehensive Monitoring Report on Romania by the European Commission (2005: 58) states, 'Increased efforts are needed in the area of privatization and restructuring. Romania needs to fully implement its privatization strategy including resolving post-privatization litigations. Romania also needs to continue the restructuring of key industries'. In 2006, the country's competitiveness still lay in traditional labour-intensive industries rather than high-tech sectors. For some considerable time, the unstable business environment and the reluctance of the government to privatize kept foreign investors away from the country. Only recently, in line with the European Commission recommendations, has the Romanian government concentrated its efforts on bringing forward the implementation of structural reforms, and the improvement of its administrative and legislative framework. As a consequence, in 2004, Romania attracted the highest amount of FDI among Hungary, the Czech Republic and Bulgaria – €4.66 billion.

The evolution of FDI flows in 2004 reflects the country's positive economic trends, the improvement of the existing investment climate, and the growing attractiveness of Romania as a destination for foreign investors. These developments have been facilitated by the closing of the process of land return, favouring the development of greenfield projects and local industrial parks, and the incentives provided to foreign investors and the elaboration of local policies aimed at attracting FDI, as well as the continuous development of national capital as an element of attracting new investments though horizontal economic relations.

Despite the steady real GDP growth of around 5 per cent per year since 2000, the level of GDP per head in purchasing power parity is only one third of the EU-25 average. Romania remains a lower-middle income country. Some 25 per cent of its population lives below the poverty line (WTO, 2005). Although low value-added goods still represent the core of Romanian exports, subcontracting by foreign companies has underpinned the growth of the most dynamic export industries. Business conditions for SMEs remain difficult due to the uneven implementation of legislation and red tape, and limited access to finance.

To summarize, the economic revival that has occurred since 2000 has not been sufficiently strong to stimulate enterprises to take on the financial and commercial risks necessary to undertake R&D. Despite the recent policy initiatives of the Romanian government, the national innovation system is still weakly developed, with low performance scores in terms of most indicators. There is no cooperation between research institutions and industry, partially because of the bad economic performance of the economy and partially because of the socialist heritage when such linkages did not exist. For example, R&D personnel, as part of the active population, is 0.33 per cent; that is, almost one quarter of the EU-15's 1.39 per cent. Funding for R&D stands at only 0.4 per cent of GDP (in the EU-25, funding for R&D is 1.95 per cent of GDP), with the public and private sectors sharing approximately half the contribution. It should also be noted that these levels are much lower than those of the early 1990s. The number of R&D personnel in the working population has also fallen 'as a consequence of the lack of funding, brain drain, migration to other employment categories and the restructuring of R&D activities during the transition period' (NASR, 2005b). Not only are the links between business and universities vague, but there is also a lack of cooperation between domestic and foreign companies. The lack of a transfer of knowledge is a worrying phenomenon, as local companies cannot benefit from the innovations of large companies. Much more remains to be done in order to promote innovation, to make Romanian R&D more responsive to the needs of the economy, and to enhance integration of Romanian researchers into international networks and programmes, particularly at EU-level.

Trade policy

Trade policies are one of the measures that heavily influence foreign companies' decisions to source locally. Registration and documentation, customs procedures, tariffs, and duties and taxes are among the factors that might force foreign enterprises to use local inputs. Protection of property rights, competition policy and stages of privatization also matter with regard to the embeddedness of FDI.

Since 1992, Romania has been gradually liberalizing its trade regime, based on multilateral rules. Trade facilitation has been given full attention, and much had been achieved by 2006. For example, customs procedures were simplified and clearance time had been substantially reduced. Continued trade policy liberalization has included the introduction of a new import/export licensing system, abolition of an import surcharge, a simplified tariff structure, and lower MFN tariffs. In line with its commitments under the WTO and the EC, Romania has redrafted or amended legislation in many areas, including customs, import licensing, standards and technical regulations, government procurement, and IPRs. In general, import licences are maintained on health, sanitary, phytosanitary, and environmental grounds, or under international conventions to which Romania is a signatory. The country has entered into 84 Bilateral Agreements on the Promotion and Reciprocal Protection of Investment and some 74 Agreements on the Avoidance of Double Taxation, largely based on OECD models. Parties to these agreements have included a wide range of non-OECD countries in addition to Romania's traditional economic partners (OECD, 2005d).

All of these improvements have positively influenced the country's trade relations. Romania's trade (exports and imports) in goods and services as a percentage of GDP rose from 60.9 per cent in 1999 to 83.5 per cent in 2004. In 2004, Romania ranked 35th among the world's merchandise exporters (considering the countries of the EC together and excluding intra-EC trade), and 27th among importers. For trade in services, the country ranked 38th among exporters and 49th among importers.[12]

FDI has been encouraged through incentive programmes for industrial parks, disadvantaged zones, and SMEs. The incentives system comprises, *inter alia*, duty and tax concessions, and state aid. Romania also promotes investment (domestic and foreign) at the local level. Romania is the largest recipient of FDI in South-East Europe, an accumulated FDI stock of US$15 billion having been forecast for the end of 2005 (OECD, 2005d).

Romania continues to harmonize its national standards with international or regional standards – in particular, with those of the EU. Currently, close to 90 per cent of EC standards have been implemented as Romanian standards. As of June 2005, 28,395 standards were in force in Romania, of which 9,014 were national standards, 15,740 were European standards, and 3,641 were ISO and/or IEC standards.

Prior to Romania's accession to the EC, goods imported into Romania were subject to four types of duty: customs tariffs, excise duties, value added tax (VAT), and a 0.5 per cent customs commission. All tariffs, applied and bound, were *ad valorem*. In an effort to simplify and harmonize its tax system with that of the EC, Romania modified its legislation on excise duties and VAT. Romania's non-tariff measures are aligned with those of the EC.

Prior to EC accession, Romania's trade agreements provided tariff preferences to 38 partners, including the 25 EC member states. As far as agricultural products were concerned, Romania had limited preferential trade agreements, which meant a high protection of agricultural products until EU accession. MFN applied tariffs (using the WTO definition) were high, on average 27.9 per cent on agricultural products in 2005 (down from 34 per cent in 1999), and 14.9 per cent on non-agricultural goods (compared with 16.3 per cent in 1999) (WTO, 2005: 32). All of these were changed to the levels of the EU external tariffs when the country joined the EU in 2007.

To summarize, Romania has a fully liberal trade regime. The country synchronized its legislation to the *acquis communitaire* in many areas, including customs, import licensing, standards and technical regulations, government procurement, and IPRs. Although it has gradually decreased the MFN tariffs on agricultural and industrial goods since 1992, domestic producers still enjoy a very protectionist regime. This is especially true for agricultural producers. The influence of the government on the economy, mainly through state-owned enterprises (SOEs), remains substantial. A number of these SOEs are sheltered from competition, and some remain a drain on public revenue (WTO, 2005). In sum, as a result of its protectionist policies Romania created the preconditions for the foreign companies to source locally rather than importing the necessary raw materials from abroad. The effectiveness of these measures is a subject of analysis in the following sections, which focus on the Romanian food industry and, in particular, on Nestlé, Unilever, and InBev.

The food industry in Romania

Overview

This brief overview of the development of the Romanian agro-food sector from the early 1990s until 2005 shows the influence the national innovation system had on the food industry. The section attempts to investigate the links that the food industry establishes with innovation actors, suppliers, and retailers; that is, to map the forces that lead to the locking-in of MNEs. It also aims at understanding the extent to which food MNEs transfer knowledge to the domestic companies – suppliers. In this respect, an analysis of the agricultural sector has been undertaken to examine the capability of local firms to benefit from FDI. As a raw material provider to the food industry, agriculture deserves attention in this section.

Romanian agriculture

With 14.8 million hectares of agricultural land, Romania is, after Poland, the second largest agricultural producer in CEE. Agriculture is one of the key sectors in the Romanian economy: it contributes around 13 per cent to GDP,[13] and employs 31 per cent of the labour force (down from 36 per cent in 1999). Foreign investment in agriculture represented 12 per cent of Romania's total foreign investment inflows in1991–2004 (OECD, 2005d).

In contrast to most other countries in the region, the share of agriculture in GDP rose substantially following the initiation of the transition process, mostly as a result of sharp declines in other sectors of the economy. Production in agriculture fell in 1990, since which time it has remained relatively stable. This is due to the relatively high level of support provided for agricultural production, in particular up until 1996, and also to the large share in production of the small-scale farming that resulted from the restitution process. This type of farming, mostly for self-consumption, has been loosely linked with the market and somewhat immune to the adverse changes in prices (OECD, 2000b).

Although important for the Romanian economy, the agricultural sector is not characterized by high productivity and quality. Land restitution has led to high land fragmentation: most farms comprise, on average, only 2 hectares. State farms and cooperatives were privatized; many of them liquidated and destroyed. Due to these problems, small-scale farmers appeared that satisfy the needs of their own families and, to a limited extent, the local markets. In the milk sector, for example, the domination of small-scale milk production has been a major impediment to further development of the sector, as small farms lack the capital for investment, and dairies face difficulties in milk collection and enforcing quality standards.

In sum, as a consequence of the heavy transition period, Romanian agriculture is still underdeveloped and many agricultural producers are not competitive in the EU market. Therefore, food MNEs that invest in Romania face difficulties in finding: (1) agricultural suppliers who are sufficiently large to satisfy their demand for raw materials; and (2) products of a sufficiently high quality to meet the MNEs' high standards and quality requirements. In this sense, the links between MNEs and domestic producers are somewhat weak. Local companies cannot benefit from foreign companies' know-how, as they do not possess the minimum capacity to absorb this knowledge. The last part of this chapter will illustrate this finding with the case studies of Nestlé, Unilever, and InBev (Romania).

The food industry

By virtue of economic activity, the bulk of FDI in Romania is concentrated in manufacturing (37.3 per cent of total investment), with metallurgy (8.2 per cent); food, beverages, and tobacco (6.5 per cent); and transport (5.1 per cent) holding significant weights.[14] The large concentration of FDI in food, beverages, and tobacco confirms the importance of this sector for the economy, and proves Romania's integration in the European and world economy. The food sector in Romania contributes some 12 per cent of manufacturing industry output and employs about 30 per cent of total manufacturing employment (DG AGRI, 2003: 33).

Compared with other CEECs, privatization in Romania has unfolded slowly and is far from finished. By the end of 2003, Romania had privatized only about 40 per cent of its large enterprises and about two-thirds of its medium-sized enterprises. Food MNEs entered the market mainly by participating in the privatization process, and are consolidating their positions through further acquisitions, mergers, and modernization and extension of the existing capacities, or even through greenfield investments.

The results of EU integration and the economic growth that has occurred since 2000 are expected to stimulate further flows of foreign investment. In addition, the food industry is expected to become highly concentrated. This is because only 68 of the 1,450 processors active in 2005 meet EU requirements, with a further 50 committed to meet the required standards some time very soon. The remaining companies will have had to close by 2007, although the Ministry of Agriculture identified another 200 that would be given a longer transition period.[15]

Most FDI in Romania comes from the EU-15. MNEs operate mainly in the packaged food industry, brewing, soft drinks, confectionery, the dairy industry, and frozen foods. Foreign investment in the dairy industry reached €120 million by 2005, and was made by large companies including Danone Romania, Friesland Romania, and Hochland Romania.[16] The large oils and fats industry saw lower investment levels of only €30 million, made mostly by the American companies Bunge and Cargill. Bunge – the owner of Unirea from 2002, when it acquired Cereol – increased its investment in 2003 through the acquisition of two important oil producers, Muntenia SA and Interoils SA. Cargill purchased two seed oil facilities from Topway Industries in 2004. By acquiring the sauces and margarine division from Topway Industries in 2002, and renaming the company Orkla Foods Romania, the Orkla Group became an important player in the Romanian packaged food industry. Kraft Foods (Romania) and Nestlé are the main players in chocolate confectionery, challenged by Kandia-Excelent, which is owned by the Julius Meinl bank. As the bakery industry is extremely fragmented and there is little demand for high value-added packaged products, FDI in this subsector has been limited. The Greek company Loulis made an exception to this trend, by investing €80 million to build a manufacturing facility in Bucharest. Vel Pitar, owned by the investment fund Broadhurst, invested €10 million in 2002–5. Processed meat was also highly fragmented: Campofrio (€20 million) and Angst made the main investments in this area.

Food MNEs are mainly interested in the domestic market. The research of Birsan *et al.* (2005) reveals that, contrary to the general perception, important investors such as Compania de Bere România SA (beer production, privatization), Kraft Europe (sweets and similar products, privatization) and Dorna Lactate SA (dairy products – part of Natural Dorna Investment Holdings SA, greenfield) do not consider labour costs and the quality of the workforce as the main reasons to invest in Romania. Rather, these companies were attracted by the Romanian market opportunities and the availability of raw materials (for the dairy products). The third section in this chapter will conclude the same for Nestlé, Unilever, and InBev; namely, that the low labour costs were an advantage but not a prerequisite for investment in Romania. The size of the market and the aim of broadening the local market for their products were more decisive factors.

To summarize, food MNEs entered Romania mainly through the privatization of large state enterprises (to a lesser degree, through greenfield investments). They were interested in local firms that had large market shares. The basic aim of the companies was to reinforce their dominant position in the European market. MNEs were following a market-seeking strategy in an effort to achieve economies of scale and scope for their highly diversified product portfolios. The MNEs preferred branches of the food industry were sugar-refining, brewing, distilling, vegetable oil, confectionery, and chocolate; that is, sub-sectors characterized by highly processed food that does not contain a high raw material content. In many cases, the resource inputs are not sourced locally, as the agricultural producers cannot offer the quality desired by the parent company. In addition, many Romanian subsidiaries do not have the authority to select suppliers themselves but, instead, are dependent on company headquarters for this decision. In this sense, one cannot observe a process of transfer of knowledge and know-how from foreign companies to the domestic producers. Romania's weak innovation system also reflects the process of collaboration between food MNEs and local research centres. As a common practice, MNEs are reluctant to internationalize R&D centres. In some cases, attracted by the national innovation institutions, they might undertake the risk to move/establish a new research centre abroad (Narula, 2003). In the food industry, in particular, such a step is even more challenging for the parent company, as the need for research can be satisfied by one R&D centre per region (Europe, Africa, South America, and so on) – thus, there is rarely a need for several research units in one region. It is, therefore, easy to understand why none of the MNEs invested in a research unit in Romania (the MNEs have such centres in their home countries in Western Europe). However, the notion of R&D is not limited only to the establishment of new research units. R&D is also related to the links between the MNEs and local research centres; that is, training of local researchers in MNE laboratories, hiring of local researchers for a particular projects, joint projects between the MNEs and the Romanian institutes, grants for Ph.D. students, and so on.

In fact, in these areas there are no such kinds of partnership between MNEs and national agricultural and food research centres. MER and the Ministry of Agriculture, Forests and Rural Development are in charge of agricultural research. The realization of concrete research projects is undertaken by the Romanian Academy for Agricultural and Forestry Sciences, which at the time of writing comprises 17 research institutes, 3 centres and 50 regional stations.[17] The coordination between all these institutions looks perfect on paper; however, something essential is missing – a link between this research structure and business, in particular between domestic and foreign food companies. As will be revealed in the next section, the MNEs admit that they do not have any contacts with Romanian researchers (except for marketing research). Actually, the absence of linkages between the knowledge institutions and business was already illustrated by the innovation system scheme presented in the first section of this chapter. The food industry does not deviate from the rule.

When talking about FDI in the food industry, one should pay attention to two variables that influence the behaviour of MNEs in a particular market. The factors that are of particular importance to the MNEs are the consumer and retail markets. As already mentioned, FDI is concentrated in the packaged food industries. This means that there should be: (1) a population with average/high disposable income, to be able to afford that type of food; (2) a developed retail market to offer these goods to the consumers; and (3) a population leading a busy lifestyle and lacking time to cook at home, preferring the semi-prepared foods offered by the MNEs.

Consumer market and retail market

Consumer market

The heavy economic reforms and the long process of transition have had a negative outcome on the disposable incomes of the population. Euromonitor International (2006d) reports that only 21 per cent of the amount Romanians spent on food for 2003 was for packaged food. The rest was for unpackaged bread, cheese, milk, biscuits, chilled meat, and oils and fats, comprising the bulk of retail food sales. This low share of packaged food within total food spending is because 45 per cent of the population lives in rural areas and the suburbs of large cities, where consumption of basic food from own household resources remained very high. Another factor that prevented the packaged food industry from developing its full potential until 2005 was the high consumption of food grown or farmed by individual households, especially meat, cheese, milk, vegetables, and honey.[18] It is also common for people living in cities to purchase fresh products directly from farms, as prices are lower when compared with those of retailers. Such products are also perceived as natural, providing better quality and nutritional value.

The perception that fresh food is healthier than packaged food increased in 2004 and 2005, when improved consumer purchasing power resulted in changes to lifestyle and purchasing habits. This led to greater concern about healthy eating. This trend was particularly noticeable in Bucharest and other large cities, where household incomes are generally higher. However, another explanation for the high sales of fresh food compared with packaged food stems from the strong cultural tradition of home cooking within most Romanian households. This resulted in professionals and medium- and higher-income consumers choosing packaged food during the working week, when convenience is the main factor in meal preparation, while retaining a preference for fresh food at weekends. Although the share of packaged food within the food industry as a whole remained low over the review period, its growth has been dynamic, as it started from a low base. It also benefited from the influence of Western lifestyles, intensive advertising, and a change in consumer habits due to economic recovery and improved levels of disposable incomes.

The marketing report by Euromonitor International (2006d) reveals that, in recent years, Romanian people have begun to become aware of the emergence of supermarkets offering processed food and imported products throughout the year, and have taken a stance in relation to it. While younger consumers living in urban areas accept the abundant products offered by supermarkets due to a lack of time and for the purposes of convenience, their older, more traditional, and sometimes more conservative counterparts demonstrate different trends. The latter still visit local markets, and refuse to buy imported products or processed food, specifically seeking out local produce; they negotiate prices with vendors, and preserve fruit and vegetables at home using traditional techniques. Because of the ageing population, the trend will be for this type of market to co-exist with the supermarkets. However, for the time being and in the near future it is more of a financial issue, as natural products sold in open-air markets are usually more affordable.[19]

The brief analysis of the Romanian consumer market shows that MNEs invested in a very large and prospective market; however, it was a market that was not familiar with packaged food. While the unfamiliarity with Western products could be overcome with extensive advertising campaigns, encouraging consumers to become used to packaged food requires a shift in the way of thinking and lifestyles that

Table 7.1 Retail sales of packaged food by distribution format, 2000–5

% Retail value retail sales price

	2000	2005
Supermarkets/hypermarkets	6.2	14.2
Independent food stores	36.2	41.0
Convenience stores	0.2	0.3
Standard convenience stores	0.0	0.0
Petrol/gas/service stations	0.2	0.3
Internet sales	–	–
Discounters	2.6	3.7
Others	54.9	40.8
Total	100.0	100.0

Source: Euromonitor International (2006d): 25–6.

normally requires years before real changes in consumer behaviour can be observed. In addition, consumer trends and habits are modelled by Western retail chains, which have only recently recorded growth.

Retail market

The Romanian retail market is still underdeveloped. Until 2000, a very limited number of multinational retailers invested in Romania. The market had been controlled by so-called 'other' shops,[20] which had 54.9 per cent of the market share (Table 7.1).

The reason for the weak retail market is the fact that Romania accounts for one of the lowest levels of consumer purchasing power in Europe. This was one of the major obstacles facing Western retailers that invested in the country, as they were not confident they would achieve sufficient returns on their investment. Market research data reveal that more than 70 per cent of Romanian people are concerned only in fulfilling their most urgent needs.[21] They buy small quantities of the most essential goods from traditional independent food stores, as well as low-margin 'others', and do not go to supermarket/hypermarket channels. Furthermore, in small urban areas and rural areas there are no supermarkets/hypermarkets.

The modern retail system appeared in Romania in 1991, when the first La Fourmi supermarket was opened in Bucharest, followed by four Mega Image supermarkets in 1994. However, the first foreign investor entered the market quite late, in 1996. This was the Metro Cash & Carry chain. Metro was followed by the Billa and Gima supermarket chains in 1999, Selgros in 2000, and Carrefour and XXL in 2001. In the period 1996–2003, the main retail companies in Romania invested €650 million, and investments were estimated to reach €1.25 billion by the end of 2005. Half of these investments were made in Bucharest, where the purchasing power is higher. Consumers with incomes higher than US$180 (€150) per month buy in larger quantities. This category of consumer (usually professionals with busy lifestyles) shops rarely, and chooses supermarkets/hypermarkets for their propensity for one-stop-shopping. The leading retailers in the Romanian market are Metro, Rewe, the Delhaize Group, Louis Delhaize, and Hiproma Angst RO.

The Romanian retail network, being underdeveloped, does not offer an acquisition target for the major multinationals. Most of the multinationals prefer to build in out-of-town greenfield locations in order to meet the population's needs for entertainment during weekends, providing both shopping and on-trade sales facilities.[22]

Since 2000, discounters have also entered the market, and witnessed excellent growth due to lower prices as well as to expansion, although their presence remained limited to a few cities. Confectionery, bakery products, dairy products, oils and fats, pasta, and chilled meat comprised the majority of this channel's sales. Delhaize's Profi was the largest chain in 2005, with 25 stores in Western and Central Romania, followed by Rewe's XXL Mega Discount, operating four stores. Discounters are expected to witness strong growth in the future, following the intention of several multinational chains, such as Tengelman's Plus and Rewe's Penny Market, to establish operations in Romania.

Multinationals have increased their share of retailing in Romania, but it remains low compared with total retail sales, due mainly to their low numbers and limited expansion plans, which are dictated by the low purchasing power. Metro and Rewe – with Selgros, Billa, and XXL Mega Discount – are the main multinationals in the Romanian market, benefiting also from first entry advantages. In any case, the 'others' channel still leads retail distribution. Hence, food MNEs have to cooperate with many local distributors in order to have their products sold in the Romanian market. This impedes MNEs' ability to plan production in the longer term. The considerable number of distributors is linked to a great variety of contracts and conditions under which the MNEs collaborate with retailers, and this is definitely not the large companies' preferred way of working; large companies are used to having a particular retailer as a global partner. In addition, the absence of strong modern retailing complicates the situation for MNEs, which alone have to influence consumer tastes through high investment in advertising.

To conclude, the large Romanian market – the second largest in accession states after Poland – attracted companies such as Danone, Unilever, Nestlé, Kraft foods, Coca-Cola, and InBev. Following a market-seeking strategy, they used privatization to acquire the largest state food enterprises, and invested in their modernization and restructuring. However, late privatization, the underdeveloped retail market, and the low purchasing power of the population negatively affected the level of investment. The analysis has revealed that there are no linkages between foreign investors and local suppliers, as local suppliers do not offer high quality agricultural inputs. There is no cooperation between business and knowledge institutions. The reasons are that: (1) the importance of such cooperation is not realized and targeted; and (2) there are no effective institutions to implement linkage creation programmes.

Bearing this analysis in mind, the empirical examples of Nestlé, Unilever, and InBev in the next section will help in the better understanding of MNEs' embeddedness in Romania.

Firm case analysis

This section presents the major empirical contribution of this chapter, and discloses the embeddedness of Unilever, Nestlé, and InBev in Romania. It is constructed from interviews conducted with the CEOs of these companies at their Romanian subsidiaries and at company headquarters. The micro-level analysis allows for the deeper understanding of the processes between the MNEs and their domestic and international partners.

Unilever (Romania)

The UK–Dutch company Unilever has in its portfolio a large variety of products, from food to home and personal care brands. Unilever supplies the Romanian market with both global and local brands, among which are the local Dero and Bona brands, and the international Omo, Sunlight, Coccolino, Domestos, and Cif brands. The company offers food brands such as Lipton tea, Rama margarine, and Magnum ice cream. Delma and Rama margarines are produced in a factory in Targu Mures, and most Knorr products in a facility based in Otopeni. However, the company's local market presence is strongest in the area of home and personal care products. In 1995, Unilever acquired Dero, the country's leading detergent manufacturer. Post-acquisition expenditure on plant modernization ranked Unilever as one of the top international investors in Romania. The factory situated in Ploiesti has been rebuilt and was renamed Dero Lever. It is now the largest detergent manufacturer in Romania, providing high standards of product quality, efficiency, and environmental impact.[23] 'Today Dero is a volume market leader and is purchased by every second household at least once per year', said Martina Kastler, Chairman of Unilever South-Central Europe, in interview with the Bucharest newspaper *The Diplomat*. She added that this requires a very good local strategy, bearing in mind that Unilever targets families with incomes below €150 per month per household (about the national Romanian average). 'Across South Europe there is still much work to do to develop our brands to the level of Romania's market shares', pointed out Ms Kastler. 'This development requires heavy investment and a range of launch and relaunch activities to keep the portfolio up to date.'[24]

Romania is Unilever's trading and production centre for South-Eastern Europe. The research tried to establish the reasons Unilever invested in the country, and exactly why Romania became the production centre for South Europe.

There were two main factors for investment in Romania: (1) the size of the market, including its growth potential; and (2) the political and economic stability of the country. The nation's attraction to Western brands also convinced the multinational to make a firm commitment to the country, where it now launches a different product almost every week. Important factors were tax incentives, the low cost of the work-force, and the proximity to other markets; however, these factors were not crucial for Unilever's investment.

Asked whether Unilever was likely to close a plant in Romania, the Managing Director, Foods, Unilever South-Central Europe, Mr E, said that, in general, this might happen if sudden hyperinflation occurred or if there were political and economic turmoil. In addition, a plant might be closed if the company undertook a process of optimization on a European basis. Romania is a part of Unilever's European business and, as such, a part of Unilever's supply chain. The manufacturing is organized on an optimal European basis and, if there is a need for restructuring, then it could be that a plant might be shut down.

The analysis of the previous section disclosed that it is difficult to find high quality suppliers in Romania, and the MNEs import many of their input sources.

Does Unilever confirm this general conclusion?

Unilever has Europe-wide contracts, with a guaranteed quality level and good prices; that is, it purchases from global suppliers. However, for many local products the company uses local suppliers, though it is not easy to find local suppliers that are able to comply with the strict Unilever quality requirements. Management admitted that, in Romania, there was no strong supply network, which made matters more difficult. Although the situation is improving, there is still much to be done. In short, it is difficult for Unilever to help local suppliers to upgrade as, put simply, there is no one to be helped. The raw material suppliers are lagging behind Western suppliers to such an extent that MNEs hardly cooperate with them at all. Those who are sufficiently competitive in terms of quality are not competitive in terms of price. Put differently, even if an MNE had the intention of sourcing locally, it is not possible.

The Romanian retail market is not developed to the same extent as the Western market. That is why it is not surprising that 60–70 per cent of Unilever's production is distributed by small local retailers. Western retailers have a 20–30 per cent share. However, Western retailers in Romania are stronger in terms of negotiation than those in Bulgaria, where the retail market is also undeveloped. Unilever prefers working with multinational retailers, as they have a clearer trade terms structure, professional store management, and greater opportunity for branded products to demonstrate strength and quality than small local retailers. Yet, local distributors also have their advantages; for example, being flexible in negotiations on trade terms. Western retailers expect higher discounts, based on their Europe-wide trading, and have a strong impact on negotiation patterns.

Does Unilever (Romania) cooperate with local branch associations, business centres, or agencies for regional development; and what is the essence of this cooperation?

Mr E, said that Romanian authorities helped in the process of creating the infrastructure to support Unilever's expansion; this is a necessary platform for the development of Unilever activities. However, it was difficult for the management staff of Unilever to point out any concrete acts of cooperation and partnership between them and the local institutions. It seems that, insofar as the local institutions do not hinder the company's work, they 'support' it.

Unilever invested in the training of its own personnel and management staff. The company transferred its management know-how, values, and experience to Romania. It has recruited young and talented people from local universities. To this extent, there is a partnership between the universities and Unilever. Yet, the cooperation finishes at this level and goes no further. Unilever does not work with the local universities on any research projects, there are no grants for Ph.D. students, and there is no student training at Unilever plants. The same situation exists as far as the specialized food and agricultural institutes are concerned. Unilever has no linkages with them.

Is the Romanian subsidiary independent from its headquarters?

According to management, this depends on the country cluster. As the regional office is in Romania, the local Unilever sites are independent from company headquarters in taking everyday decisions; however, this is not the case for Bulgaria. Yet, for strategic decisions, the Romanian office is also dependent on company headquarters.

Will levels of investments undertaken by Unilever (Romania) catch up with those of Unilever in Hungary and the Czech Republic?

The management has been positive that the parent company will keep investing in Romania. The large market, with a population of 22.5 million people, is a good target for the company. In addition, Romania has a strategic location in Europe at the crossroads of traditional commercial roads, which affords the opportunity of reaching over 240 million potential consumers within a radius of 1,000 kilometres. Therefore, Unilever will continue to develop in the country.

To summarize, Unilever entered the Romanian market in the mid-1990s, attracted by the opportunities for growth that the Romanian market offered. The company acquired plants and invested in them through modernization and restructuring. Unilever trained its employees and management staff. It also contributed to the development of the consumer market. The local economy, however, cannot benefit further from the knowledge and capital the MNE possesses. The local raw material suppliers are not sufficiently competitive to provide high quality materials for the company and, hence, Unilever cannot help them upgrade. There is weak cooperation between the company and the specialized agro-food institutions. Furthermore, there are no initiatives from the local and national authorities to encourage such a partnership.

InBev (Romania)

InBev has two enterprises in Romania and around 700 employees. The plant in Ploiesti is a joint venture with Efes Group called Interbrew Efes Brewery. The plant in Blaj, Bianca Interbrew Bergenbier, was inaugurated in May 1995. The Proberco plant from Baia Mare was bought by Interbrew in August 1994. The latter two became Interbrew (Romania) in December 2002.

> How did Interbrew decide which local state companies to acquire when it entered the local market?
> Were the privatization schemes clear?
> Did InBev close any enterprises in the process of restructuring?

The ex-General Manager of Interbrew Romania, Mr C, currently the President of the Business Unit (BU) of InBev, answered these questions.[25] He has been working at Interbrew since 1996 and recalls very well the first steps of the company in the Romanian market. He explained that the local companies acquired by Interbrew were selected by the external growth teams in order to match the needs of Interbrew in terms of capacity, technology and profitability. Romania was, at that time, a country with great potential, a country with a population of 22 million where the beer market was fragmented; at that time, there were 40 local producers and no clear market leader. He explained that, when acquired by Interbrew, both plants (Blaj and Baia Mare) were already private, following a clear privatization process. No enterprises were closed in Romania in the process of restructuring. Since 1996, Interbrew had invested more than €140 million in its Romanian plants to bring them up to the required standard.

> What were the challenges that Interbrew faced in the first years of investment and later on?

The greatest difficulty was the volatility of the business climate: devaluation and inflation were hard to predict, and this negatively affected the profitability of their business. In addition, the legislative framework was not clear, and management could not make long-term decisions. Mr C believes that the situation improved over the last few years and that, at the time of writing, there is a competitive and more predictable environment in the beer industry.

> How does InBev work with suppliers?
> Does it use local or global suppliers?
> Are there good suppliers for the brewing industry?

As in the case of Unilever, InBev also faces difficulties in finding good local suppliers. He explained that Interbrew's strategy has always been to use the best available suppliers that match their needs. When the company acquired local breweries, it mainly established new suppliers and did not stick to the old network of suppliers. However, he pointed out, 'if the previous ones were competitive and could adapt to our requirements, we would have taken them into consideration'.

The company uses 68 per cent foreign suppliers for packaging and raw materials, and 32 per cent local suppliers. For marketing, it relies mainly on local suppliers, the ratio being 80 per cent to 20 per cent in favour of local suppliers. In Romania, InBev does not have a very strong supplier network, due to the fact that the country is an emerging market. But the situation started to change gradually from 2004 and production is moving locally for some InBev suppliers as well (for example, Ball Packaging, Vetro Pack, and so on). Mr C mentioned that the company's largest supplier is a foreign supplier. The malt supplier is local but, due to a confidentiality agreement, InBev has not disclosed its identity. To sum up, InBev works with foreign suppliers because there is no strong supply network available in Romania. In order to keep the partnership with its already established good local partners, InBev makes long-term agreements with them.

InBev's portfolio in Romania is comprised of locally produced beers: two local brands (Bergenvier and Noroc), one regional brand (Lowenbrau), and two global brands (Stella Artois and Beck's). Bergenbier has a brand identity based on male friendship, and this image is supported through sponsorship of the Romanian national football team. In addition, InBev also imports and distributes the Belgian specialties Leffe and Hoegaarden. Bergenbier is the centrepiece product of InBev's portfolio, the strongest beer brand in Romania, as well as one of the strongest Romanian brands that exists in the market in general. Company strategy is based on the existence of a strong portfolio, with strong brands in the segments in which they are situated: 'This portfolio of brands and packages allows InBev to address the needs of the consumer, in all its complexity given by his needs, momentum and its consumption availabilities. We are not moulding the consumer by the structure of our products; on the contrary, we address customer needs with products and packages that bring him complete satisfaction', explained Mr C. That is the key to the success of the company in the local market.

InBev is present with brands for every segment – from the super-premium range all the way down to the most affordable. Together, Stella Artois and Beck's ensure dominance in the premium sector; Bergenbier acts in the medium sector; while Noroc, next to Bergenbier Q-Pack, is the most present brand in InBev's portfolio in a plastic package. When talking about the future, the manager says that the company's portfolio is constantly dynamic. InBev keeps its focus on what consumers inform the company, so that it is always there to meet their needs. In short, InBev plays a crucial role in the development of the Romanian consumer market. The company offers high quality products in a wide range of packages, with different tastes and available to all possible sectors – none of which existed in 1993.

InBev's products reach the consumers by means of a good sales team. The company works exclusively with local distributors. Mr C referred to the statistics of 2005, when 'the sales via multinational retails represented only 5.4 per cent of our total sales volume.' Multinational retailers help a great deal in the process of presenting a particular product to the market, and he expressed his hope that, in the near future, the percentage of sales by Western retailers would double.

Does InBev collaborate with local knowledge institutions?

Mr C explained that the company works with local universities. It recruits personnel from the Academy of Economic Studies in Bucharest and all its branches from the Polytechnics University of Bucharest and Dunarea de Jos University of Galati. In addition, it invests in the training of employees by paying for their participation in master programmes. InBev has brought a great deal of expertise and know-how to Romanians. Romania is one of the rare cases in CEE where Romanians manage the entire organization. Furthermore, at the time of writing many Romanians are working in management positions or have coordination roles for the Balkans or the South-East European zone. However, cooperation with universities finishes here. There is no initiative from the universities or the research institutes to deepen their contacts with InBev. Nor do the government or the local institutions encourage the creation of linkages between business and academia. There are no programmes to stimulate linkage creation between suppliers and MNEs, and no initiatives to motivate the business to invest in research. In short, the local economy could have benefited far more from the multinational company if there had been a properly functioning national innovation system. Mr C said that it might happen in the future that InBev would create an R&D centre in CEE if this were more economically efficient. Hence, the country that offered the best conditions would benefit the most.

Would EU accession have an impact on InBev's policies?
Were there any prospects of plant closures?

Management thought that Romania's accession to the EU would definitely have an impact on the company's business, and this impact would be a positive one. Free trade with the EU would facilitate the work of the company and would allow for the full integration of InBev (Romania) into InBev's global supply chain; no plant closures in Romania were foreseen.

To sum up, Interbrew came to Romania in the mid-1990s, driven by a market-seeking strategy. It invested more than €140 million to renovate and modernize its two plants in the country. In addition, the company invested in improving the skills and capabilities of its management staff and workers. The company contributed a great deal to the development of the Romanian consumer market by offering high quality products that satisfy the demands of the different market segments. This required considerable effort, bearing in mind the underdeveloped retail market in Romania. The extent of this involvement with the local retail market is re-emphasized by mentioning again that, in 2005, only 5 per cent of the company's sales were by Western retailers. In addition, the unstable political and business climate did not offer many opportunities for the company to create linkages with the local business actors and institutions. There are very vague linkages between InBev and the local suppliers. InBev's biggest supplier is a foreign company. And, in general, the company works mainly with foreign suppliers, as it is difficult to find good local resources. It was anticipated that EU membership would lead to the full integration of InBev (Romania) in InBev's global supply chain. This means that it would be much easier for the company to satisfy its needs for raw resources from its global suppliers, as there would be no import restrictions. However, Romania is a large market with a long agricultural tradition and, in the future, it could be that local suppliers upgrade, with the support of national institutions and EU funds. In this case, it would be highly likely that a Romanian supplier could become a regional supplier for InBev. The efforts of the national and local institutions to help domestic companies to upgrade are therefore crucial in establishing this opportunity. The same conclusion is valid as far as scientific research is concerned. InBev has weak linkages with local universities and research institutes. Fundamentally, local institutions do not encourage this kind of cooperation. Romania has a very weak innovation system, and linkages between the different innovation actors only exist on paper. In this sense, one cannot say that InBev is locked into the Romanian economy. However, the great potential of the Romanian market and the specificity of the brewing industry (beer is not easily transportable) suggest that, if local actors and government pursued a strategy to embed Inbev, they might be able to attach the company successfully to the Romanian economy.

Nestlé (Romania)

Nestlé (Romania) owns the largest Romanian wafer plant, Joe, based in Timisoara, and another plant at the head office in Bucharest. In 2006, the company had a total of 600 employees in Romania, approximately 350 in Timisoara and 250 in Bucharest. There are additional employees involved in the company's distribution network. An ice cream plant was acquired as a result of Nestlé's global acquisition of the Greek based Delta Ice Cream.

The Timisoara plant is located approximately 400 kilometres from Bucharest and produces Joe brand wafers and coffee sticks, which are used for single-serve coffee. However, production is mainly concentrated on the Joe wafers, as this is the most famous local brand. The success of the Joe brand in particular can be explained by the snacking habits of Romanian consumers and Nestlé's aggressive advertising campaign, combined with the wide availability of Joe chocolate coated wafers at low prices.

Since 2004, Nestlé Romania has produced a Joe brand dessert to complement the biscuits. Nestlé has boosted its Romanian production capacity with the installation of a new chocolate wafer production line at the Timisoara unit, also going under the Joe label. The investment reflects the rapid growth of the Romanian snack market, as reported by Bogdan Tudorache.[26] 'We have invested an undisclosed amount in the new production line and know-how in a bid to expand sales of our Joe lines, sold mainly on the domestic market', said Paul Nuber,[27] Managing Director of Nestlé (Romania). Nestlé planned to invest around €3.5 million in its Romanian business between 2005 and 2007, and Nuber said that although this investment was not particularly great in terms of value, it was nonetheless important to help the company increase its share in the wafer market.

The Timisoara plant accounts for approximately 50 per cent of the total production of Nestlé (Romania). The Romanian wafers market is worth some €40 million per annum (Nestlé with its Joe brand), while the wider confectionery market is valued at around €150 million. Nestlé's production at the Timisoara plant, which concentrates largely on the Joe brand, is said to top 12,000 tonnes annually, equivalent to sales of between €25–30 million. However, about 20 per cent of the Timisoara factory production is exported. 'Generally we are exporting Joe Milky and Joe Crunch wafers to neighbouring countries in Central Europe – specifically Hungary, the Czech Republic and Bulgaria', said Mrs Klara Wrenger, Plant Manager, Nestlé (Romania).[28] The plant also produces the Bulgarian waffle Mura and the Hungarian Boci, explained Mr Nuber. The company is hoping to increase production to meet both the domestic and export markets, which are both very important to growth.

The continued demand for Joe brand products led to sales increases of about 25 per cent during the course of 2005. Nestlé (Romania) reported more than €80 million of turnover in 2005. That is as a result of the diversified product portfolio[29] and a strong marketing campaign. 'In 2006, we shall continue to offer our consumers ever varied and finest quality products', Nestlé Romania Managing Director Paul Nuber said. In 2005, sales of breakfast cereals climbed 40 per cent from 2004, while the pet food division grew 10 per cent.

The Joe Company was a locally owned greenfield plant built in the mid-1990s by a Romanian entrepreneur, Mr Florentin Banu. Nestlé bought the company in 2001 to acquire a critical mass, and since then has invested more than €10 million in production and marketing, as it wishes to dominate the all-important wafer market in the region. There were no classical privatization schemes as in the other CEECs. Nestlé is a leader on the Romanian confectionery market (it has around 35–40 per cent of the market), followed by Naty (European Foods) and Alka, the biggest producer of sunflower seed snacks.

According to Mr Nuber, the reason for the better embeddedness of Nestlé in Hungary and the Czech Republic is the fact that, thanks to the openness of their economies, Nestlé started its business much earlier in those countries than in Bulgaria and Romania. He explained, 'Romania lost out on its reform start and foreign investors at the beginning of the 1990s', and added, 'In Romania, there was no real privatization process.' This only happened in 2001, when Nestlé acquired its Romanian plant. In comparison, Nestlé entered Hungary in 1992, Czechoslovakia in 1992, and Bulgaria 1995. In absolute amounts, the investments in Hungary and the Czech Republic are greater than those in Bulgaria and Romania.

According to Mr Nuber, the unclear privatization schemes were the reason for Nestlé's late entry into Romania. James Gallagher, CEO of Nestlé for CEE, added some other factors that impeded investment in the country; namely, the authorities' persistence in overregulating everything and imposing restrictions. He stressed that 'ridiculously high import duties are applied to some of our products to bring revenue in to government'. For example, regarding coffee in Romania, €5 per kilogram on the gross weight, including packaging and even pallets. 'But such high rates just encourage smuggling and the government just doesn't understand that halving the rate would almost certainly bring more revenue', Mr Gallagher noted. 'Probably they don't want to understand, since there are so many vested interests profiting from this situation.' When asked to comment on the role of the government, Mr Gallagher pointed out that for three years they had been trying to resolve a dispute concerning ownership of the access road to Nestlé's factory, since local government and national government could not agree between them. He added that, as a country with a population of 22 million, Romania clearly has major potential for development, but 'Nestlé still has a long way to go to get to the size of business it would like'.

In most recent years, 'Romania is beginning to catch up', Mr Nuber said. However, further reforms and much more foreign investment are needed for this purpose – there should be improvements in the area of taxation, labour law and the judicial system. The good news is that since 2005 things are moving in the right direction, and the EU plays an important role in this process, the General Manager concluded.

As far as suppliers are concerned, Nestlé (Romania) uses both global and local suppliers. For example, the company sources flour and sugar locally, because of high import tariffs. The company finds it more profitable to use local suppliers than to import the products from another country in the region. Some of the local suppliers are foreign companies that had acquired local enterprises. In terms of volume, local suppliers have a greater share; in terms of value, global suppliers have the dominant share. The company helps local suppliers upgrade, as Nestlé has high food quality standards. It helps mainly by assisting in growing the know-how, rather than financially. When choosing suppliers, Nestlé selects those that can offer the highest quality at the best price but, of course, trade regulations have a decisive role, as they give preference to local suppliers.

Mr Nuber considers the Romanian plant to be completely integrated into the Nestlé global network. This implies that, with Romania's membership in the EU, the company will be even more deeply integrated in Nestlé's global supply chain. The General Manager pointed out that Romania is characterized by a considerable spectrum in the quality of suppliers – from top performers to very bad ones. So, in order to have competitive domestic suppliers, the Romanian government has to make efforts to encourage technological upgrading and innovativeness in local companies.

Nestlé has a very large distribution network. It sells to everyone in order to dominate the market. About 70–75 per cent of production is distributed through local retailers. Actually, the retail market is divided between 60 per cent local retailers and 40 per cent foreign retailers. In other words, in Romania the local retailers are dominant and it therefore makes perfect sense that Nestlé chose them as its preferred partner.

To the question:

Is it possible that Nestlé might move an R&D centre to Romania?'

Mr Nuber said, 'I do not think this will happen.' According to him, there are no reasons for Nestlé to invest in such a centre in Romania. The internationalization of R&D in CEE is not one of 'Nestlé's policies, as there are such centres through out Europe and worldwide. Nestlé (Romania) works with some of the local laboratories for regular checks, but not with any research institutes. Therefore, we do not observe very strong links between the company and local knowledge institutions. The company cooperates with the University of Bucharest and Timisoara to recruit personnel, but does work on any projects with Romanian researchers.'

When asked:

How EU membership will reflect Nestlé's policies in Romania?

the General Manager of the company responded very generally, saying that this could only have a positive impact on Nestlé – thus leaving a considerable room for interpretation.

To sum up, Nestlé entered the Romanian market ten years later than it entered the other CEE countries, due to the unstable economic climate until 2000, and the existing administrative and bureaucratic obstacles to FDI, the inflexibility of the labour market, taxes, the state of the judiciary, and corruption. The company invested in new production lines and technical equipment in both its plants. Despite recent growth, the company still faces many difficulties while working with the local and national authorities. The protectionist trade regime forced the company to work with the local suppliers; however, this will have changed with the country's entry into the EU, all protectionist measures having been removed. Even so, Nestlé imports many raw materials due to the fact that: (1) they are not grown locally – coffee, for example; and (2) there are no suppliers that satisfy Nestlé's high quality standards. The company distributes its products through all possible channels, using both local and Western retailers. Nestlé creates aggressive advertising campaigns to acquaint consumers with the launch of new products. The company has contributed a great deal to the development of the Romanian consumer market. Nestlé works with young and energetic people recruited from

Romanian universities. However, it does not cooperate with Romanian researchers; the company relies on its Western R&D centres. There is a lack of initiative from the local universities and institutions to cooperate with the multinational.

Conclusion

This chapter discussed the linkages existing between the different actors of the national innovation system and MNEs. In particular, it focused on the food industry within the national innovation system and empirically presented the cases of Nestlé, Unilever, and InBev in Romania.

The first section concluded that a national innovation system is merely a notion in Romania. The costs of political and economic reforms had a negative impact on national research institutions, characterized by a lack of resources and a reduced number of researchers. In principle, there never were strong linkages between business and universities because all the enterprises were previously state-owned and specialized sector institutes had conducted research. At the beginning of the 1990s, there was reorganization of sector institutes; some closed, and others were left to survive on sparce state subsidies. In any case, they could not compete with Western research centres and could not offer high quality research to the foreign investors that entered the country.

The second section analyzed the food industry in Romania. It revealed that the agricultural sector is highly fragmented, and that there are not many producers of high quality raw materials. There are no programmes that encourage the creation of linkages between suppliers and MNEs. This section also analyzed the Romanian consumer and retail market, and underscored the great contribution MNEs make to the development of the consumer market, especially given that numerous local retailers dominate the retail market. The low purchasing power of the population stimulated MNEs to concentrate on local products. Many global brands have also been imported to satisfy the needs of consumers with higher expectations.

The third section examined the linkages between Nestlé, Unilever, and InBev and the local actors. It revealed that none of the three companies had any kind of collaboration with knowledge institutions, apart from recruiting personnel from universities. MNEs do not support any Ph.D. students with grants; do not participate in any scientific projects, and do not train students in their factories; neither are their managers invited to lecture at the universities. They explained the absence of such activities as being the result of an absence of initiatives by the local or national governments to encourage partnership between business and the research centres. This section also concluded that Romania does not have a strong supply network, and that MNEs face problems in finding good quality suppliers. The high import tariffs forced them to source locally; however, in many cases this was impossible due to the absence of good input resources. None of the managers said that they plan any plant closures in the future; however, as an outcome of global restructuring and cost optimization measures this option is not excluded. Yet, Romania is the second largest market in CEE after Poland, and all the food MNEs are attracted by the growth opportunities it offers. In this respect, if the national absorptive capacity increases, these companies could contribute much more to increasing the competitiveness of the local economy.

Part IV
Conclusion

8
Conclusion

The focus of this last chapter is to give a comparative overview and derive the major conclusions from the book. The first section summarizes the empirical findings of the comparison between the policies of food MNEs Nestlé, Unilever, and InBev in Hungary, the Czech Republic, Bulgaria, and Romania. It highlights the impact of EU integration on MNEs' strategies in Hungary and the Czech Republic. The second section returns to the theoretical framework of the book in order to link the conclusions of the book to the literature on MNEs and economic development. This section places the food industry within the broader context of other industries, thus showing that MNEs in many sectors go through major reorganizations and restructurings in Europe, and how it is very challenging to embed them in a particular economy.

Conclusions from the comparative case studies

A huge literature is dedicated to the positive role of multinational enterprises and FDI on host economies' productivity and exports. Scholarly work on the transformation of CEECs has given a specific flavour to this literature by generating knowledge about restructuring efforts by post-Communist states and the role of multinationals in the context of EU integration.

It is important to record that this literature established that FDI *per se* does not guarantee increased competitiveness and economic growth in the long term, and that what matters is the ability of the country to embed FDI. In this light, the book asked:

What determines beneficial MNE embeddedness?

This research question was answered by focusing on the agro-food sector. It is a sector with great importance to the local economy as an employer and GDP contributor – one that has received little attention from scholars, however. The book discussed the strategies of the largest food MNEs as one of the major determinants for embeddedness. The analysis was based on interviews with CEOs at their headquarters: Nestlé (Vevey, Switzerland), Unilever (Rotterdam, Holland), and InBev (Leuven, Belgium).

The book presented the importance of transnational strategies as a factor that shaped the policies of local CEE subsidiaries, and determined their level of embeddedness (Chapter 2). It found that the claim that MNEs treated their subsidiaries equally in all four countries did not stand up to the empirical evidence. This claim related to their relationships with company headquarters – including the freedom to choose local suppliers, the opportunity to undertake their own marketing campaigns and create linkages with domestic knowledge institutions. The interviews, conducted at the subsidiaries of Unilever, Nestlé, and InBev in Hungary and the Czech Republic at the beginning of 2005, suggested an alternative understanding of the parent–subsidiary relationship. It appeared that not all the subsidiaries had the same status within the global production networks of the companies. For example, the Hungarian and Czech subsidiaries turned out to be less dependent on company headquarters; they could take decisions about local suppliers, they received greater funds for the modernization of their plants, and they had larger product portfolios than the Bulgarian and Romanian subsidiaries (the size of the product portfolio is a criterion for the power of a certain affiliate). In other words, the Hungarian and Czech subsidiaries could have been considered as contributing more to local development than their counterparts in Bulgaria and Romania. Given that, in all cases, company headquarters underlined that they had an the same attitude to all of their subsidiaries, the challenge that subsequently arose was to identify the factors that influenced the companies' strategies in the countries, causing them, ultimately, to behave differently to different subsidiaries.

Innovation system literature gives an answer: it claims that what makes the crucial difference is the absorptive capacity of the country, including the role of formal and informal institutions, and the role of economic actors.

Chapter 3 explained why the Hungarian and Czech subsidiaries were able to choose local suppliers. It was simply that these two countries underwent a successful process of restructuring in the agro-food sector and had managed to preserve their supplier networks. Therefore, MNEs had competitive partners with whom they could cooperate. In Bulgaria and Romania, the reforms were significantly delayed because of political disagreement, and multiple changes in legislation and regulations. In other words, it was not that MNEs had different attitudes to their subsidiaries as far as suppliers were concerned, but simply that Bulgarian and Romanian subsidiaries did not source locally, as the gap between local firms and MNEs was too large.

Empirical Chapters 4, 5, 6 and 7 depicted the innovation systems of the four countries and the level of development of the food industry. Chapters 4 and 5 examined the cases of Hungary and the Czech Republic, and revealed the importance of national government and business organizations with regard to the embeddedness of MNEs. In Chapter 5, it became clear that, among all of the new member states, the Czech food industry was the best prepared for EU accession. The government had invested in the sector, as had the domestic firms themselves in order to comply with all EU regulations. All food-processing companies had met EU requirements prior to accession. The general conclusion was that the Czech Republic had one of the most competitive and dynamic food industries of the CEE countries. This explained why Czech subsidiaries were embedded more deeply in the local economy. Hungary's position was similar to that of the Czech Republic. The interviews with governmental officials showed that, by the 1990s, Hungary had a policy of strengthening the competitiveness of local enterprises and embedding MNEs. In order to root foreign companies, the government applied broad policy measures – such as high tariffs and customs duties, rules of origin, joint venture requirements, and so on. Tax incentives were introduced to stimulate firms to spend more on R&D. Moreover, the government initiated numerous programmes that encouraged the establishment of linkages between FDI and local companies. That seemed a plausible explanation for why MNEs established stronger production networks in Hungary than they have done in Bulgaria and Romania.

In order to test the plausibility of these explanations, interviews were conducted at the subsidiaries of Nestlé, Unilever, and InBev in Hungary and the Czech Republic. The conversations with the managers of the local affiliates took place in 2005 and 2006; that is, shortly after these two countries joined the EU. However, the argument that these companies were highly embedded in both countries was challenged by EU membership. Their actions following EU expansion in 2004 revealed a different picture, as far as the embeddedness of MNEs was concerned. Food companies that seemed to be embedded in these countries closed plants (completely or partially) and moved production to neighbouring economies, including other EU member countries. Given the higher or comparable costs of production in other EU countries, explanations that suggest their actions were motivated by a desire for cheap labour or cheap raw materials can be ruled out immediately. The next section examined in greater detail the question as to what provoked MNEs to leave particular CEECs.

Having completed the research, I adopt an explanation that draws largely from strategic management literature. This literature states that the worldwide competitiveness of MNEs requires efficiency, centralized management of their international business units, standardized products, focus on core businesses, and economies of scale and scope. The search for synergies between the different subsidiaries that form the global structure of food MNEs leads to restructuring operations. As there are no longer any trade barriers in the EU, no protectionist measures from governments, and the logistics regarding goods are improved, MNEs can follow their efficiency strategies much more easily:

> Trade liberalization reduces the need for FDI to jump tariff barriers and intensifies competition in existing activities. It also increases the size of accessible markets, including for export activities. Both can lead to changes in the factors determining location. TNCs have to restructure their activities and deploy their assets to achieve 'best practice' levels, reducing their presence where competitiveness is difficult to achieve and raising it where it is possible. This involves shifting production and marketing sites in line with costs, logistics and reliability factors. It also involves relocating such functions as R&D, financial management, procurement and strategic decision-making between countries to maximize corporate efficiency. (UNCTAD Report, 2001: 5)

In this sense, the decision of a food multinational to close a plant is based on motives for efficiency.

Since 2004, the Czech Republic has completely liberalized its trade regime. Cheap import goods entered the country and producers faced fierce competition. The strong retail sector did not allow for dramatic increases of food prices and, hence, the producers had to invest a great deal in order to optimize their production processes: a number of local companies went bankrupt and others had to be restructured, including the subsidiaries of MNEs. Nestlé, Unilever, and InBev chose to implement their global restructuring plans in order to keep their leading market positions (regionally and globally). Their optimizations plans led to plant closures, employee lay-offs, and redirection to global suppliers rather than local ones. The impact of EU membership on Hungary proved to be comparable to that of the Czech Republic; namely, it allowed for an intensification of the processes of restructuring and optimization.

This allows for a general conclusion suggesting that, after EU enlargement, the idea of an MNE's 'embeddedness' might be seriously questioned in any country (Western or CEE) from the Union. Of course, some of the plant closures in CEE would have happened even if the countries had not joined the EU, in the cases of M&A or global divestments of some activities. However, the economic integration of Central and Western Europe was the major force that provoked and facilitated the processes of company restructuring. Actors such as national governments and institutions were simply unable to interfere. Countries such as Hungary and the Czech Republic seem to have been able to 'root' food multinationals in the local economies: MNEs invested heavily in local plants, they were market leaders, and they sourced products locally. In addition, national governments put their efforts into the improvement of national innovation systems, and the encouragement of the links between local and foreign companies, and between business and academia. Yet, it seems that these efforts were not enough to keep food MNEs in the local CEE economies. There is strong business logic behind this: the competition has become much stronger following EU enlargement and, in order to be competitive, companies have to be efficient. It seems that to be efficient does not correspond with the idea of embeddedness in a given economy. It should also be noted that none of companies studied in this book had an R&D centre in any CEEC, and that there were no plans to create such a centre in the near future. The reason was not the scarcity of highly qualified personnel to operate such centres; neither was the reason the absence of effective protection of IPRs: it was simply a question of strategic need. Company headquarters did not have such needs at the time and, hence, they did not consider the option of opening such centres in CEE in general. However, R&D is also related to the links between the MNEs and the local research centres; that is, the training of local researchers in the MNEs' laboratories, hiring of local researchers for a particular project, joint projects between MNEs and local institutes, grants for Ph.D. students, and so on. Such type of partnerships between MNEs and the national research centres and universities did not exist either, and further governmental efforts are needed in these areas.

In short, the factors that determine the level of embeddedness for food MNEs seem to be the companies' global strategies and host country characteristics, such as the size of the market. Chapters 6 and 7 examined the innovation systems of Bulgaria and Romania, and their role in embedding the local subsidiaries of Nestlé, Unilever, and InBev. The chapters discussed the governments' inability to concentrate on the development of strong innovation systems. For both countries, the effects of EU membership remain to be seen, as they only achieved full membership of the EU in January 2007. However, I also expect restructurings to happen there. As Romania is a large market with high growth opportunities, it is hard to believe that any of the multinationals would leave the country completely; however, with regard to Bulgaria this possibility is not excluded. The question as to whether the national innovation systems have any influence over the level of embeddedness of MNEs is irrelevant for these two countries, simply because Bulgaria and Romania have very weak innovation systems, which were never an important factor in the development of their local economies. The local authorities and the national governments have not introduced even half the number of programmes and measures that were undertaken by the Central European countries in order to embed FDI.

In conclusion, it should be noted, that the book has been based on limited case studies and does not allow for strong generalizations. However, it leads to some useful insights. Bearing in mind that Hungary and the Czech Republic had the strongest innovation systems in the CEECs and still did not manage to keep MNEs in the local economies, the book questions the 'power' of the innovation system to lock multinationals into host economies. The role of innovation systems is even more questionable in a liberal trade regime such as the EU. However, this does not mean that the level of development of the national innovation system does not matter with regard to attracting FDI, or to the transmission of knowledge to local firms. The higher the absorptive capacity of the domestic economy, the higher the benefits achieved from MNEs.

Relating the studies to the literature on MNEs, regional integration, and national innovation systems

This study analyzed the strategies of Nestlé, Unilever, and InBev in four CEE economies. It relates to and builds on a sizeable body of work on FDI embeddedness. It tried to make an original contribution by combining its analysis of the strategies of the largest food MNEs with the knowledge of national innovation systems of transition economies. The findings of this book confirm the argument that economic growth does not necessarily mean economic development. A high rate of economic growth says little about the entrepreneurial and innovative capacities within an economic area (Crouch *et al.*, 2004). Spillovers from FDI are regarded as one of the most practical and efficient means by which industrial development and upgrading can be promoted (Narula and Dunning, 2000). These include knowledge spillovers, and linkages from multinationals to domestic firms in host countries. 'Through these externalities, FDI inflows can potentially break the vicious circle of underdevelopment (as evident in low savings, low investment and low growth poverty traps) by easing capital, technology, knowledge constraints in the host economy' (Narula and Portelli, 2004: 5). It is positively confirmed that the effects of FDI are smaller in the least developed countries due to the existence of a threshold for externalities. A project coordinated by Lorentzen (2006a) systematically compares the technological capabilities of an African economy with those of a few Latin American economies. His team conducted micro-level research that presented the direct contribution resource-based activities made to the knowledge intensification of the economy as a whole. The results from the six case studies showed that knowledge intensification is 'a possible answer to the resource curse potentially bedeviling resource-intensive economies' (Lorentzen, 2006a: 22). The author hypothesizes that knowledge intensification can even take place in the absence of foreign technology and with weak systemic interactions, but only from a particular level of economic development. This implies that countries need a certain level of education, infrastructure, and health to benefit from investment flows (OECD, 2002). As Narula (2005) successfully explains, benefiting from FDI requires an exhaustive plan to build up domestic absorptive capacity and upgrade the quality of location advantages. Alvarez and Marin (2007) argue the same; namely, that absorptive capacities are vital in order to understand the impact of FDI on developing countries. They stress the importance of institutions and government in the attraction of FDI, as well as in the promotion of the conditions for the generation of positive external effects. An MNE's decision to locate important sections of the firm's value chain in one particular country is a result of the host government's struggle for local investment (Jarillo and Martinez, 1990). In line with this, Lall and Narula (2004) underline the crucial role governments have in developing and promoting a proactive industrial policy. They argue that FDI does not provide growth opportunities unless there is a domestic industrial sector that has the necessary technological capacity to profit from the externalities of MNE activity. Narula and Marin (2005) support this statement, arguing that market forces cannot substitute for the role of governments in developing and promoting a proactive industrial policy. With regard to this, innovation policy and innovation governance become key challenges for governments wishing to create flexible and dynamic economic environments (OECD, 2005a). Put differently, what matters in order to attract FDI and to have a potential for positive spillover effects are the level of human capital, national R&D expenditures, and the institutional and regulatory features of the host economies (Lorentzen, 2005). Analyzing humic substances in South Africa, with particular focus on pharmacological aspects, Lorentzen (2006b) concludes that good governmental intentions and highly developed local scientific capabilities are not sufficient to guarantee beneficial outcomes in favour of making the most of resource-intensive sectors if there are no effective institutions. Institutional stability can be seen as a determinant factor for attractiveness (Clarke 2001). While internationalizing their activities abroad, MNEs consider various local conditions in the host economy – such as domestic suppliers, industries, and country-level factors (Shimizu *et al.*, 2004). Akbar (2005) highlights the significant role played by public policy in shaping competitiveness. Poor public policy, he argues, can lead to loss of competitiveness and FDI flows; for example, a continuing micro-level bureaucracy can cause problems for subsidiaries, while an appropriate public policy can lead to significant gains in response to a country's attempts to attract inward FDI. In sum, 'When foreign and local inputs match well, technology diffusion may take place' (Lorentzen and Barnes, 2004: 466).

Christensen *et al.* (1996) also emphasize the great importance of national innovation systems. They find that industry is heavily dependent on external sources of technology, such as suppliers and public laboratories. In this context, 'The process of innovation, through which technologies are created and used, is more and more a collective endeavor, shaped by institutional and knowledge-sharing systems' (OECD, 1997: 18). Holl and Rama (2007a), using a unique data set questionnaire survey collected in three major electronic centres in Spain, show that attracting FDI contributes to local and regional economic development. However, they strongly underline that the three electronics clusters existed before most MNEs arrived, which is an argument in favour of the importance of the absorptive capacity of the local economy. In other words, subsidiaries of MNEs play a positive role at the local level when clusters and networks already exist; that is, when there is already good capacity for local firms to enjoy FDI spillover effects. 'Foreign electronics R&D plants are attracted by a dynamic socioeconomic environment, accompanied by a certain degree of technological specialization at the regional level' (Holl and Rama, 2007b: 8). Sternberg and Arndt (2001: 380) confirm the findings of Holl and Rama, and argue that,

'Political programmes intended to increase the innovativeness of regions must always begin with the innovation activities of local firms.' It should be noted that there is a considerable difference between improving production capacity and the development of technological capability and engagement in innovation (Lorentzen and Barnes, 2004).

Governments in Central, Eastern, and South-Eastern Europe have realized that, in order to achieve sustainable economic growth and to foster regional economic development, it is crucial to encourage entrepreneurial spirit. One way to do so is by building clusters. In CEE, cluster creation has been largely driven by foreign investment, with homegrown clusters emerging slowly (OECD, 2005b). Hungary is a good example of a country where, between 1995 and 2007, several clusters have appeared – in the automotive industry, logistics, construction, and tourism. The frontrunner in this development was the Pannon Automotive Cluster (PANAC), whose main mission was to embed MNEs in Hungary by increasing the level of their interaction with local companies (OECD, 2005b). In order to achieve this goal, the government focused on improving the quality of Hungarian suppliers; that is, on increasing the absorptive capacity of the local economy.

The phenomenon of clustering has also been present in the Czech Republic. In established industrial areas – Moravia, for example – clusters have been created in traditional sectors such as metallurgy and engineering. Apart from these, very strong clusters appeared in the automobile industry. Czech suppliers increased their competitiveness and became part of the international supply networks of large international firms such as Volkswagen/Skoda. In short, cluster creation is claimed to be the correct strategy for Central and Eastern European countries to embed FDI successfully by identifying and building on local competitive advantages (OECD, 2005b). However, this still leaves the question:

Has it been successful?

This book has shown that, as far as MNEs in the food industry are concerned, the role of governments has not been crucial to the embedding of MNEs within the local milieu. It should be noted, however, that these results became obvious after CEECs joined the EU, when MNEs began major processes of internal reorganization. The CEE economies had been closed for years and, in those circumstances, MNEs were locked in the local economies following political rather than economic imperatives. When the trade barriers were removed, economic factors gained importance, and MNEs began to integrate their European activities.

EU integration helped lower production costs and reduced cross-border transport costs; it led to intra-regional product and process specialization, made further economies of scale possible, and enabled multi-product firms to exploit fresh economies of scope, which motivated global companies to reorganize their production networks (Dunning, 1992; Hogenbirk and Narula, 1999). Using data on subsidiaries in the Nordic countries, Benito *et al.* (2003) concluded that deep integration, such as with the EU, played a significant part in determining differences in both scope and the level of competence of subsidiaries.

This study has shown that the factors that mattered for MNE embeddedness were corporate strategies. Pushed, on one hand, by strong global competitive forces, and, on the other hand, by national governments to invest locally, to create employment, and to transfer advanced technology, MNEs adopt higher levels of integration and differentiation in their strategies (Martinez and Jarillo, 1991). The cases of Nestlé, Unilever, and InBev confirmed the findings of authors such as Bartlett and Ghoshal (1989), Ghoshal and Nohria (1989), Jarillo and Martinez (1990), and Harzing (2000), who argued that subsidiaries of transnational companies were locally responsible, operated as a network, and built cost advantages through economies of scale. These affiliates have lower production and R&D content than products sold by subsidiaries of multi-domestic companies (Harzing, 2000). In other words, the book confirmed previous literature on subsidiary management (see Martinez and Jarillo, 1991); namely, that there is a lower expectation that subsidiaries of transnational and global companies will generate technology spillovers as they have little autonomy in shaping their technological behaviour within the structure and strategy of the corporation as a whole. As Ghoshal and Bartlett (1988: 370) argue, 'subsidiaries with a low level of local autonomy neither created nor diffused innovations'.

The following questions arise:

Can we generalize the conclusions made for food MNEs?
Is it possible to embed MNEs in a particular economy?
Can national and local governments lock in FDI through innovation policies and the creation of clusters?

Analyzing the networking relationships of 184 electronics companies (both foreign and domestic), Holl and Rama (2007b) discovered that FDI plants are not deeply embedded in Spanish clusters; that is, the relative levels of regional sourcing, sales, and cooperations are below those of clustered domestic plants. The authors argue that the relatively lower level of embeddedness of MNEs limits the potential of FDI plants to stimulate development and innovation at the regional level. Their research demonstrated that the most R&D intensive FDI plants tend to remain isolated, and they avoid not only R&D collaboration with other companies, but also outsourcing linkages. The larger and more R&D intensive firms prefer extra-regional (not regional, within the cluster) linkages (Holl and Rama 2007a). In short, Holl and Rama's study for the electronics industry reveals that it is very difficult to embed large MNEs within local clusters.

What is the picture in other industries and in the other European countries?
Are MNEs from other industries embedded in CEE?
Do MNEs reorganize and restructure only in CEECs or is this a more general trend all over Europe?
Do MNEs close plants and leave Western European countries in the same way as they do in CEE?
Are the countries with strong innovation systems capable of locking in MNEs?
What provokes MNEs to restructure, and why?

'Given the current policy debate throughout Europe, it is impossible to ignore the issue of globalization and restructuring.'[1] At present, there is only one source of data on restructuring available at the European level, and that is the European Restructuring Monitor (ERM). ERM is 'a tool designed to provide a quick overview of restructuring activities in Europe and their employment consequences'.[2] It should be noted that it is beyond the scope of this study to examine the process of restructuring from its social perspective; rather, the goal is to look at restructuring from the companies' perspective. A better understanding of the pressure that restructuring imposes on states and public authorities is required; however, not many studies deal with this issue.

Lazonick (2004: 579) identifies five possible forms of restructuring: buy-out, outsourcing, relocation, downsizing and bankruptcy. Huws and Ramioul (2006: 19) explain that restructuring initiatives take place in the context of a takeover or merger, a decision to outsource, a major technological change, a strong upturn or downturn in the market, or some other variable that makes it difficult to isolate the dynamic features (motivation or impacts) of any specific restructuring measure. In a nut-shell, corporations are not stable and homogenous entities; rather, they are very dynamic and are held together by elaborate webs of contracts that are in a continuous process of renegotiation (Huws and Ramioul, 2006).

To return to the question:

> Are MNEs embedded in Western Europe and do 'external' factors keep them in a given location?

The evidence shows that it is difficult to talk about the 'embeddedness' of MNEs in any industry. The *ERM Quarterly* (European Foundation for the Improvement of Living and Working Conditions, 2007) reports large restructurings in all sectors of the European economy. Reorganizations are observed not only in traditional industries, but also in services: telecommunications, postal services, banking and insurance, and public administrations.[3]

Let us take the automobile sector, for example. Some of the largest MNEs – such as PSA Peugeot Citroën, Bosch, Seat, Ford, and Volkswagen – underwent global optimization plans, shutting down plants all over Europe and moving to new destinations in CEE, India, or China during the period 2002–6 (European Foundation for the Improvement of Living and Working Conditions, 2007).[4] Countries' innovation systems were not a factor in any way capable of stopping automobile giants from shutting down their Western European plants; moreover, countries could not even anticipate what was going to happen.

A detailed analysis of Volkswagen gives a good clue as to the factors that pushed most of the companies in the sector to restructure. The first reason was the Western European automotive market itself – a market that is largely saturated and struggling with excess capacity. In addition, export opportunities had also been limited, due to the US$ exchange rates and high import duties in growth markets. It was a question of strategic importance for Volkswagen to ensure its competitive production and utilization of capacity at plants in Western Europe. At the same time, it should be noted that Volkswagen's Western European plants had not been running at full capacity, despite a rise in market share. In this environment, Volkswagen had to find a strategy in order to secure the quality, innovation, and economic efficiency of its brand over the long term. To deal with this, the company initiated restructuring of its entire group of companies and brands, the various models' production processes, and new single plants for a new series. Thousands of jobs at Spanish, Portuguese, and Belgian factories were to be cut and some of the models production was to shift back to German factories, which were only running at about 70 per cent capacity (VW Press release, 21

November 2006).[5] Volkswagen's strategic focus is on the growth markets of the future – Russia, India, and China (European Foundation for the Improvement of Living and Working Conditions, 2006a).[6]

The chemical industry witnessed several instances of worldwide restructuring at the beginning of 2007. Companies such as Michelin (20,000 job cuts), Pfizer (10,000 job cuts), Bayer (6100 job cuts), Perlos (4000 job cuts), and Astra Zeneca (3000 job cuts) initiated dramatic reorganizations. The reasons for these restructurings varied. In the cases of Michelin and Pfizer, it was part of the worldwide business strategies of these companies to retain competitiveness; in the case of Bayer, it was the outcome of a merger with Schering; and, in the case of Perlos, Finland, it was the result of offshoring activities to Asia (European Foundation for the Improvement of Living and Working Conditions, issue 1, 2007).

The transport sector is a third example where one can observe the impact of globalization over companies' business strategies. In 2007, Airbus, one of the world's leading aircraft manufacturers, developed a restructuring plan known as 'Power 8'. The plan encompassed the sales and closures of three plants, and a search for industrial partners to take over three more facilities producing fuselage and wing parts. The company had been under pressure to cut costs because of financial losses caused by delays in orders and development problems with an airliner model.

The next example is the IT sector and the restructuring within the world's IT leader – IBM. For years, IBM was ahead of its competitors, as it was the only company that made global offers to its clients. However, partnerships and mergers were creating global competitors. In addition, there was a trend of 'offshoring' towards CEECs as well as South-East Asia. All these factors explain the worldwide reorganization of IBM. The company has consistently implemented plans to adapt and safeguard its competitiveness in response to its passage from an industrial organization to a service company, and to smoothe the path of its efforts to adapt to a fast changing economic environment. In a nutshell, the restructuring of IBM France in 2006, which involved 12 companies, came within the scope of a broader plan decided on by the IBM Corporation. This plan impacted on around 13,000 staff in Europe and the USA, whereas, at the same time, the group's workforce in Asia (India, in particular) was growing exponentially.[7] It is interesting to note that, in 2003, IBM withdrew its investments from Hungary, moving its hard disk drive plant from Hungary to China.[8]

These are just a few of the examples of sectors where, between 2002–6, large MNEs closed plants in Western Europe, moving either to CEE Europe or to India and China. It seems that the process of restructuring – which has been discussed for the food industry in CEE – is running throughout Europe and in all sectors. My observation is in line with Benito *et al.* (2003), who analyze the effect of EU integration on MNEs' strategies, and conclude that restructuring has occurred in a variety of firms across many industries. Obviously, MNEs cannot be considered 'embedded' even in Western Europe, which is characterized by industrial relations traditions, and has strong innovation systems and stable regulatory regimes.

A recent project (AgriE), begun in 2006, completed in 2008 and funded by the European Social Fund (ESF) in cooperation with 10 European partners is devoted especially to analyzing the problems of restructuring in the EU.[9] The project focuses on 26 case studies of companies present in more than 10 sectors, and aims at examining the dynamics of restructuring at the European level. The project was completed in 2008, but has not yet brought forward any policy recommendations or reached any general conclusions, however, some of the preliminary conclusions deserve attention.

The AgriE study reveals that the duration of restructuring varied from one country or sector to another during 2002–6: for example, a lengthy process in countries such as Germany, and a swift process in the United Kingdom; a lengthy process in the industrial sector, and a swift process in sectors such as telecommunications. Forms of restructuring are also tending to develop: 56.4 per cent of job losses occur in cases of internal reorganizations. The new international division of labour, which is one of the factors contributing to the toughening of competition at the international level, is accelerating restructuring and producing new actors: Indian or Chinese multinationals are now breaking into the merger and takeover game (AgriE refers to the case of Arcelor–Mittal). In short, the general context of restructuring, and the business strategy of the firm at world and European levels have to be identified in order to be understood. Special attention has to be given to European regulations, which condition the implementation of company strategies. Globalization, strong competition, pressures on price cost, increases in prices of raw materials, development of supply chains, and IT technologies, are some of the factors that force MNEs to reorganize their activities. The emergence and development of new information and communication technologies seemed to be the cause of restructuring in only a few cases. In most cases, however, reduction in production costs, increase in benefits, and reduction of losses could only be achieved by relocating production to other countries. AgriE summarizes that the different levels of regulation in Europe should be linked, external competition rules should be examined, and competition in Europe and outside Europe should be compared. In short, the essential reason for restructuring is an adaptation to the economic and competitive environment influencing the activities and organization of the company.

To conclude, for many sectors, it seems that national institutions cannot do a great deal to embed MNEs in local economies. Empirical studies prove that companies' international business strategies are the most powerful factor to have an impact on the locking in of subsidiaries in the host economy. However, it is still difficult to predict the strategy that MNEs will pursue, since it is based on the speed with which these complex and sophisticated choices are made in order to preserve competitive advantage. I believe that all these issues will be analyzed in greater depth by other scholars in order to identify those factors and mechanisms that can embed MNEs – if, indeed, this is at all possible. It seems that in the area of globalization – which is characterized by constant change, flexibility and dynamism – it is very ambitious to talk about the embeddedness of FDI. MNEs aim to be globally competitive, which requires innovativeness, consideration for the future and, very often related to these, processes reorganizations and restructurings. A company that seems to be locked into a particular economy might be forced to leave the country because of different market or competition drivers. In this sense, a country or region appears to be a good location for a particular company might become a poor location in the future. This does not mean that there is no need for focused national and regional policies to improve countries' growth and competitiveness. Stable economic and political environments, tax policies, high quality local suppliers, and good knowledge institutions are all factors that will retain importance for attracting FDI and creating positive conditions for spillover effects. The challenge is how to grasp the knowledge that foreign firms bring, whether they stay permamently or only for a short while.

Appendix

Questionnaires

Questionnaire to the headquarters

1   Do you have an investment strategy plan for the whole of Central and Eastern Europe that predetermines the investments in the different countries?

(a)	Yes. (If so, what are the main factors influencing that plan?);
(b)	No, we decide at the time and at the place whether to invest or not, and how much to invest.

2   Can a subsidiary in any Central and Eastern European Country be closed at any point, free from constraints; and, if so, why would that happen?

(a)	Price of labour force increases;
(b)	The purchasing power of the population decreases;
(c)	Strong local competitors;
(d)	Other.

3   Are the retailers in some CEE countries stronger than in the others in their influence over companies' policies, and in which countries?

(a)	Bulgaria;
(b)	Romania;
(c)	Hungary;
(d)	Czech Republic;
(e)	Poland.

What is the nature of that influence?

4   Which retailers are preferable partners for the company in CEE?

(a)	Local retailers;
(b)	Multinational retailers – (Billa, Tesco, Metro, etc.) and why?

5   Do you plan closer cooperation with the local research institutes or universities?

(a)   Yes, because we need a highly qualified labour force;
(b)   Yes, because we rely on them for routine sanitary and health/hygiene control;
(c)   Yes, because we rely on them for more elaborated research, and ideas for innovation and development;
(d)   No, we do not need them, because we have a research institute in Western Europe;
(e)   No, we do not work with them, because the research institutes are not developed and cannot offer anything new as products or ideas.

6   Do you receive help from the local branch associations, business centres, or agencies for regional development? If so, what did/do they do for you?

(a)   Help you in developing the local infrastructure;
(b)   Participate in seminars and workshops organized by them where you discuss common strategies for the industry's development with the local firms;
(c)   Other.

7   Do you use local banks (including branches of Western banks) and, if so, why?

(a)   To get credit from them;
(b)   Just to make transactions.

8   What is the strategy of the parent company towards suppliers?

(a)   Prefers to work with its global suppliers from Western Europe;
(b)   Prefers working with local suppliers;
(c)   Depends on the cost of local suppliers;
(d)   Depends on the cost and quality the local suppliers offer;
(e)   Other.

On what does this strategy depend?

9   What is your strategy towards local competitors?

(a)   Try to cooperate with large competitors;
(b)   They are, in general, too small and are of no interest to us;
(c)   We acquire some of them;
(d)   Other.

10   Who distributes your production?

(a)   Large Western retailers;
(b)   Large local retailers;
(c)   Small local retailers.

11   Why do you prefer this specific form of distribution?

(a)   Because it is your global partner (for Western retailers);
(b)   Because it has a large market share;
(c)   Other.

12   What was the basic reason for investing in the country?

(a)   Tax incentives the government gave to FDI;
(b)   Local market;
(c)   A cheap labour force;
(d)   Proximity to other markets;
(e)   Educated labour force and the knowledge-based region.

13   What is the national/regional government doing to keep you in a particular country?

(a)   We have been invited to participate in the national strategy for the development of food industry;
(b)   Good relationships with local authorities help us in our work;
(c)   We do not collaborate with regional and national authorities.

14 **Are CEE subsidiaries independent in decision-making from headquarters?**

(a) Yes, they are independent, but only in taking everyday decisions;   (b) They have to complement their governing decisions with the Executive Director of the parent company;   (c) No, they are completely dependent on the parent company;   (d) In some countries they are relatively more independent than in other CEE countries. (If this is the case, why?)

15 **What kind of relationship do you have with the local trade unions?**

(a) We consider them to be an important partner and reach mutually beneficial agreements;   (b) They have insignificant power in CEE and we consider them unimportant;   (c) In general, we do not have a policy of cooperation with trade unions;   (d) Depends from country to country.

16 **What is your investment strategy for CEE in the future?**

(a) Large long-term investments;   (b) Flexible short-term investments;   (c) In some places in CEE we have long-term investments; in others, short-term. (If so, can you please explain on which factors your decision depends);   (d) Other.

17 **Which brands do you produce in your subsidiary?**

(a) Home and personal care;   (b) Foods;   (c) Both of them.

Questionnaire to the subsidiaries

1 Can you tell me how many enterprises you have and how many employees you have?
  What are the names of your enterprises? (Some historical information if you have any.)

2 Do you think that Hungarian and Czech subsidiaries are much better developed (that is, the company has invested more in them), than those in Bulgaria and Romania?
  If yes, why?

3 How did your company decide which local state companies to acquire when you entered the local market?
  Were the privatization schemes clear?
  Did you close some enterprises in the process of restructuring?
  If yes, why?

4 What difficulties did you face in the first years of investment in the country?

5 The company uses local and global suppliers. Can you please show the percentages of these two for your affiliate (for example, 60 per cent local and 40 per cent foreign)?
  Which suppliers are local – those providing raw materials, packaging, some other products? (Which?)
  Are your biggest suppliers local or foreign?
  Why you have chosen a global supplier?

6 Do you have backward linkages with local suppliers?
  How do you help local suppliers to upgrade?

7 Do you have regional brands?
  Do you intend to turn a local brand into a regional one?
  Why and which one?
  What local products you produce and do you have mother company's global products in your portfolio?

8 Do you consider your subsidiary integrated in the parent company's global network?

9   Which countries you consider having strong supplier networks (Romania, Bulgaria, the Czech Republic, Hungary)?
Why do you think this is the case?

10 How do you think the company contributed to the local development?

11 What is the percentage ratio between local retailers and multinational retails you use?
Which retailers do you use to a greater extent?

12 What can motivate the parent company to internationalize its R&D centres in CEE and can this happen in your country?

13 With which universities do you collaborate to recruit personnel?
Do you use domestic research institutes for marketing research or some other type of research for example?

14 How does the government help (or not help) you?
Do you think EU accession will have an influence over companies' policies in your country?

15 When you acquired an enterprise in CEE, did you use the suppliers that the state enterprise used before, or did you establish new suppliers?

16 Do you intend to close a plant and, if yes, what are the reasons for this?

Tables

Table A.1   Employment in agriculture, hunting, forestry, and fishing

Bulgaria, % of employed population	2000	2001	2002	2003	2004
Employment in agriculture, hunting, forestry and fishing	26.6	26.3	26.1	10.1	10.5

Sources: International Labour Organization, Euromonitor International (electronic database).

Table A.2 Livestock numbers, '000 head

Bulgaria	1992	1993	1994	1995	1996	1997	1998	1999	2000	2001	2002	2003	2004	2005
Asses	329.41	303.03	297.16	275.63	281.25	286.87	225.02	220.50	207.70	209.50	196.69	196.70	191.00	187.59
Cattle	1310.50	973.73	750.40	638.24	631.74	582.06	611.72	671.00	682.00	639.80	634.54	635.00	607.60	591.36
Goats	552.74	611.22	676.43	795.44	833.33	848.74	966.11	1048.00	1046.00	970.30	898.56	900.00	827.90	785.26
Horses	114.27	113.71	113.18	133.05	150.52	170.47	126.20	133.40	141.00	140.30	150.69	151.00	155.10	157.68
Pigs	3141.40	2679.70	2071.30	1986.20	2140.00	1500.40	1479.70	1721.00	1512.00	1144.00	1013.70	1000.00	983.30	967.80
Sheep	6703.40	4814.30	3763.20	3397.60	3383.00	3019.60	2847.50	2774.00	2549.00	2286.00	2418.50	2400.00	2335.00	2288.20

Sources: UN Food and Agriculture Organization, FAOSTAT, Euromonitor Plc (2006).

Table A.3 Cereal production, '000 tonnes

Bulgaria	1992	1993	1994	1995	1996	1997	1998	1999	2000	2001	2002	2003	2004	2005
Cereals	6559.6	5666.0	6409.1	6514.0	3379.5	6151.6	5344.8	5237.2	5268.4	6084.7	6768.4	3819.0	4463.0	5468.0

Sources: UN Food and Agriculture Organization, FAOSTAT, Euromonitor International (electronic database).

Table A.4   Average age of Bulgarian population

Bulgaria	2000	2001	2002	2003	2004	2005
Mean age of population	39.1	39.3	39.9	40.1	40.2	40.4
Mean age of male population	37.8	38.1	38.6	38.8	38.9	39.0
Mean age of female population	40.4	40.6	41.2	41.5	41.5	41.7

Source: National Statistical Institute.

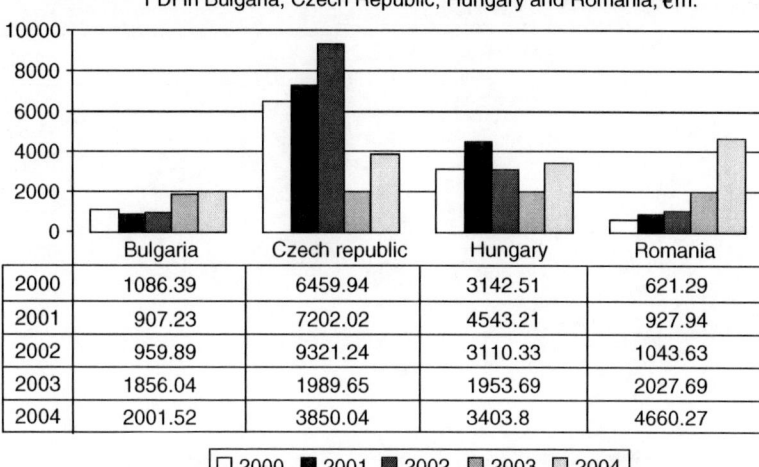

Figure A.1 FDI in Bulgaria, Hungary, the Czech Republic and Romania, 2000–4
Source: Euromonitor International (electronic database).

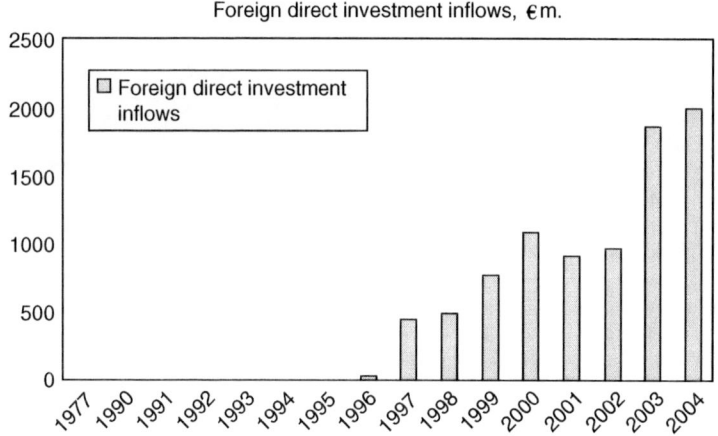

Figure A.2 FDI inflows trend, Bulgaria, 1997–2004
Source: UNCTAD, Euromonitor Plc (2006).

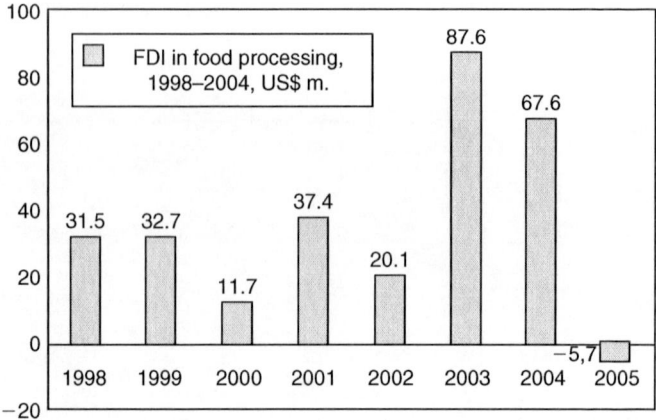

Figure A.3 FDI in food processing, Bulgaria, 1998–2004, US$m.
Source: Bulgarian National Bank.

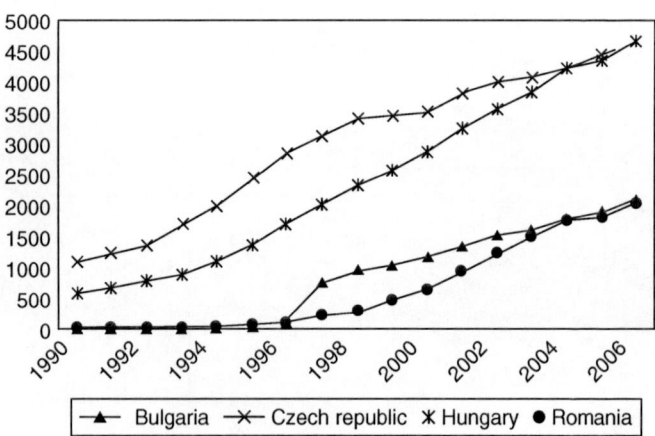

Figure A.4 Annual disposable income in Bulgaria, the Czech Republic, Hungary, and Romania
Source: National Statistical Institute.

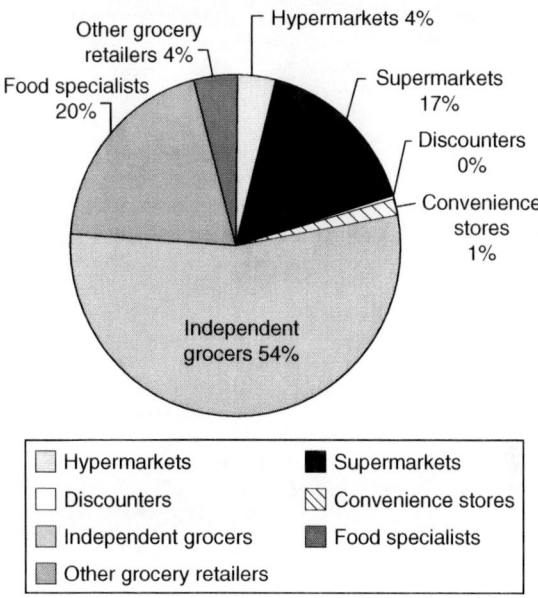

Figure A.5 Grocery retailer share, Bulgaria, 2005
Source: National Statistical Institute.

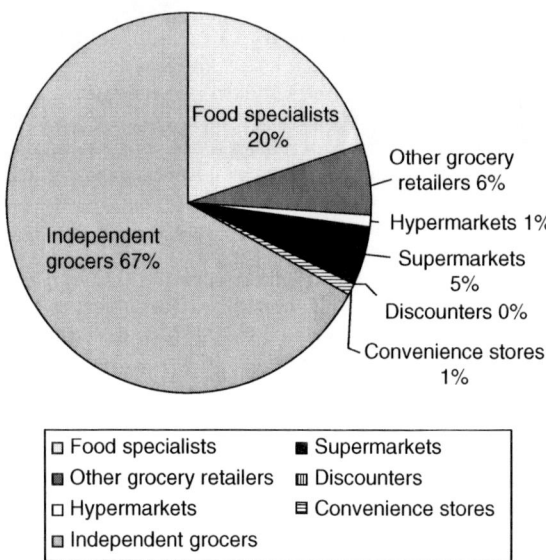

Figure A.6 Grocery retailer share, Bulgaria, 2000
Source: National Statistical Institute.

Notes

Introduction

1. Beneficially embedded MNEs are multinational companies that are part of the national system of innovation; that is, they collaborate with local research institutes, universities, financial institutions, business organizations and also contribute to local development by helping domestic companies to upgrade.
2. I understand shallow integration to be integration where multinationals stand as 'cathedrals in the desert'; that is, they do not help local companies to upgrade and do not cooperate with them. Deep East–West integration is such a form of integration, where we observe strong patterns of production networks; multinational companies, by means of being linked to local agencies, research institutes and regional authorities, create conditions for local economic development.
3. As Charles Ragin notes, 'the goal of exploring diversity is best served by a comparative approach' (Ragin 1994: 52).
4. See CIAA, 'Food and Drink Statistics', available at http://www.ciaa.be/uk/library/statistics/ceecs.htm
5. Significant in terms of contribution to the industrial value added and employment of the countries.
6. Alexander Yotsev, head of the Association of the Food and Beverage Industry said that some 70 per cent of the Bulgarian food industry firms will have to be closed after the country joins the European Union because they do not match the EU standards, 24 September 2003, available at http://www.bgnewsnet.com/story.asp?st=1691, date accessed: March 2004.
7. Hirschhausen and Bitzer (2000: 9) argue that 'in industries like food processing, technology transfer from the West has become the predominant vehicle for technological catch-up'.
8. For more information, see OECD (2001) *Challenges for the Agro-Food Sector in European Transition countries*, available at: http://www.oecd.org/document/42/0,2340,en_2649_34489_2026986_1_1_1_1,00.html (accessed May 2007).
9. Confederation of the Food and Drink Industries of the EU (CIAA) (2006) *Data and Trends of the European Food and Drink Industry*: 18, available at: http://www.ciaa.eu/documents/brochures/Data_&_Trends_2006_FINAL.pdf (accessed 21 May 2007).

1 The Analytical Framework

1. Narula defines absorptive capacity as the ability to catch up economic units (firms or countries) to absorb, internalize and utilize the knowledge potentially made available to them. Absorptive capacity can be decomposed into four constituent parts: firm-sector absorptive capacity, basic infrastructure,

advanced infrastructure, and formal and informal institutions (Lall and Narula, 2004).

2. Knowledge institutions consist of public research institutes, universities, organizations for standards, intellectual property protection, and so on; that is, bodies that enable and promote the development of science and technology.

3. See Krueger (1990), McKenzie and Lee (1991), and Stopford and Strange (1991).

4. As, for example, described by Dunning (1993) and Loree and Guisinger (1995).

5. Leading edge industry clusters, according to Birkinshaw and Hood (2000), are those clusters in which the share of world cluster exports is more than double the average for that country.

6. Birkinshaw (1996: 467) defines a subsidiary mandate as 'a business, or element of a business, in which the subsidiary participates and for which it has responsibilities beyond its national market'.

7. Dunning, J.H. (1993).

8. FDI inflows into the 10 EU accession countries from Central and Eastern Europe rose by 69 per cent in 2004, to $20 billion, with Poland, the Czech Republic and Hungary, in that order, receiving the largest FDI inflows. Re-invested earnings accounted for more than half of the FDI flows to these countries, whereas equity investments in new projects and privatization sales were the dominant forms of FDI in Slovakia, Latvia and Lithuania (UNCTAD, World Investment Report 2005: 84).

9. The case studies of the project are Dobrogea SA, bakery in Romania; Groupe Souffle in Romania, the malt industry, Eridania Beghin–Say; General Bottlers in Poland; United Biscuits in Hungary; Tesco in the Czech Republic.

10. These are the segments more closely linked to agriculture.

11. What Bartlett and Ghoshal define as a transnational strategy is what M.E. Porter defines as a global strategy in his book *On Competition* (1998).

12. In Bulgaria, InBev preserved the beers Astika, Slavena, Kamenitza, Shumensko; in Romania, Bergenbier, Noroc, Efes; in Hungary, Borsodi Sor, Borsodi Barna, Borsodi Bivaly, Borsodi Polo.

13. Typical tasks include the coordination of production and logistics; making key decisions about the brand portfolio (the mix of global, regional and local brands), product introductions, the development of regional brands and advertising campaigns; the setting up of operations; the selection and training of local managers; and the provision of on-the-spot support to local teams' marketing activities.

14. Euromonitor International (2006e) *Packaged Food, Nestlé SA*.

15. Helen Wallace (2001:18–20) discerns three kinds of pattern, when she discusses the development of linkages across Europe: function, territory and affiliation. In the functional linkage she defines three types: those promoted by and in relation to the EU, those emerging around groups of neighbours; and those stimulated by private actors. The last type of linkage is my main focus. Why is it important? My interpretation of Wallace is that there are elements of organic linkages already observable between the East and West in the form of production and investment, and these are important because, as she puts it, 'in the absence of synergy we might find the

discourse of Europeanization becoming an obstacle, rather than a stimulus to transnationalism, let alone a support for modernization' (2001: 20).

2 The Global Strategies of the Food Companies and their Impact on the CEE Region

1. Euromonitor International (2006f), *Unilever Group – Packaged Food*, February.
2. Unilever Group, at: www.unilever.com
3. Unilever 2006 Results Presentation by Patrick Cescau – Unilever Group Chief Executive, London, Thursday 8 February 2007, available at: http://www.unilever.com/Images/ir_Q4%202006%20Results%20speech_tcm13-84121.pdf (accessed: May 2007).
4. Unilever Group, *Adding Vitality to Life*, 2006 Annual Report and Accounts, available at: http://www.unilever.com/Images/ir_06_annual_report_en_tcm13-88803.pdf (accessed May 2007).
5. *Ibid*: *Packaged Food*, Unilever Group (2006): 16.
6. Bestfoods was a landmark acquisition in 2001, and effectively redefined Unilever's position in packaged food with its portfolio of powerful brands, including Knorr and Hellmann's.
7. In March 2000, Unilever signed an exclusive licensing agreement with Vera Wang, a reputed designer of luxury bridal and evening wear, to develop the designer's first fragrance. In addition, Unilever holds global licences with Valentino, Cerruti and Lagerfeld, and added Nautica to its portfolio of global fragrance licences in 1999. However, the company sold this business to Coty in 2005.
8. See *Packaged Food*, Unilever Group (2006): 22.
9. Euromonitor International (2006a) *Beer – InBev*, April: 7.
10. Euromonitor International (2006a) *Beer – InBev*, April: 28–9.
11. *Ibid*: 17.
12. *Ibid*: 17.
13. Euromonitor International, (2006e) *Packaged Food – Nestlé SA*, March: 1.
14. Euromonitor International (2006e) *Packaged Food – Nestlé SA*, March: 7.
15. *Ibid*: 8.
16. *Ibid*: 10–12.
17. *Ibid*: 20.
18. Interviews with Best Foods Europe President and Vice-president conducted at the company's headquarters in Rotterdam, Holland, September 2004.
19. Interview with the Corporate Affairs Office, Leuven, Belgium, November 2004.
20. OECD (2005) 'Country Fact Sheet – Bulgaria, Investment Compact for South East Europe'.
21. Interview with Mr Gallagher, Nestlé CEO for CEE region, Vevey, Switzerland, November 2004.

3 Privatization and Restructuring in the Agro-Food Industry

1. Restitution involves the return of property to its rightful owners. Transformation is the process of converting collective farms into other corporate or legal

structures not based on collective property. Transformation also includes the process of confirmation of property rights over land and other assets that had never been collective property, but remained, in law, the property of individuals throughout the communist period. Privatization is the transfer of ownership of state property to private hands and is distinct from the process of restitution, by which state property also changes hands but reverts to those with a historical claim to ownership (OECD (1995) 'Review of Agricultural Policies: The Czech Republic': 14).

2. The Second Act extended the deadline retrospectively by ten years – from 8 June 1949 (the date of the first collectivization measures) to 1 May 1939 (the date of the first anti-Jewish legislation) – to include mainly Jewish property confiscated during the war years, but also the postwar land reform. The Third Act extended restitution to cover those who had suffered loss of freedom or life for political reasons (including deportation, forced labour and so on during the war) between 11 March 1939 (the introduction of compulsory membership of the paramilitary youth organization) and 23 October 1989 (the declaration of the Hungarian Republic), while the Fourth Act was intended to serve as a facilitator for the other three (Swain 1994: 7).

3. The nine ways by which the vouchers could be used were:

   - To buy agricultural land
   - To buy a flat owned by local authorities
   - To obtain a pension supplement
   - To participate in the 'pre-privatization' of shops and restaurants
   - To buy shares in the privatization of certain state companies
   - To participate in 'decentralized privatization'
   - To use as security for certain government credits
   - To purchase shares in Employee Share Ownership Programmes
   - To invest in certain state investment funds.

   The first three uses for the vouchers were restricted to individuals personally entitled to restitution. Anyone who obtained vouchers, by whatever means (such as purchase on the secondary market), could use them for the other six purposes (Swain, 1994).

4. As the generations changed and new people came into agriculture, the proportion of member-owned land gradually fell, being 35 per cent privately owned at the beginning of the 1990s.

5. OECD (1994). *Review of Agricultural Policies: Hungary*: 61.

6. Voucher privatization was conducted in two waves, the first in 1992 and the other in 1994. All adult citizens were offered a voucher worth 1000 'bidding' points for a nominal fee. The vouchers could be used to bid for the shares of companies listed for privatization. Individuals could invest their points in investment funds that could also bid for shares. Each wave consisted of a number of rounds in which prices were adjusted administratively according to supply and demand (OECD, 1995: 21).

7. The largest confectionary enterprise (Ceske Cokoladovny) was privatized with the participation of Nestlé (Switzerland) and BSN (France), which invested around US$70 million. Unilever bought one of the four large companies producing soaps and vegetable fats. Rieber & Son from Norway invested

in Vitana Bysice, which produces dehydrated foodstuffs for fast cooking. Although many foreign breweries were looking for joint ventures with well-known Czech breweries, so far most of the Czech breweries have limited their cooperation to the joint marketing of products (OECD, 1995: 100).

8. In fact, 'associations' are cooperatives, but of the non-Stalinist variety.

9. The land reform carried out after World War II restricted farm size per family to 5 hectares. Therefore, restitution during the post-socialist regime was affected by this land reform.

10. The legislative and institutional framework for foreign direct investment was established as early as 1991. The 'Law on Foreign Direct Investment' provided for tax rebates and allowed for the repatriation of profits to foreign direct investors. However, bureaucratic rigidities and an unstable economic and legal environment left many potential investors undecided. Inflows of foreign capital grew from 1995, as the privatization programme created improved opportunities for investment (OECD, 2000b: 91).

11. Republic of Bulgaria, Ministry of Agriculture and Forestry Annual Report 2000: 4, available at http://www.mzgar.government.bg/MZ_eng/OfficialDocuments/Agry_report/Agry_report_2000.htm

12. Council for Mutual Economic Assistance (this included Bulgaria, Cuba, Czechoslovakia, German DR, Hungary, Mongolia, Poland, Romania, USSR, and Viet Nam.)

13. See Minty and Fuchs (2002) 'Agricultural Situation in the Candidate Countries', Country Report on Bulgaria, European Commission Directorate-General for Agriculture, available at: http://europa.eu.int/comm/agriculture/external/enlarge/publi/countryrep/bulgaria.pdf: 21

4   Strategies of MNEs in Hungary

1. Other fiscal measures are:

   - Tax credits on investments, including R&D investments (rate depends on volume, company size and geographic location)
   - Tax free employment of PhD, MSc or MBA students (up to the official minimum wage) in the field of educational and research activities and other services closely related to these activities
   - Option to create tax-free investment reserves, including R&D investments
   - Tax allowance for corporate donations to organizations of public benefit supporting R&D activities
   - Tax credit for individual donors supporting R&D activities
   - Tax credit off personal income tax after the creation of intellectual property; in addition, the Research and Technological Innovation Fund with fiscal incentives like credits toward the innovation contribution to be paid by companies.

2. Interview with Mr Tamas Balogh, Director, Innovation Department, Ministry of Economy and Transport, Republic of Hungary, January 2006, Budapest.

3. TrendChart Newsletter, September 2006, 'Hungary: 2005 R&D Statistics' published, available at: http://www.trendchart.org/tc_article.cfm?ID=3452&NEWSID=19.

4. Trendchart, Country Report, 'Hungary 2005': 34, available at: http://trend chart.cordis.lu/reports/documents/Country_Report_Hungary_2005.pdf
5. Interview with Mr Jozsef Urban, Project Manager, Marketing Department, AMC, Budapest, Hungary, April 2005.
6. Despite strenuous efforts, I was unable to arrange interviews with the Food Association or the Hungarian Agricultural Chamber. Subsequently, after several interviews with foreign producers, it became clear that food companies do not recognise these institutions as being dynamic and efficient organizations.
7. Interview with Laszlo Kallay, Ministry of Economy and Transport, Budapest, Hungary, April 2005.
8. The Széchenyi Plan was a medium-term development programme for the Hungarian economy for the period 2001–6. The objectives of the programme were to maintain economic growth and to improve the international competitiveness of the Hungarian economy. It stimulated five major areas:

- Housing
- Bridge and highway construction
- Development of the small and medium-sized enterprise sector
- Tourism
- Innovation and R&D (particularly in the field of information technology).

9. NORT devises R&D and innovation programmes, and manages international R&D cooperation in bilateral and multilateral relations, as well as supervising the network of Hungarian science and technology attachés. NORT's activities are guided by the Research and Technological Innovation Council. This 15-strong committee is appointed by the Prime Minister. The Council makes the major strategic decisions: what sort of RTDI policy schemes should be launched by NORT, and how much funding is to be earmarked for the EU Structural Funds, as well as those launched by NORT, and funded by national sources specific schemes.
10. Food and Drink Europe.com, Lidl Planning Hungarian Rollout, 7 January 2004, available at: http://www.foodanddrinkeurope.com/news/ng.asp?id=s48848-lidl-planning-hungarian, date accessed: May 2007.
11. Government of Canada (2005), 'Past, Present & Future Report', Hungary, November.
12. GFK Marketing Agency, 'The Results of the Project "Shopping Monitor Central and Eastern Europe"', 7 February 2006, available at: http://www.gfk.at/de/default.aspx?path=/de/press/releases/reader.aspx&msg=943&lng=EN&ctr=204 (accessed May 2007).
13. Euromonitor International (2005), *Packaged Food in Hungary*, January.
14. CEE FoodIndustry.com, 'Central Europe: Hypermarkets poised for Rapid Growth', 24 February 2004, available at: http://www.cee-foodindustry.com/news/ng.asp?n=50123-central-europe-hypermarkets (accessed May 2007).
15. *Népszabadság*, 24 January 2006.
16. *Budapest Sun*, 9–15 June 2005.
17. Interview with former Vice-chairman of Unilever Hungary and South Central Europe, Budapest, Hungary, January 2006.
18. Since June 2006, the Hungarian subsidiary has been running three factories.

19. Hungarian Competition Authority, available at: http://www.gvh.hu/index.php?id=4021&l=e
20. Interview with Unilever Chairman – Hungary, Croatia, Slovenia, October 2004.
21. Interview with InBev Communications Director – Hungary, Budapest, 2006.
22. Interview with Nestlé Human Resources Managing Director, Hungary, Budapest, 2006.

5   Strategies of MNEs in the Czech Republic

1. WTO definition.
2. TDC Trade.com (2007) *Market Profiles Czech Republic*, available at: http://www.tdctrade.com/mktprof/europe/mpczech.htm
3. CzechInvest was established by the Ministry of Industry and Trade (MIT) in November 1992. Its task was to promote the Czech Republic internationally to ensure a sustained inflow of foreign direct investment that would support industrial restructuring and development. Between 1992 and 2004, CzechInvest became a development agency through the implementation of programmes supported by both the MIT and the EU. Among these are the investment incentives system, the industrial zones and supplier development programmes, which are among MIT's most successful instruments in strengthening Czech industrial competitiveness. For more details, see www.czechinvest.org
4. The programme was co-funded by the EU's Phare programme.
5. CzechInvest Agency, www.czechinvest.cz
6. The FFDI was founded in 2000 as a successor to the Business Association, developing the Association's activities since 1995 and established in order to defend the interests of the food industry members. At the time of writing, the FFDI represents, on the basis of Act No. 110/97, Foods and Tobacco Products. Information is available at www.foodnet.cz
7. Interview with Mr Miroslav Koberna, Director, Federation of the Food and Drink Industries, Czech Republic, April 2005, Prague, the Czech Republic.
8. Each shop must obtain a Hazard Analysis Critical Control Points (HACCP) certificate, without which food cannot be sold. However, if the state inspection identifies an obvious breach of the HACCP system, it cannot revoke the certificate and subsequently halt the possibility of selling food – not even for the most serious offences.
9. CEE Foodindustry.com (2005) 'Czech Republic leading CEE Pack', 15 March 2005, http://cee-foodindustry.com/news/ng.asp?id=58726&n=wh11&c=%23emailcode
10. Food and Drink Europe.com, 'Czech Food Industry Demands Marketing Support to Survive', 17 March 2005, Anthony Fletcher, http://www.foodanddrinkeurope.com/news/ng.asp?id=58764-czech-food-industry (accessed 20 March 2007).
11. European Foundation for the Improvement of Living and Working Conditions (2004), http://eurofound.europa.eu/emcc/publications/2004/sf_fd_1.pdf (accessed 28 March 2007).

12. Food Manufacture, *Czech out the Future*, 7 January 2005, available at: http://www.foodmanufacture.co.uk/news/fullstory.php/aid/982/Czech_out_ the_future.html (accessed 15 April 2006).

13. Actually, Czechs are at the top of the European Commission's working hours list with an average 42-hour week.

14. *Ibid*: Food Manufacture (2005).

15. GFK marketing agency, Czech Republic, available at www.gfk.cz

16. GAIN Report (2004), 'Czech Republic Retail Food Sector – Market Update', EZ4005.

17. Euromonitor International (2006b), *Packaged Food in the Czech Republic*, February.

18. CEE Foodindustry.com, 'Czech Focus: Conditions Good for Foreign Investment', 17 March 2005, available at: http://cee-foodindustry.com/news/ng. asp?id=58794&n=wh11&c=%23emailcode

19. The only food that saw significant price increases was sugar, which rose in current value prices by 25 per cent.

20. Nestlé press release, 30 June 2004, Prague, ORION factory in Prague – Modřany closes down in October; Olomouc becomes the home of the ORION brand.

21. *Czech Business Weekly*, 'Big Changes Brewing', Sean B. Carney, 27 February 2006, at: http://www.cbw.cz/phprs/2006022711.html

22. 'Staropramen Brewery to Merge Prague Units, Close Branik', at: http://www. financninoviny.cz/english/index_view.php?id=174721 (accessed 19 April 2006).

23. Interview with the Corporate Communications Manager of Unilever, Prague, the Czech Republic, 2005.

24. Interview with Unilever CEO, Prague, the Czech Republic, 2005.

25. Cokoladovny reported sales of CZK 11.4 billion in 1997 (around CHF 500 million).

26. EBRD press release, 'EBRD Sells its Stake in Czech Chocolate Company; First Exit from Mature Equity Investment', 6 December 1995, http://www.ebrd.com/new/pressrel/1995/129dec06.htm (accessed 23 May 2007).

27. Interview with Mr Martin Walter, Corporate Affairs Manager, Nestlé Cesko, 6 February 2006.

28. Nestlé press release, 30 June 2004, Prague.

29. The group controls the Prazdroj and Gambrinus breweries in Plzeň, the Velkopopovicky Kozel brewery in Velké Popovice (near Prague), and the Radegast brewery in Nošovice (in north Moravia).

30. 30th European Brewery Convention Congress, 'Czech Beer', Prague 14–19 May 2005, press release.

31. It brews traditional domestic brands such as Staropramen Lager, Staropramen Light, Staropramen Black, Staropramen Garnet, Ostravar, Vratislav, Branik and Mestan.

32. Interview with InBev management, Prague, Czech Republic, March 2006.

33. Pivovary Staropramen Annual Report (2003).

34. Financni Noviny.Cz, 'Staropramen Brewery to Merge Prague Units, Close Branik', at: http://www.financninoviny.cz/english/index_view.php?id= 174721 (accessed 19 April 2006).

35. *Czech Business Weekly*, 'Big Changes Brewing', Sean B. Carney, http://www.cbw. cz/phprs/2006022711.html (accessed 27 February 2006).

6   Strategies of MNEs in Bulgaria

1. European Commission, European Trend Chart on Innovation, 'Annual Innovation Policy Trend and Appraisal Report, Bulgaria 2004–2005'.
2. For more information, see Dutta *et al.* (eds) (2006).
3. The Networked Readiness Index (NRI) shows the country's degree of prepa- ration to participate in and benefit from information and communication technology (ICT) developments. The component index identifies key areas where a nation is under- or over-performing.
4. National Innovation Strategy of Bulgaria, available in Bulgarian at: http:// www.mi.government.bg/doc_pub/Investment-strategy-JUNE-2005.pdf
5. European Commission, European Trend Chart on Innovation, 'Annual Innovation Policy Trend and Appraisal Report, Bulgaria 2004–2005', DG Enterprise, European Commission: 16.
6. 'National Innovation Fund Bulgaria', available at: http://www.bepc. government. bg/en/innovation.asp (accessed 17 May 2006).
7. 'Investment Promotion Law', *State Gazette*, 2004, no.37.
8. *Ibid*: 'Annual Innovation Policy Trend and Appraisal Report, Bulgaria 2004– 2005'.
9. Corporate Income Tax Law; *State Gazette* no.102; 20 December 2005.
10. In 2005, the average applied duty on agricultural products was 22.6 per cent (EU 17.6 per cent) and 8.6 per cent on industrial products (EU 3.7 per cent). The applied rates for industrial products are lower than bound rates but significantly higher than in the EU. See OECD/Investment Compact – Bulgaria Enterprise Policy Performance Assessment 2004 (http://www.investmentcompact.org and http://www.ced.bg)
11. 'Bulgaria Invest Agency, Bulgaria Fact Sheet 2005', available at: http:// investbg.government.bg/
12. Crops produced in Bulgaria include:

   • cereals – wheat, barley, maize, oats
   • industrial and oil-bearing crops – of which sunflower, sugar beet, cotton, and tobacco dominate
   • grapes and wine
   • vegetables and fruit – mainly tomatoes, potatoes, green and red peppers, cucumbers, apples, plums, cherries, peaches, apricots, and berries
   • The main livestock production involves cattle, sheep and goats, pigs, poultry, rabbits, horses, bees, and silkworms.

13. Ministry of Economy and Energy, Bulgaria.
14. Invest Bulgaria Agency, available at: http://investbg.government.bg/
15. Interview with the Managing Director, Foods, Unilever South Central Europe, Sofia, 2004.

16. Interview with Unilever Group Vice-President Central and Eastern Europe, May 2006.
17. He was a member of the acquisitions decision-making team
18. InBev produces the brands Kamenitza (in light, dark, white, extra and non-alcoholic brews), Astika, Burgasko Pivo, Pleven, Slavena, Stella Artois, Beck's and Staropramen brands in three breweries in Bulgaria.
19. Interview Inbev General Manager, Kamenitza, Bulgaria, 2006.
20. Interview with Mr Yannis Lazaridis, Country Manager Nestlé Bulgaria, April 2006, Sofia, Bulgaria.

7 Strategies of MNEs in Romania

1. The SII gives an 'at a glance' overview of aggregate national innovation performances and is calculated using the European Innovation Scoreboard, an instrument developed by the European Commission under the Lisbon Strategy to evaluate and compare the innovation performance of the member states.
2. European Commission, European Trend Chart on Innovation, 'Annual Innovation Policy Trends and Appraisal Report 2004–2005': Romania, available at: http://trendchart.cordis.lu/reports/documents/Country_Report_Romania_2005.pdf (date accessed 12 July 2006).
3. The highest concentration of innovating firms was found in the Bucharest Region (848 firms), and the lowest concentration in the West Region.
4. University professors, however, often hold posts at both universities and other research institutions.
5. MER was created by the merger of the former Ministry of National Education with the former National Agency for Science, Technology and Innovation, according to Government Ordinance 2/2001.
6. The National Plan for R&D and Innovation especially promotes R&D projects that:

   - support the development of new products, technologies and services in industrial firms in partnership with R&D organizations
   - are based on joint funding from enterprises and the government's programme budget.

7. The programme was approved by the government in 2005 and promotes the development of a high quality and competitive research potential, infrastructures and activities, from the viewpoint of better correlation with the priorities specific to the European Research Area, including those promoted by the future EU Framework Research Programme for 2007–13 (FP7).
8. INFRATEH is a programme that promotes technology transfer and innovation, especially at regional level, and includes: technical assistance and information centres, technology transfer centres, incubators, S/T parks, and so on. During 2004, nine technology transfer centres and incubators, and five S&T parks were authorized to function in various regions of the country.

9. For comparison, the ranking of the other three countries is Bulgaria: 58th place, Hungary: 39th, and the Czech Republic: 38th.
10. 'Colliers Real Estate Review: Romania 2005', available at: www.colliers.com
11. *Ibid*: 'Annual Innovation Policy Trends and Appraisal Report', Country Report for 2005, Romania: 11.
12. WTO Statistics Database (2006), 'Country Trade Profiles: Romania', available at: http://stat.wto.org/CountryProfile/WSDBCountryPFReporter.aspx?Language=E
13. In addition, the food industry accounted for about 13 per cent of total industrial output in 2004, and for 10.2 per cent of industrial employment.
14. National Bank of Romania, 31 December 2005.
15. Euromonitor International (2006d) *Packaged Food in Romania*: 13.
16. Euromonitor International (2006d) *Packaged Food in Romania*: 12.
17. Standing Committee on Agricultural Research Portal, available at: http://ec.europa.eu/research/agriculture/scar/index_en.cfm?p=1_ro
18. Euromonitor International (2006d) *Packaged Food in Romania*: 1.
19. Euromonitor International (2005b) *Consumer Lifestyle in Romania*: 63.
20. Other shops are:

- Kiosks
- Markets selling predominantly groceries
- Food and drink souvenir stores
- Regional speciality stores
- Health food stores, selling predominantly food or beverages (rather than predominantly vitamins and dietary supplements)
- Organic food and drink stores
- Delicatessens
- Direct home delivery; for example, milk, meat from farm/dairy.

21. Euromonitor International (2004d) *Retailing in Romania*: 8.
22. Euromonitor International (2004d) *Retailing in Romania*: 37.
23. Unilever Romania, http://www.archi-web.com/unileverromania/rom.htm (accessed 15 December 2007).
24. *The Diplomat* – Bucharest, 'Dutch Courage', April 2005, http://www.thediplomat.ro/business_0405.htm
25. Interview with the ex-General Manager of Interbrew Romania, 2002–05; since 2006, a Business Unit President in charge of Croatia, Hungary, Slovakia, Czech Republic, Bucharest, Romania, 27 April 2006.
26. Bogdan Tudorache, 'Nestlé Expands Romanian Biscuit Production', http://confectionerynews.com/news/ng.asp?id=58956&n=wh13&c=%23emailcode
27. Interview with Mr Paul Nuber, General Manager, Nestlé Romania, Bucharest, Romania, March 2006.
28. See CEE FoodIndustry.com, 'Nestlé Romania Invests in Wafers', http://www.bakeryandsnacks.com/news/ng.asp?id=52849-nestle-romania-invests
29. The Nestlé Romania portfolio includes:

- Coffee (Nescafé Brasero, Nescafé Classic, Nescafé Gold)
- Instant cocoa (Nesquik)
- Wafers (Joe)
- Chocolate bars (Lion)
- Cooking products (Maggi condiments and soups)
- Baby food (Nan, Beba, Nestlé)
- Cereals and baby food in jars for newborns, breakfast cereals (Nesquik, Chocapic, Cini Minis, Fitness, Kangus, Cheerios, Corn Flakes, Gold Flakes)
- Cereal bars (Nesquik, Chocapic, Fitness, Cini Minis)
- Pet food (Purina, Friskies, Darling, Gourmet).

8 Conclusion

1. European Foundation for the Improvement of Living and Working Conditions (2006b), 'Restructuring and Employment in the EU: Concepts, Measurement and Evidence', www.eurofound.eu.int
2. European Restructuring Monitor, available at: http://www.eurofound.europa.eu/emcc/erm/index.php?template=home
3. Blas-Lopes, E. (2007) 'Synthesis Report – Brussels Seminar', available at: http://www.fse-agire.com
4. European Foundation for the Improvement of Living and Working Conditions (2007) *European Restructuring Monitor Quarterly* (ERM), 1, spring.
5. VW press release, 'Restructuring of Volkswagen Brussels', 21 November 2006, available at: http://www.volkswagen-media-services.com/medias_publish/ms/content/en/pressemitteilungen/2006/11/21/restructuring_of_volkswagen.standard.gid-oeffentlichkeit.html
6. European Foundation for the Improvement of Living and Working Conditions (2006) *European Restructuring Monitor Quarterly*, 4, winter.
7. AgriE project, 'IBM Case Study, Alpha Team', available at: http://www.fse-agire.com
8. For more information see the web page of the Anticipating for an Innovative Management of Restructuring in Europe (AgriE) project, available at: http://www.fse-agire.com
9. For more information, see the web page of 'Anticipating for an Innovative Management of Restructuring in Europe (AgriE) project, available at http://www.fse-agire.com

Bibliography

Akbar, Y. (2005) 'Shifting Competitiveness, Evolving MNE Strategies and EU Enlargement: The Case of Hungary', Jean Monnet/Robert Schuman Paper Series, 5 (22), July 2005.

Alfranca, O., R. Rama and N. von Tunzelmann (2005) 'Innovation in Food and Beverage Multinationals', in R. Rama (ed.), *Multinational Agribusinesses* (New York: Food Products Press).

Alvarez, I. and R. Marin (2007) '*National Systems of Innovation and the Attraction of FDI: Does This Relation Matter?*', Paper presented at the conference 'Four Decades of International Business at Reading', 16–17 April 2007, Reading, UK.

Association of Hungarian Brewers, 'Annual Report 2004', available at: http://www.merlin.hu/referenciak/mssz/2004eves.pdf (accessed May 2007).

Association of Hungarian Brewers, 'Annual Report 2003', available at: http://www.merlin.hu/referenciak/mssz/2003eves.pdf (accessed May 2007).

Association of Hungarian Brewers, 'Annual Report 2001', available at: http://www.merlin.hu/referenciak/mssz/2001eves.pdf (accessed May 2007).

Bacskai, T. R. Nagy, T. Ay, Cs. Bazso, K. Apatini, M. Kismarty, H. Laki, T. Laky, and G. Szucs (eds) (2005) *State of Small and Medium-sized Business in Hungary: Annual Report 2005*, Hungarian Institute for Economic Analysis, Hungary.

Bacskai, T. R. Nagy, T. Ay, Cs. Bazso, K. Apatini, M. Kismarty, H. Laki, T. Laky, and G. Szucs (eds) (2002) *State of Small and Medium-sized Business in Hungary: Annual Report 2002*, Hungarian Institute for Economic Analysis, Hungary.

Bartlett, C.A. and S. Ghoshal (1989) *Managing Across Borders: The Transnational Solution* (Boston, MA: Harvard Business School Press).

Benito, G.R.G., B. Grogaar and R. Narul (2003) 'Environmental Influences on MNE Subsidiary Roles: Economic Integration and the Nordic Countries', *Journal of International Business Studies*, 34: 443–56.

Bergman, E., G. Maier and F. Todtling (1991) *Regions Reconsidered: Economic Networks, Innovation, and Local Development in Industrialized Countries* (London, NY: Mansell).

Biacs, P.A. (2003) 'The Future of Food Industry in the CEE and NIS', Expert Papers, Technology Foresight Summit Budapest, 27–29 March 2003, available at: http://www.unido.org/file-storage/download/?file_id=10567 (accessed May 2007).

Birkinshaw, J. (1996) 'How Multinational Subsidiary Mandates are Gained and Lost', *Journal of International Business Studies*, 27 (3): 467–95.

Birkinshaw, J. and C. Bouquet (2006) 'Voices that Count: How Foreign Subsidiaries Gain Positive Attention from Corporate Headquarters', Strategic and International Management Working Paper.

Birkinshaw, J. and N. Hood (2000) 'Characteristics of Foreign Subsidiaries in Industry Clusters', *Journal of International Business Studies*, 31, (1): 141–54.

Birkinshaw, J. and A.J. Morrison (1995) 'Configurations of Strategy and Structure in Subsidiaries of Multinational Corporations', *Journal of International Business Studies*, 26 (4), (4th qtr, 1995): 729–53.

Birsan, M., C. Moraru, R. Cramarenco and S. Andrei (2005) 'Contribution of FDI to the Privatisation in the Manufacturing Sector in Romania: Success and Failure Stories', available at: http://www.tbs.ubbcluj.ro/studia/articol_7_2_2005.pdf (accessed: 22 November 2006).

Borensztein, E., J. De Gregorio and J.W. Lee (1998) 'How Does Foreign Direct Investment Affect Economic Growth?', *Journal of International Economics*, 45: 115–35.

Christensen, J.L., R. Rama and N. von Tunzelmann (1996) *Industry Studies of Innovation Using CIS Data: Study on Innovation in the European Food Products and Beverages Industry*, EIMS SPRINT, 1996, for the European Commission.

Clarke, G. (2001) 'How the Quality of Institutions Affects Technological Deepening in Developing Countries', World Bank Policy Research Working Paper WPS2603.

Crookell, H. (1990) *Canadian–American Trade and Investment under the Free Trade Agreement* (Westport: CT: Quorum Books).

Crookell, H. (1986) 'Specialization and International Competitiveness', in H. Etemad and L.S. Dulude (eds), *Managing the Multinational Subsidiary* (London: Croom Helm).

Crouch, C., C. Trigilia, H. Voelzkow and P. Le Galès (2004) *Changing Governance of Local Economies – Responses of European Local Production Systems* (Oxford: Oxford University Press).

Dunning, J.H. (2002) *Global Capitalism, FDI and Competitiveness: The Selected Essays of John H. Dunning* (Cheltenham, UK; Northampton, MA: Edward Elgar).

Dunning, J.H. (ed.) (2000) *Regions, Globalization and the Knowledge Based Economy* (Oxford: Oxford University Press)

Dunning, J.H. (1993) *Multinational Enterprises and the Global Economy* (Wokingham, Berkshire: Addison Wesley).

Dunning, J.H. (1992) 'Trans-Atlantic Foreign Direct Investment and the European Community', *International Economic Journal*, 6 (1): 59–82.

Dutta, S., A. Lopez-Claros and I. Mia (eds) (2006) *Global Information Technology Report 2005–2006: Leveraging ICT for Development* (World Economic Forum Reports) Palgrave Macmillan.

Eden, L. (2001) 'Regional Integration and Foreign Direct Investment: Theory and Lessons from NAFTA', in M. Kotabe, P. Aulakh and A. Phatak (eds), *The Challenge of International Business Research* (London, UK: Edward Elgar)

Edquist, C. (2002) 'Innovation Policy – A Systemic Approach', in D. Archibugi and B. Lundvall (eds), *The Globalizing Learning Economy* (Oxford: Oxford University Press).

Edquist, C. (1997) *Systems of Innovation: Institutions and Organizations* (London: Pinter).

Estrin, S. and K. Meyer (eds) (2004) *Investment Strategies in Emerging Markets* (Aldershot, UK and Northampton, MA, USA: Edward Elgar).

Euromonitor International (2006a) *Beer – InBev*, April.

Euromonitor International (2006b) *Packaged Food in the Czech Republic*, February.

Euromonitor International (2006c) *Packaged Food in Hungary*, May.

Euromonitor International (2006d) *Packaged Food in Romania*.

Euromonitor International (2006e) *Packaged Food – Nestlé SA*, March.

Euromonitor International (2006f) *Unilever Group – Packaged Food*, February.

Euromonitor International (2005a) *Packaged Food in Hungary*, January.

Euromonitor International (2005b) *Consumer Lifestyle in Romania*.

Euromonitor International (2004a) *Retailing in Bulgaria*.

Euromonitor International (2004b) *Retailing in Romania*.

Euromonitor International (2003) *Shopping Habits and Consumer Lifestyles*.

European Commission (2005) *Romania – 2005 Comprehensive Monitoring Report*, Brussels, 25 October 2005, SEC (2005) 1354.

European Commission (2004a) *European Innovation Scoreboard* SEC (2004) 1475

European Commission (2004b) *Regular Report on Bulgaria's Progress Towards Accession*, Brussels, 6 October 2004, SEC (2004) 1199.

European Commission, European TrendChart on Innovation, 'Annual Innovation Policy Trends and Appraisal Report 2004–2005: Romania', available at: http://trendchart.cordis.lu/reports/documents/Country_Report_Romania_2005.pdf (accessed 12 July 2006).

European Commission, TrendChart on Innovation, 'Annual Innovation Policy Trends and Appraisal Report 2004–2005: Hungary', available at: http://trendchart.cordis.lu/reports/documents/Country_Report_Hungary_2005.pdf (accessed 12 July 2006).

European Commission, European TrendChart on Innovation, 'Annual Innovation Policy Trend and Appraisal Report 2004–2005: Bulgaria', available at: http://trendchart.cordis.lu/reports/documents/Country_Report_Bulgaria_2005.pdf (accessed 12 July 2006).

European Commission, European TrendChart on Innovation, 'Country Report Czech Republic 2002–2003', available at: http://trendchart.cordis.lu/reports/documents/Czech_Republic_CR_September_2003.pdf (accessed: May 2007).

European Foundation for the Improvement of Living and Working Conditions (2007) *European Restructuring Monitor Quarterly*, 1, spring.

European Foundation for the Improvement of Living and Working Conditions (2006a) *European Restructuring Monitor Quarterly*, 4, winter, 2006.

European Foundation for the Improvement of Living and Working Conditions (2006b) 'Restructuring and Employment in the EU: Concepts, Measurement and Evidence', available at www.eurofound.eu.int (accessed May 2007).

Freeman, C. (2002) 'Continental, National and Sub-national Innovation Systems – Complementarity and Economic Growth', *Research Policy 31*: 191–211.

Freeman, C. (1987) *Technology Policy and Economic Performance: Lessons from Japan* (London: Pinter).

Freeman, C. and F. Louca (2001) *As Time Goes By* (Oxford: Oxford University Press).

GAIN (2005) *Supermarkets Expansion in Bulgaria*, GAIN Report BU 5003, USDA Foreign Agricultural Service.

GAIN (2004) *Czech Republic Retail Food Sector – Market Update*, EZ4005, USDA Foreign Agricultural Service.

GAIN (2002) *Czech Republic: Food Processing Ingredients Sector*, EZ2002, USDA Foreign Agricultural Service.

Ghoshal, S. (1993) 'Horses For Courses: Organizational Forms For Multinational Corporations', *Sloan Management Review*, 34 (2), winter.

Ghoshal, S. (1987) 'Global Strategy: An Organizing Framework', *Strategic Management Journal*, 8: 425–40.

Ghoshal, S. and C.A. Bartlett (1988) 'Creation, Adoption and Diffusion of Innovations by Subsidiaries of Multinational Corporations', *Journal of International Business Studies*, Fall: 365–88.

Ghosal, S. and N. Nohria (1993) 'Horses for Courses: Organizational Forms for Multinational Corporations, *Sloan Management Review*, 34 (2), winter: 23–34.

Ghoshal, S. and N. Nohria (1989) 'Internal Differentiation within Multinational Corporations', *Strategic Management Journal*, 10 (4): 323–37.

Government of Canada (2005a) 'Marketing Report: *Agri-Food Past, Present & Future Report – Hungary*', November 2005, Agri-food Trade Service, Canada, available at: http://atn-riae.agr.ca/europe/4079_e.pdf (accessed 12 March 2006).

Government of Canada (2005b) 'Marketing Report: *Agri-Food Past, Present & Future Report – Czech Republic*', October 2005, Agri-food Trade Service, Canada.

Gupta, A.K. and V. Govindarajan (1991) 'Knowledge Flows and the Structure of Control within Multinational Corporations', *Academy of Management Review*, 16: 768–92.

Hanisch, M. and I. Boevsky (1999) 'Political, Institutional and Structural Developments Accompanying Land Reform and Privatisation in Bulgarian Agriculture', *Südosteuropa, Zeitschrift für Gegenwartsforschung*, 48 (7–8), Munich, available at: www.agrar.hu-berlin.de/wisola/ipw/KATO/papers/suedost.pdf

Harzing, A. (2000) 'An Empirical Analysis and Extension of the Bartlett and Ghoshal Typology of Multinational Companies', *Journal of International Business Studies*, 31 (1): 101–21.

Harzing, A. and N.G. Noorderhaven (2006) 'Knowledge Flows in MNCs: An Empirical Test and Extension of Gupta and Govindarajan's Typology of Subsidiary Roles', *International Business Review*, 15 (3): 195–214.

Hastenberg, J. (1999) *Foreign Direct Investment in Hungary: The Effects on the Modernization of the Manufacturing Industry and the Demand for Labor*, Ph.D dissertation, Faculty of Geographical Sciences, Utrecht University.

Hirschhausen, C. von and J. Bitzer (eds) (2000) *The Globalization of Industry and Innovation in Eastern Europe: From Post-Socialist Restructuring to International Competitiveness*, (Cheltenham, UK; Northampton, MA: Edward Elgar).

Hogenbirk, A. and R. Narula (1999) 'Globalization and the Small Economy: The Case of the Netherlands', *MERIT RM*, 1999–02.

Holl, A. and R. Rama (2007a) 'The Spatial Patterns of Networks, Hierarchies and Subsidiaries', European Network on the Economics of the Firm (ENEF), Discussion Paper, available at: http://www.enef.group.shef.ac.uk/papers/HollRama.pdf

Holl, A. and R. Rama (2007b) 'An Exploratory Analysis of Networking, R&D and Innovativeness in the Spanish Electronics Sector', European Network on the Economics of the Firm (ENEF), Discussion Paper 2007, available at: http://www.enef.group.shef.ac.uk/papers/HollRama2.pdf

Huws, U. and M. Ramioul (2006) European Foundation for the Improvement of Living and Working Conditions, 'Globalization and the Restructuring of Value Chains', in U. Huws (ed.), *The Transformation of Work in the Global Knowledge Economy: Towards a Conceptual Framework*, WORKS project, http://www.worksproject.be/documents/WP3synthesisreport-voorpublicatie.pdf

InBev (2006) *Annual Report 2006*, available at: http://www.inbev.com/annualreport 2006/our_global_vision.cfm (accessed May 2007).

Invest Bulgaria Agency (2006) *Bulgaria Investment Guide 2006*.

Isobe, T. and D.B. Montgomery (1998) 'Strategic Roles and Performance of Japanese Subsidiaries', *Stanford GSB Research Paper* 1507, Stanford, CA.

Jarillo, J.C. and J.I. Martinez (1990) 'Different Roles for Subsidiaries: The Case of Multinational Corporations in Spain', *Strategic Management Journal*, 11: 501–12.

Kovács, K. (1997) 'Agricultural Protection And Agricultural Interests In Hungary: The Burden of Transformation of Hungarian Agriculture in the 1990s', Centre for Central and Eastern European Studies, Working Paper 43, Rural Transition Series, University of Liverpool.

Krueger, A. (1990) 'Economists' Changing Perception of Government', *Weltwirtschaftliches Archive*, 126 (3): 417–31.

Krugman, P. (1994) *Rethinking International Trade* (Cambridge, MA: MIT Press).

Krugman, P. (ed.) (1986) *Strategic Trade Policy and the New International Economics* (Cambridge, MA: MIT Press).

Lall, S. and R. Narula (2004) 'FDI and its Role in Economic Development: Do We Need a New Agenda?', MERIT Research Memorandum 2004-019.

Lazonick, W. (2004) 'Corporate Restructuring', in P. Thompson, P. Tolbert, R. Batt and S. Acroyd (eds), *Oxford Handbook of Work and Organization* (Oxford: Oxford University Press).

Levitt, T. (1983) 'The Globalization of Markets', *Harvard Business Review*, May–June: 92–102.

Lopez-Claros, A., M. Porter and K. Schwab (eds) (2006) *Global Competitiveness Report 2005–2006: Policies Underpinning Rising Prosperity* (Palgrave Macmillan).

Loree, D.W. and Guisinger, S.E. (1995) 'Policy and Non-policy Determinants of US Equity Foreign Direct Investment', *Journal of International Business Studies*, 26 (2): 281–300.

Lorentzen, J. (2006a) *Innovation in Resource Based Technology Clusters: Investigating the Lateral Migration Thesis*, available at: http://www.hsrc.ac.za/Document-1841.phtml

Lorentzen, J. (2006b) 'Muti from Coal: Science and Politics of Humic Substance Research in South Africa', in J. Lorentzen (project coordinator), *Innovation in Resource Based Technology Clusters: Investigating the Lateral Migration Thesis*, Employment Oriented Industry Studies (HSRC Press).

Lorentzen, J. (2005) 'STARSTRUCK: Economic Impact of DaimlerChrysler on the Eastern Cape', *HSRC Review*, 3 (2): 6–7.

Lorentzen, J. and J. Barnes (2004) 'Learning, Upgrading and Innovation in the South-African Automobile Industry', *European Journal of Development Research*, 16 (3): 465–98.

Lundvall, B. (2002) 'Innovation Policy in the Globalizing Learning Economy', in D. Archibugi and B. Lundvall (eds), *The Globalizing Learning Economy* (Oxford: Oxford University Press).

Lundvall, B. (ed.) (1992) *National Systems of Innovations* (London: Pinter).

Martinez, J.I. and J.C. Jarillo (1991) 'Coordination Demands of International Strategies', *Journal of International Business Studies*, 22 (3): 429–44.

McKenzie, R.B. and D.R. Lee (1991) *Quicksilver Capital* (New York: The Free Press).

Meyer, KE. and Y.T.T. Tran (2006) 'Market Penetration and Acquisition Strategies for Emerging Economies', *Long Range Planning*, 39 (2).

Meyer, K.E. and C. Jensen (2003) 'Foreign Investor Strategies in view of EU Enlargement', in: H.-J. Stuting, W. Dorow, S. Blaszejewski and F. Claasen, (eds),

Change Management in Transformation Economies: Integrating Strategy, Structure and Culture (London: Palgrave Macmillan).

Ministry of Agriculture and Forestry, Bulgaria (2000) *Annual Agricultural Report 2000*, available at: http://www.mzgar.government.bg/MZ_eng/Official Documents/Agry_report/Agry_report_2000.htm (accessed May 2007).

Ministry of Agriculture and Rural Development, Hungary (2005) *The Hungarian Agriculture and Food Industry in Figures*, Department of International Relations, available at: http://www.fvm.hu/doc/upload/200601/stat_2005_angol.pdf (accessed May 2007).

Ministry of Agriculture of the Czech Republic (2003) *Summary Report on Agriculture, Food Industry, Forestry and Water Management*.

Minty, P. and Fuchs, C. (2002) 'Agricultural Situation in the Candidate Countries', Country Report on Bulgaria, European Commission Directorate-General for Agriculture, available at: http://europa.eu.int/comm/agriculture/external/enlarge/publi/countryrep/bulgaria.pdf: 21

Mowery, D. and T. Simcoe (2002) 'Is the Internet a US invention? – An Economic and Technological History of Computer Networking', *Research Policy 31*: 1369–87.

Narula, R. (2005) 'Globalization, EU Expansion and Consequences of MNE Location', MERIT Research Memoranda Series, 2005–003.

Narula, R. (2004) 'Understanding Absorptive Capacities in an "Innovation Systems" Context: Consequences for Economic and Employment Growth', MERIT Research Memoranda Series, 2004–003.

Narula, R. (2003) *Globalization and Technology* (Cambridge: Polity Press).

Narula, R. (2002) 'Innovation Systems and "Inertia" in R&D Location: Norwegian Firms and the Role of Systemic Lock-in', *Research Policy 31*: 795–816.

Narula, R. (2001) 'Multinational Firms, Regional Integration and Globalizing Markets: Implications for Developing Countries', *Research Memoranda 035*, Maastricht: MERIT Research Memoranda, 2001–035.

Narula, R. and J. Dunning (2000) 'Industrial Development, Globalisation and Multinational Enterprises: New Realities for Developing Countries', *Oxford Development Studies*, 28 (2).

Narula, R. and A. Marin (2005) 'Exploring the Relationship between Direct and Indirect Spillovers from FDI in Argentina', *MERIT Research Memoranda* 2005–024.

Narula, R. and A. Marin (2003) 'FDI spillovers, Absorptive Capacities and Human Capital Development: Evidence from Argentina', MERIT Research Memoranda 2003–16.

Narula, R. and B. Portelli (2004) 'Foreign Direct Investment and Economic Development: Opportunities and Limitations from a Developing Country Perspective', MERIT Research Memoranda 2004–009.

Nelson, R. (2006) 'What Makes an Economy Productive and Progressive? What are the Needed Institutions?', LEM Papers Series 2006/24, Laboratory of Economics and Management (LEM), Sant'Anna School of Advanced Studies, Pisa, Italy.

Nelson, R. (2002) 'Technology, Institutions and Innovation Systems', *Research Policy 31*: 265–72.

Nelson, R. (1993) *National Innovation Systems: A Comparative Analysis* (Oxford, New York: University Press).

Niosi, J. (2002) 'National Systems of Innovation are "X-efficient" (and X-effective). Why Some are Slow Learners', *Research Policy 31*: 291–302.

Niosi, J., P. Saviotti, B. Bellon and M. Crow (1993) 'National Systems of Innovations: In Search of a Workable Concept', *Technology in Society*, 15: 207–27.

North, D.C. (1990) *Institutions, Institutional Change and Economic Performance* (Cambridge: Cambridge University Press).

O'Donnell, S.W. (2000) 'Managing Foreign Subsidiaries: Agents of Headquarters, or an Interdependent Network?', *Strategic Management Journal*, 21: 525–48.

OECD (2006) *Factbook 2006: Economic, Environmental and Social Statistics* (Paris: OECD).

OECD (2005a) *Governance of Innovation Systems: Synthesis Report* (Paris: OECD).

OECD (2005b) *Business Clusters: Promoting Enterprise in Central and Eastern Europe* (Paris: OECD).

OECD/Investment Compact for South-East Europe (2005c) 'Country Fact Sheet: Bulgaria', available at: http://www.oecd.org/dataoecd/27/31/36454652.pdf (accessed May 2007).

OECD (2005d) *Investment Policy Review: Romania* (Paris: OECD).

OECD (2002) *Foreign Direct Investment for Development* (Paris: OECD).

OECD (2000a) *Review of Agricultural Policies: Bulgaria* (Paris: OECD).

OECD (2000b) *Review of Agricultural Policies: Romania* (Paris: OECD).

OECD (1997) *National Innovation Systems* (Paris: OECD).

OECD (1995) *Review of Agricultural Policies: The Czech Republic* (Paris: OECD).

OECD (1994) *Review of Agricultural Policies: Hungary* (Paris: OECD).

Patel, P. and K. Pavitt (1994) 'The Nature and Economic Importance of National Innovation Systems', 14, *STI Review*, Paris: 9–32.

Pearce, R. (1999) 'Multinationals and Industrialization: The Basis of 'Inward' Investment Policy', University of Reading, Discussion Papers 279.

Pearce, R. (1992) 'World Product Mandates and MNE Specialization', *Scandinavian International Business Review*, 1 (2): 38–57.

Pivovary Staropramen, *Annual Report 2003*.

Porter, M.E. (1998) *On Competition* (Boston: Harvard Business School Press).

Quelch, J.A., E. Joachimsthaler and J.L. Nueno (1991) 'After the Wall: Marketing Guidelines for Eastern Europe', *Sloan Management Review*, 31 (4): 82–93.

Ragin, C. (1994) *Constructing Social Research: The Unity and Diversity of Method* (Thousand Oaks, CA: Pine Forge Press).

Rasiah, R. (1994) 'Flexible Production Systems and Local Machine Tool Subcontracting: Electronics Component Multinationals in Malaysia', *Cambridge Journal of Economics*, 18: 279–98.

Rodrik, D., A. Subramanian and A.Trebbi (2002) 'Institutions Rule: The Primacy of Institutions over Geography and Integration in Economic Development', NBER Working Paper 930.

Roth, K. and A. Morrison (1992) 'Implementing Global Strategy: Characteristics of Global Subsidiary Mandates', *Journal of International Business Studies*, 23 (4): 715–36.

Sapir, A., P. Aghion, G. Bertola, M. Hellwig, J. Pisani-Ferry, D. Rosati, J. Viñals, and Helen Wallace (2003) *An Agenda for a Growing Europe: Making the EU Economic System Deliver*, available at: http://www.iue.it/ECO/internal/ws-papers/papers2003-04/NO%20SIGNATURE%20complete%20report.pdf (accessed May 2004).

Schuh, A. (2000) 'Global Standardization as a Success Formula for Marketing in Central and Eastern Europe?', *Journal of World Business*, 35 (2):
133–48.

Schuh, A. and E. Damova (2001) 'Market Entry and Marketing Strategies of
Western FMCG-Firms in Bulgaria', in P. Chadraba and R. Springer (eds), *Proceedings of the 9th Annual Conference on Marketing and Business Strategies for Central
and Eastern Europe* (Vienna: WU-Wien Eigenverlag).

Schuh, A. and H. Holzmüller (2003) 'Marketing Strategies of Western Consumer
Goods Firms in Central and Eastern Europe', in H.-J. Stuting, W. Dorow,
F. Claassen and S. Blazejewski (eds), *Change Management in Transition Economies –
Integrating Corporate Strategy, Structure and Culture* (New York: Palgrave
Macmillan).

Shama, A. (1995) 'Entry Strategies for U.S. firms to the Former Soviet Bloc and
Eastern Europe', *California Management Review*, 37 (3): 90–109.

Shimizu, K., M.A. Hitt, D. Vaidyanath and V. Pisano (2004) 'Theoretical Foundations of Cross-border Mergers and Acquisitions: A Review of Current Research
and Recommendations for the Future', *Journal of International Management*, 10:
307–55.

Sternberg, R. and O. Arndt (2001) 'The Firm or the Region: What Determines the
Innovation of European Firms?', *Economic Geography*, 77 (4): 364–82.

Stopford, J. and S. Strange (1991) *Rival States, Rival Firms: Competition for World
Market Shares* (Cambridge: Cambridge University Press).

Swain, N. (1997a) 'Agricultural Restructuring and Rural Employment in Romania:
the Rebirth of Family Farming?', Central and Eastern European Studies Working
Paper 40, Rural Transition Series, University of Liverpool.

Swain, N. (1997b) 'Agricultural Restructuring and Rural Employment in Bulgaria:
The Rebirth of Family Farming?', Central and Eastern European Studies Working
Paper 41, Rural Transition Series, University of Liverpool.

Swain, N. (1994) 'Agricultural Privatisation in Hungary', Central and Eastern
European Studies Working Paper 32, Rural Transition Series, University of
Liverpool.

Szanyi, M. (2001) 'Policy Consequences of FDI, Linkage Promotion Opportunities
in Hungary' (Geneva: UNECE/EBRD).

Tozanli, S. (2005) 'The Rise of Global Enterprises in the World's Food Chain',
in R. Rama (ed.), *Multinational Agribusinesses* (New York: Food Products Press).

UNCTAD (2005) *World Investment Report 2005 – Transnational Corporations and the
Internationalization of R&D* (New York and Geneva: United Nations).

UNCTAD (2001) *World Investment Report 2001 – Promoting Linkages* (NY and
Geneva: United Nations).

Unilever Group (2007) *Unilever 2006 Results Presentation by Patrick Cescau, Unilever
Group Chief Executive*, London, Thursday 8 February 2007, available at:
http://www.unilever.com/Images/ir_Q4%202006%20Results%20speech_tcm13-
84121.pdf (accessed May 2007).

Unilever Group, *Adding Vitality to Life: 2006 Annual Report and Accounts*,
available at: http://www.unilever.com/Images/ir_06_annual_report_en_tcm13-
88803.pdf (accessed May 2007).

Unilever Group, *Adding Vitality to Life: Unilever Annual Review and Summary Financial Statement 2004*, available at: http://www.unilever.com/Images/Annual_
Review_Eng_04_tcm13-11959.pdf (accessed May 2007).

Vass, A. (2005) *Private Sector Interaction in the Decision Making Processes of Public Research in Romania*, Draft document provided to the policy mix peer review team.

Wallace, H. (ed.) (2001) *Interlocking Dimensions of European Integration* (New York: Palgrave Macmillan).

White, R.E. and T.A. Poynter (1984) 'Strategies for Foreign Owned Subsidiaries in Canada', *Business Quarterly*, summer: 59–69.

Williamson, O. (1975) *Markets and Hierarchies: Analysis and Antitrust Implications* (New York: Free Press).

WTO (2005) *Trade Policy Review – Romania*, Report by the Secretariat WT/TPR/S/155, 24 October (Geneva: World Trade Organization).

WTO (2003) *Trade Policy Review – Bulgaria*, Report by the Secretariat, WT/TPR/S/121, 15 September (Geneva: World Trade Organization).

WTO (1998) *Trade Policy Review – Hungary*, Report by the Secretariat, WT/TPR/S/40, 7–8 July (Geneva: World Trade Organization).

WTO (1996a) *Trade Policy Review – Czech Republic*, Report by the Secretariat, WT/TPR/S/12, 6–7 March (Geneva: World Trade Organization).

WTO (1996b) *Protocol of Accession Bulgaria*, WT/ACC/BGR/5, 1 December (Geneva: World Trade Organization).

Xu, Bin (2000) Multinational Enterprises, Technology Diffusion and Host Country Productivity Growth, *Journal of Development Economics*, 62: 477–93.

Yip, G.S. (1989) 'Global Strategy … In a World of Nations?', *Sloan Management Review*, 31 (1), fall: 29–41.

Yoruk, D.E. and N. von Tunzelmann (2002) 'Network Realignment and Appropriability in the CEE Food Industry', Working Paper 24, University of Sussex.

Internet sources

AgriE project, IBM case study, Alpha team, available at: http://www.fse-agire.com

Anticipating for an Innovative Management of Restructuring in Europe (AgriE) project, http://www.fse-agire.com (accessed May 2007).

Blas-Lopes, E. (2007) 'Synthesis Report – Brussels Seminar', http://www.fse-agire.com (accessed May 2007).

Bulgarian National Bank, http://www.bnb.bg

CEE FoodIndustry.com, 'Czech Focus: Conditions Good for Foreign Investment', 17 March 2005, http://cee-foodindustry.com/news/ng.asp?id=58794&n=wh11&c=%23emailcode (date accessed: 20 May 2007).

CEE FoodIndustry.com, 'Central Europe: Hypermarkets Poised for Rapid Growth', 24 February 2004, available at: http://www.cee-foodindustry.com/news/ng.asp?n=50123-central-europe-hypermarkets (accessed 20 May 2007).

CEE FoodIndustry.com, 'Czech Republic Leading CEE Pack', 15 March 2005 http://cee-foodindustry.com/news/ng.asp?id=58726&n=wh11&c=%23emailcode (accessed: May 2007).

CEE FoodIndustry.com, *Nestlé Romania invests in Wafers*, 16/06/2004, available at: http://www.bakeryandsnacks.com/news/ng.asp?id=52849-nestle-romania-invests (accessed: 20 May 2007).

CIAA (Confederation of the Food and Drink Industries of the EU) 'Data and Trends of the European Food and Drink Industry', available at: http://

www.ciaa.eu/documents/brochures/Data_&_Trends_2006_FINAL.pdf (accessed 21 May 2007).

CIAA (Confederation of the Food and Drink Industries of the EU) 'Food and Drink Statistics', available at: http://www.ciaa.be/uk/library/statistics/ceecs.htm (accessed December 2004).

'Colliers Real Estate Review Romania 2005', available at: www.colliers.com (accessed: May 2007).

Confectionary News.com, 'Nestlé Expands Romanian Biscuit Production', Bogdan Tudorache, 24 March 2005, available at: http://confectionerynews.com/news/ng.asp?id=58956&n=wh13&c=%23emailcode (accessed May 2006).

Czech Business Weekly, 'Big Changes Brewing', Sean B. Carney, 27 February 2006, available at: http://www.cbw.cz/phprs/2006022711.html (accessed: May 2007).

CzechInvest Agency, available at: www.czechinvest.org

CzechInvest, *The Czech Food Sector (2007)*, available at: http://www.czechinvest.org/data/files/czech-food-sector-102-en.pdf (accessed May 2007).

DG AGRI (2003) 'Key Developments in the Agro-Food Chain and on Restructuring and Privatisation in the CEE Candidate Countries', available at: http://ec.europa.eu/agriculture/publi/reports/agrifoodchain/2002_en.pdf (accessed May 2007).

DG AGRI (2002a) *Agricultural Situation in the Candidate Countries: Country Report on Romania*, available at: http://ec.europa.eu/agriculture/external/enlarge/publi/countryrep/romania.pdf (accessed May 2007).

DG AGRI (2002b) *Agricultural Situation in the Candidate Countries: Country Report on Bulgaria*, available at: http://europa.eu.int/comm/agriculture/external/enlarge/publi/countryrep/bulgaria.pdf (accessed May 2007).

European Foundation for the Improvement of Living and Working Conditions (2004) *The Future of the Food and Drink Sector*, available at: http://eurofound.europa.eu/emcc/publications/2004/sf_fd_1.pdf (accessed 28 March 2007).

European Restructuring Monitor, available at: http://www.eurofound.europa.eu/emcc/erm/index.php?template=home (accessed May 2007).

Federation of Food and Drink Industries of the Czech Republic (FFDI), available at: www.foodnet.cz

Financni Noviny.Cz, *Staropramen Brewery to Merge Prague Units, Close Branik*; available at: http://www.financninoviny.cz/english/index_view.php?id=174721 (accessed 19 April 2006).

Food and Drink Europe.com, available at: http://foodanddrinkeurope.com/ (accessed May 2007).

Food and Drink Europe.com, 'Czech Food Industry Demands Marketing Support to Survive', Anthony Fletcher, 17 March 2005, available at: http://www.foodanddrinkeurope.com/news/ng.asp?id=58764-czech-food-industry (accessed May 2007).

Food and Drink Europe.com, 'Lidl Planning Hungarian Rollout', 7 January 2004, available at: http://www.foodanddrinkeurope.com/news/ng.asp?id=48848-lidl-planning-hungarian (accessed May 2007).

Food Manufacture (2005) 'Czech out the Future', 7 January 2005, available at: http://www.foodmanufacture.co.uk/news/fullstory.php/aid/982/Czech_out_the_future.html (accessed 15 April, 2007).

Food Production Daily, electronic newspaper, 'Czech food industry demands marketing support to survive', 17 March 2005, available at: http://www.food productiondaily.com/

GFK Marketing Agency, Czech Republic: www.gfk.cz

GFK Marketing Agency, 'The results of the project 'Shopping Monitor Central and Eastern Europe', 7 February 2006, available at: http://www.gfk.at/de/default. aspx?path=/de/press/releases/reader.aspx&msg=943&lng=EN&ctr=204 (accessed May 2007).

Hungarian Competition Authority, available at: http://www.gvh.hu/index.php? id=4021&l=e (accessed May 2007).

Hungarian Investment and Trade Development Agency (ITDH), *Food Processing*, http://www.itdh.hu/itdh/nid/foodprocessing (accessed May 2007).

Hungarian Investment and Trade Development Agency (ITDH), *Exporting Hungary*, available at: http://193.202.83.133:8080/itdh/nid/export (accessed January 2006).

InBev, available at: www.inbev.com

Invest Bulgaria Agency, available at: http://investbg.government.bg/

Invest Bulgaria Agency, *Bulgaria Fact Sheet 2005*, available at: http://investbg. government.bg/

Ministry of Economy and Energy, Bulgaria, available at: http://www.mi.government.bg

NASR, Romania (2005a) *Policy Mix Peer Review, Romania*, June 2005, available at: http://www.mct.ro/ancs%5Fweb/index.php?action=view&idcat=21 (accessed May 2007).

NASR, Romania (2005b) *R&D and Innovation Policies in Romania*, Report of the Policy Mix Review Team, September 2005, available at: http://www.mct.ro/ancs%5 Fweb/index.php?action=view&idcat=21? (accessed May 2007).

National Bank of Romania, available at: http://www.bnro.ro/def_en.htm (accessed May 2007).

National Innovation Fund, Bulgaria, available at: http://www.bepc.government. bg/en/innovation.asp (accessed 17 May 2006).

National Innovation Strategy of Bulgaria, available in Bulgarian at: http://www.mi. government.bg/doc_pub/Investment-strategy-JUNE-2005.pdf

Nestlé, available at: www.nestle.com

OECD/Investment Compact (2004) *Bulgaria Enterprise Policy Performance Assessment 2004*, available at: http://www.investmentcompact.org and http://www.ced.bg (accessed May 2007).

OECD (2001) Challenges for the Agro-Food Sector in European Transition countries, available at: http://www.oecd.org/document/42/0,2340,en_2649_34489_2026986_1_1_1_1,00.html (accessed May 2007).

Payne, William F. and Istvan Feher (2002) *Food Industry Market Development in Hungary: Meeting the European Economic Union Challenge*, available at http://www.nssa.us/nssajrnl/22-2/htm/14.htm (accessed May 2005).

Standing Committee on Agricultural Research Portal, available at: http://ec.europa. eu/research/agriculture/scar/index_en.cfm?p=1_ro (accessed May 2007).

TDC Trade.com *Market Profiles: Czech Republic*, available at: http://www.tdctrade. com/mktprof/europe/mpczech.htm (accessed May 2007).

The Diplomat – Bucharest, 'Dutch Courage', April 2005, available at: http://www.thediplomat.ro/business_0405.htm (accessed May 2005).

TrendChart Innovation Policy in Europe, TrendChart Romania, available at: http://trendchart.cordis.lu/scoreboards/scoreboard2005/Romania.cfm (accessed May 2007).

Unilever Group, www.unilever.com

Unilever Romania, available at: http://www.archi-web.com/unileverromania/rom.htm (accessed May 2007).

WTO Statistics Database (2006), *Country Trade Profiles, Romania*, available at: http://stat.wto.org/CountryProfile/WSDBCountryPFReporter.aspx?Language=E (accessed May 2007).

Yotsev, A., 'Bulgarian Food Industry Firms will have to be closed after the Country Joins the European Union because They Don't Match the EU Standards', 24 September 2003, http://www.bgnewsnet.com/story.asp?st=1691 (accessed: March 2004).

Interviews by the author

Balogh, Tamas, Director, Innovation Department, Ministry of Economy and Transport, Budapest, Hungary, January 2006.

Corporate Affairs Office, InBev, Leuven, Belgium, November 2004.

Gallagher, James, Nestlé CEO for CEE region, Vevey, Switzerland, November 2004.

General Manager of Interbrew Romania for 2002–05, since 2006 a Business Unit President in charge of Croatia, Hungary, Slovakia, Czech Republic, Bucharest; Romania April 2006.

InBev Communications Director, Budapest, Hungary, February 2006.

InBev General Manager Kamenitza, Bulgaria, 2006.

InBev Management, Prague, Czech Republic, March 2006.

Kallay, Laszlo, Ministry of Economy and Transport, Budapest, Hungary, April 2005.

Koberna, Miroslav, Director, Federation of the Food and Drink Industries, Prague, Czech Republic, April 2005.

Nestlé HR Manager, Budapest, Hungary, February 2006.

Lazaridis, Yannis, Country Manager, Nestlé Bulgaria, Sofia, Bulgaria, April 2006.

Nuber, Paul, General Manager, Nestlé Romania, Bucharest, Romania, March 2006.

Official from MER, Bucharest, Romania, June 2006.

Švajcr, Vít, Director of Supplier Development Department CzechInvest, Prague, Czech Republic, April 2005.

Unilever Chairman – Hungary, Croatia, Slovenia, October 2004.

Unilever Corporate Communications Manager, Prague, Czech Republic, April 2005.

Unilever CEO, Prague, Czech Republic, April 2005.

Unilever Former Vice-chairman of Hungary and South as Eastern Europe, Budapest, Hungary, January 2006.

Unilever Managing Director Foods, South Central Europe, Sofia, Bulgaria, December 2004.

Unilever President Best Foods Europe, Rotterdam, The Netherlands, November 2004.

Unilever Group Vice-President Central and Eastern Europe, Rotterdam, The Netherlands, May 2006.
Unilever Vice-president Best Foods Europe, Rotterdam, The Netherlands, September 2004.
Urban, Jozsef, Project Manager, Marketing Department, AMC, Budapest, Hungary, April 2005.
Walter, Martin, Corporate Affairs Manager, Nestlé Cesko, Prague, Czech Republic, February 2006.

Press releases

EBRD Press Release, *EBRD sells its stake in Czech chocolate company; first exit from mature equity investment*, 6 December 1995, available at: http://www.ebrd.com/new/pressrel/1995/129dec06.htm (accessed 23 May 2007).
Nestlé Press Release, Prague, 'ORION Factory in Prague – Modřany closes down in October; Olomouc becomes the home of ORION brand', 30 June 2004, Prague.
30th European Brewery Convention Congress Press Release, *Czech Beer*, 14–19 May 2005, Prague.
VW Press release, *Restructuring of Volkswagen Brussels*, 21 November 2006, available at: Press release http://www.volkswagen-media-services.com/medias_publish/ms/content/en/pressemitteilungen/2006/11/21/restructuring_of_volkswagen.standard.gid-oeffentlichkeit.html

Newspapers

Budapest Sun, 9–15 June 2005.
Bulgarian State Gazette, Investment Promotion Law 2004, issue 37.
Bulgarian State Gazette, Corporate Income Tax Law issue 102.
Népszabadság, 24 January 2006.
TrendChart Newsletter, September 2006, 'Hungary: 2005 R&D Statistics Published', available at: http://www.trendchart.org/tc_article.cfm?ID=3452&NEWSID=19

CDs

AMC CD (2005) Collection of Hungary's Traditional and Local Agricultural Products.

Index

266   *Index*